# THE
# FIRST
# VCs

THE MOVING TRUE STORY OF
FIRST WORLD WAR HEROES
MAURICE DEASE
AND SIDNEY GODLEY

# THE
# FIRST
# VCs

MARK RYAN

First published 2014

The History Press
The Mill, Brimscombe Port
Stroud, Gloucestershire, GL5 2QG
www.thehistorypress.co.uk

British Library Cataloguing in Publication Data.
A catalogue record for this book is available from the British Library.

ISBN 978 0 7509 5451 8

Typesetting by Thomas Bohm, User design
Printed in Great Britain

# Contents

# Acknowledgements

First, thanks must go to John Mulholland, who was going to write this book himself until his considerable energies had to be diverted elsewhere. Imagine my relief and joy when he very generously offered to hand over all his own research and writings on the subject, giving me a free run to pick and choose as I pleased, to use whatever I wanted from his collection.

John was the man who introduced Major Maurice French (Maurice Dease's nephew) to Colin Godley at Westminster Hall in 2003. Like Maurice Dease, John attended Stonyhurst College, and has remained as moved as I am by the story of both men. He has been a rock throughout the process. Consider that he was writing his excellent biography of Bill Speakman, VC, *Beyond the Legend* while fielding all kinds of questions from me, and you get a measure of the man's patience and intellectual capacity. I continued to pick John's brains to the very end, and fulfilled my promise to let him view the first draft of the manuscript so that he could give his own feedback. This has proved invaluable, as I knew it would, since John isn't afraid to go straight to the point when he sees something which can be improved or needs correcting. Thank you so much, John, you deserve all your success in life.

Next, I want to thank Colin Godley, who has been a great supporter of his grandfather Sidney's memory for a good number of decades. Colin and his charming wife Linda invited me into their home in Stepney Green with a typical East End welcome, and were always helpful with their many insights. It is a testament to their determination to preserve Sidney's memory that they have kept many documents and photographs in superb condition, ready to pass down to the next generation, so that they too can remember their relative with pride and affection. Colin even retrieved a precious BBC recording of his grandfather from 1954, so we could actually hear the great man speak of his ordeal. I was so lucky to be able to benefit from this direct Godley family collection and will always be grateful for their hospitality.

Meanwhile, Sidney Godley's daughter, Eileen Slade, and her son, Andy, were also a sheer delight to interview. It was an emotional experience to hear Eileen speak of her father so proudly, and recall times between the wars that she still remembered so clearly. She can be very proud of herself that she spoke so movingly of Sidney and brought his final years to life so vividly. Accounts of life before, during and immediately after the Second World War are very precious; we should cherish them and collect them while we can.

The determination of Major Maurice French to preserve everything relating to the Dease story so perfectly was also deeply impressive. It made me feel so lucky to have such extensive source material to draw upon. Major French made me feel most welcome in his house right at the very start of the process, and it was a delight to pore over photograph albums and documents which remain in such fine condition after all these years. Major French helped me up to the moment when the manuscript was handed to the publisher, and again I will always remain grateful.

Having read through the book yourself, I hope you will agree that what the Godley and Dease families preserved for us, in terms of documentary material, was quite extraordinary. To put the best of these collections together in one book was surely worthwhile, and it is something that future generations can now cherish forever when they look back at the men who won the very first VCs of the First World War.

To all the authors who have previously written about Mons, I salute your superb research and excellent accounts; I hope I have acknowledged you all as I draw on some of your material. Distinguished historians and authors have all added to the picture down the years; it would be personally satisfying to me if future authors felt my material worthy of their attention in any small way, as they add their own contribution to this subject.

Thanks to The History Press editor, Jo DeVries, for the support she showed by commissioning the book.

Last but definitely not least, I would like to thank my son Luca, 9 years old at the time of writing, who didn't see me as often as he should have done while I tried to get this story right. I hope you never have to experience war, my son, and I hope you never feel you have to do anything to put yourself in the firing line. Appreciate the value of peace among nations and find a way to contribute to that peace.

Mark Ryan
2014

# Introduction: VC – and Human Being

The tears are streaming down his face, some of them seeping into his thick moustache. It is Easter 1939 and Sidney Frank Godley is standing in Saint Symphorien Military Cemetery, 3 miles south-east of Mons. Almost a quarter of a century has passed since horror swept through here and drove men to acts of desperate and extraordinary bravery and brutality. The Belgians are putting up a plaque to commemorate those moments. The man crying is Sidney to his family and Frank when he is with the other veterans, who are collectively known as 'The Old Contemptibles'. Sidney has a softer side and he's afraid to go to the dentist. Frank is the Victoria Cross winner who wasn't scared to take on the German army alone. They are the same man, of course. Today he is honouring the fallen and he can't stop the tears. Sidney Godley's family are standing beside him. His daughter Eileen, son Stanley and wife Nellie try to understand what he is going through. They haven't seen him like this before. Not in public. The emotion suppressed as a soldier on active service is coming through now, in peace time. And there is no shame in it. If Sidney Frank Godley doesn't have the right to cry, no one does.

'I should be there,' he says, staring at a patch of ground next to the grave of a very special man. It is the final resting place of Lieutenant Maurice James Dease, whose younger sister Maud is also on this trip. Dease and Godley are forever linked by history, for Maurice also won the Victoria Cross, the highest military accolade for valour, on that fateful day. Godley was a private in the 4th Battalion, Royal Fusiliers, part of a machine gun detachment commanded by Dease. On 23 August 1914, they made a defiant stand and kept hundreds of Germans at bay for as long as they could in the opening battle of the First World War.

Standing there in tears, Godley remembers the intensity of that battle, the men's realisation that they had been targeted. What an awful feeling that must have been, knowing that the enemy were deliberately concentrating their fire on this single point, this one bridge, and the men defending it. Maurice Dease, the most popular officer in the regiment, crying out above the fizzing sound of flying metal, urging his team to keep their machine guns going at all costs. Each man fighting for his life, yet knowing all the time that, the more they fought, the more sure they were to die. They must all have come to that conclusion, sooner or later. Those machine guns had become a magnet for the shells and bullets of a relentless enemy, who had whipped up such a deadly storm of fire that there was little hope of escape. It wasn't a question of whether you were going to be hit, it was when. Yet no man backed down. Not when they were led by an officer they all adored: Lieutenant Dease, a man who wouldn't give in.

Maurice Dease, trying for all he was worth to ignore the thud of the bullets as they ripped into his flesh, willing himself to blank out the searing pain so he could continue to do his job. Loveable Maurice, who refused to leave his men as they died one by one around him, after battling so heroically against overwhelming odds. Conscientious Dease, who never let his men do anything that he wasn't prepared to do himself – even die – ignoring the pleas of his commanding officer to have his wounds treated at a field hospital towards the rear. Back to the machine guns, they must never fall silent, so back Maurice went, time and again, until silence swamped everything.

'I should be down there,' repeats Godley, VC, still crying.

And, if Sidney hadn't been a cross-country runner, a footballer and cricketer, an all-round sportsman of supreme fitness and a beneficiary of the most incredible good fortune, he would have been down there. For death was sure to come calling, he knew that much when he stepped forward as the last man alive who knew how to fire a machine gun, clearing the bodies of friends out of the way as he took over. All alone against the might of the German army; the few left alive retreating, Godley the man making it possible, yet painfully, scarily alone. What a sickening feeling, knowing he couldn't hold them for much longer, firing until the last, realising he would be overrun, firing some more. When a shell skinned his back and a bullet entered his skull, Sidney knew death had arrived, yet it hadn't taken him. Another man who wouldn't give in; why wasn't he dead?

'I should be down there with him,' says Godley again, staring at the spot where Dease lay.

As she pictures the scene in 2013, Eileen's eyes are glistening too. It is almost 100 years after her father lived that day for the first time, the day which forever defined him. 'He pointed to the ground next to Dease and kept saying he should be down there with him, and then he turned to me and he was absolutely in tears,' she said. Eileen, 91 years old, is sitting in the corner of her front room in Clacton-on-Sea. The surprise and compassion are still visible in her strong features as she sees her father's turmoil all over again. Even if Sidney had succeeded in blanking out the worst of those memories, any number of little things could have set him off when he returned to such an emotionally charged place.

'The local children had put small bunches of daffodils on all the graves. They called them "Easter Lilies", and it was beautiful,' Eileen remembered. Her face lit up when she was reminded of the moment when two children had casually gone up to the front line to give her father something to eat and drink, just before the fighting started back in 1914. They had treated it like an adventure, almost like a picnic.

'"The innocence of a child". That's what dad used to say: "The innocence of a child". He loved that innocence and he was a wonderful dad. I think it was because he had such a hard time himself when he was small. Anyway, my dad remembered those two children at Mons. And, when we went back in 1939, he found those same two children, or they found him. They had grown up by then, of course. My dad hugged them so hard he almost squeezed them to death.'

Remembering what a fine and dashing man Maurice Dease was could only have added to the poignancy of the moment. Yet Dease was just as worried about what would happen to his beloved dog Dandy and the horses he also knew by name, when he went off to war. Like Godley, Dease had a soft side; but, as he showed at Mons, he could be extraordinarily tough and brave when it mattered. In fact, his courage is almost beyond our modern-day comprehension. If ever we found ourselves fighting a war and were struck by a bullet, wouldn't most of us hope a medic could get us out of there quickly enough to save our lives? That's not the way Dease or Godley reacted. They didn't think of their own safety at all.

Due to that courage, Maurice didn't live to have children or grandchildren, but his nephew – also named Maurice – has lovingly preserved his photographs and writings to keep his memory alive. Maud Dease, the hero's sister, learned to live with her grief sufficiently well to have a family. So the memories and the documents, the letters and photographs were passed down through the generations. The mischievous sense of humour, the bubbly character that made Lieutenant Maurice Dease, VC, so special are still there for all to see: the love for life, for people, horses and dogs are all apparent. There are even photographs of Dandy the fox terrier, who had become unofficial battalion mascot long before the build-up to war. Warm-hearted – that was Irish-born Maurice; a fine human being who forced himself to defy pain and behave almost as a super-human might on that terrible day back in 1914, until the reality of his mortality finally held sway.

Sidney Frank Godley, VC, survived and on a couple of occasions even spoke to members of the media about what had happened. But interviews were such formal affairs, even in the 1950s, and you didn't learn much about the real man and what made him tick. Luckily, he had children and grandchildren, who offer more depth with their insights and memories. Over the years, Sidney's living body gave up clues to those descendants about what it had been through as Private Frank Godley. His grandson Colin Godley remembers running a child-sized hand softly over the top of his head one day. 'I was just a little boy and I remember feeling this odd bump on the top of his head, like there was something hard in his skull that wasn't his skull. I recall the strange sensation but then I thought no more of it.'

Eileen has a more visual memory from her own childhood. In 2013 she still chuckled at the thought. 'I still remember my dad's back and all these darker patches of skin in many places. I was a little child when I saw it for the first time and I thought to myself: "Why is dad's skin dark here and light there? And why isn't my skin like that?" Later on he explained a bit about it, though he never told me exactly where the skin came from, he just smiled.'

That patchwork skin points to another remarkable part of this story, one which invites us to ask ourselves rather a dark question. If you stumbled across a badly wounded enemy soldier, who had in all probability just cut down many of your friends in the prime of their lives, wouldn't you be tempted to put him out of his misery? How far would you go to save his life, and then ensure future quality of life? Would you go so far as giving your enemy a series of intricate skin grafts, while millions were being slaughtered on both sides of the war?

The unusual generosity of the Germans certainly left Sidney's daughter flummoxed when she was a small child. 'I couldn't understand how he came to have these brown patches on his back, when I didn't have them on mine. Where dad had skin grafts, his back finished up brown. I can't remember how many there were, but quite a few.'

Unfortunately, the Germans weren't finished with causing wars, and they hadn't finished causing personal pain to Sidney Godley, either. As he led his daughter out of the St Symphorien Cemetery during that Easter of 1939 and headed home, happy that a commemorative plaque was now firmly nailed into Nimy railway bridge, he didn't know they were just months away from another world war.

There was talk of another war, but people wouldn't be stupid enough to start this madness all over again, surely? Sadly, the Germans would soon come pouring across Belgium and over the canal once again. They would bomb London far more than last time. And during the Second World War Sidney would have new and terrible reasons to shed fresh tears.

This is a story of violence and compassion in equal measure; humanity and inhumanity. Two men who happened to be caught up in the very worst of the First Battle of Mons, at Nimy railway bridge just outside the town. They couldn't have imagined they were about to win the first Victoria Crosses of the Great War. Sidney Frank Godley, an Arsenal fan who didn't like going to the dentist, and Maurice James Dease, a bird-watcher and horse-lover. They were ordinary, very likeable human beings, who did extraordinary things. Somewhere in their childhoods they developed steely streaks which helped them rise to the challenge in a crisis. Yet the childhoods of Dease and Godley could hardly have been more different.

The original plaque on Nimy bridge, dedicated to the Royal Fusiliers and the first VCs of the First World War, Dease and Godley.

# Privilege and Pain

What makes someone want to join the army? What makes them take a deliberate, carefully considered decision to adopt a career path that could end their life prematurely or traumatise them forever? For Maurice Dease and Sidney Frank Godley, the reasons weren't so very different from some of the motives for young people joining up today. Godley joined because he wanted to belong to something, because he had never quite belonged, not even to his own family. Maurice joined because he already had a sense of belonging, because an admired family member had joined before him.

'I think uncle Maurice always wanted to be a soldier like his uncle Gerald. They were close.' That simple, innocent statement from his nephew, Major Maurice French, a Korean War veteran, explains better than any other why Maurice Dease would find himself in a hail of bullets on 23 August 1914. It could be argued that his uncle Gerald had a lot to answer for, though naturally he wished his nephew no harm.

Gerald had been an adjutant in the 4th Militia Battalion of the Royal Fusiliers. He had served in the regiment from 1874 to 1892 and reached the rank of major. Gerald never saw action. So there were no tales of senseless carnage and despair from the influential uncle; no first-hand accounts of almost-impossible bravery either. Neither, perhaps, were there any protective warnings about what could happen if history swept up young Maurice in a tide of international tension and dropped him in the wrong time and place. Even if there had been such warnings, however, you get the feeling that Maurice would probably still have joined up. It is what young men of a certain stock and upbringing did in those days. Some still do.

Gerald Dease was a wealthy, powerful, charismatic figure in Maurice's native Ireland. He was county sheriff for County Westmeath in 1909, and Commissioner for National Education in Ireland. He had applied his natural authority far and wide in his day, becoming ADC to the governor of Tasmania, Lord Gormanston. Therefore, if Uncle Gerald had done something as a young man, it would have seemed to Maurice worth doing himself. After all, Maurice Dease was already linked to his uncle in a very special way.

Although Gerald had married Florence Helen Marley on 3 June 1896, he was almost 42 by then. The marriage was destined to produce no children, so Maurice was his heir. One day Gerald's spectacular stately home at Turbotston, Co. Westmeath, with its glorious hunting grounds, would belong to Maurice, if, of course, he lived that long. There was no obvious reason to suppose he wouldn't because, as the nineteenth century became the twentieth, there was no inevitability of a First World War. There were always tensions, of course, yet no hint that a global conflict was going to engulf almost everything and everyone. If Maurice's time in the army was relatively brief and drew him into no desperate battles from which he couldn't fight his way out, it could be seen as a distinguished stepping stone, a dashing interlude before he returned to the idyllic life in the Irish countryside. A soldier's existence would give him the adventures all young men craved; he might travel far and wide like Uncle Gerald. It sounded manly, exciting, even righteous. When he'd had his fill, the glorious setting of Turbotston awaited him, with its rolling green hills and enchanting woods. You didn't have to stay in the army forever. Show what you could do in your prime, come out before you reached middle age; then you could enjoy the rest of your life and all your lucky circumstances promised you. That seems to have been the general game plan. Put most simply, Maurice Dease had fallen under the spell of Gerald, and it would determine his destiny. They hunted together on horseback, the boy and the powerful older man. They probably talked of wars that Gerald hadn't been in but wished he had, such as the Boer War. You can just imagine Maurice hanging on Gerald's every word, while the boy's father, Edmund, looked on fondly and his mother, Katherine, was left to accept that boys will be boys. Had Maurice fallen under the spell of any relative other than Gerald, things might have been very different. Maurice French explained:

> I don't think there were any soldiers before that; there might have been but there certainly weren't any Royal Fusiliers. The soldiers were Uncle Gerald, Uncle Maurice and me. Uncle Maurice was a gentle soul,

I think. But that didn't exclude a desire to join the army. The way of thinking was completely different back then.

Maurice Dease was born in Gaulstown, Coole, Co. Westmeath, Ireland, on 28 September 1889. He was the only son of Edmund Fitzlawrence Dease, JP, and Katherine Dease, of Mullingar, Co. Westmeath. She was the eldest daughter of Maurice Murray of Beech Hill, Cork. Maurice Dease's grandfather was James Arthur Dease, JP, DL, Vice-Lieutenant of Cavan. It was a distinguished family from the upper echelons of Irish Catholic society. Indeed, the Dease family tree could be traced all the way back to Thomas More, executed by Henry VIII and well-known even to non-historians after the film *A Man for All Seasons* came out in the 1960s. While none of their family homes was quite as spectacular as Gerald's Turbotston, all were exceedingly comfortable. At such family retreats Maurice spent many happy years, the first nine of his childhood.

He adored the countryside and the pursuits that went with it. From his earliest years he went riding, and had a beautiful grey pony called Kitty. Maurice French, his nephew, still had all the photos in 2013 to illustrate what a lovely childhood Maurice had enjoyed over a century earlier. Major French had heard all the stories from his mother, Maud, Maurice Dease's sister:

> When he was a boy he was mad keen on hunting. His father was the man who ran the Westmead Hounds, so my Uncle Maurice grew up on ponies. His Uncle Gerald was very keen on hunting too. Maurice loved riding the ponies and horses above all. And he enjoyed shooting, partridges and that sort of thing, I expect. And I think, because my mother used to fish, he would have fished a bit too. Maurice was very much a country boy.

At the age of 9, he was suddenly transported into a very different world, at least during term time;, he was sent away to a preparatory school in Hampstead. There was nothing callous about it; this was simply the done thing among many in upper-class Irish society. Major French explained, 'It was the norm for well-to-do Catholic families to send their children across to English public schools to be educated.'

Maurice's first English school was St Basil's, Frognal Hall – afterwards known simply as Frognal Park School. The Deases were related to the Liddells, who already had a boy called Aiden at the same prep school. Like Maurice, Aidan Liddell would go on to win a posthumous Victoria Cross as machine gun officer of his battalion. While such terrible tests of character were still a world away, the process of toughening up had already started with their separation from their parents at such a tender age. Fortunately, figures of authority at such schools were also capable of remembering just how young their charges were. Before long Frognal was taken over by a certain Miss Maloney, who later became Mrs Ware. Maurice considered her to be so warm and caring that he never forgot her kindness. And he was in particular need of such qualities in 1899 and 1900, after he contracted scarlet fever and measles, and spent weeks in the school infirmary.

He was already resilient enough to get over these setbacks, and more than ready to idolise those whose bravery on far-flung battlefields captured the imagination of many a schoolboy. From a postcard he sent to his father on 2 October 1900, it is clear that he was already attracted to matters military. The postcard is a picture of an infantryman directing a cavalry officer during the Boer Wars. Maurice, who had just turned 11, is brief and to the point:

> Thank you very much for your letter and chocolates you sent me for my birthday. We played football yesterday morning and it was a very good game. I have very little news to tell you now as I told it all to mother yesterday. MD.

The year 1902 was a landmark in the childhood of Maurice Dease. He experienced his first hunt on the back of his pony, Kitty, on 13 January. The Westmeath Hounds met at Turbotston, the home of his beloved Uncle Gerald, and they rode the hunt from Pakenham Hall, the beautiful home of the Earls of Longford. The military pasts of important family and friends couldn't be forgotten, and the way the Pakenhams led their lives might also have influenced Dease to make decisions which would cut short his life. Major French reflected:

> A lot of those Irish boys at that time went into the Royal Fusiliers for one reason or other. The Pakenham family was another who chose that route. They were neighbours in Mullingar, and Pakenham Hall became known as Tullynally Castle. They weren't Catholics at that stage; they'd been Catholics and then lapsed, but a lot of them were Royal Fusiliers.

The fact that Maurice was a page boy at the wedding of Lord Longford – who was also destined to be killed in the First World War – indicated the strong relationship between the families. And such established families weren't going to shy away from playing their part when the fighting began. Men who could in theory have stayed out of the war on the safer side of the Irish Sea chose instead to put themselves in the firing line, and paid the ultimate price.

Maurice always seemed to follow his conscience; he was a staunch Catholic from beginning to end. He took his first Communion on 14 June 1902 at the Dominican Church, Haverstock Hill, London. But it was back in Ireland during the summer holidays that he was confirmed in the private chapel of the bishop's palace in Mullingar. Even someone so deeply religious had no trouble reconciling army life with his Catholic faith. Sometimes you had to fight for what was right. And in the eyes of the British and the English-educated, Britain was always right.

If Maurice Dease was well on the way to becoming a Royal Fusilier even before he reached his teens, it could be argued that Sidney Frank Godley was destined to join him in the regiment because of things that had happened to him when he was even younger.

The Godly family (the spelling of the surname only changed when Sidney joined the army and the recruiting officer put the 'e' in it) was no stranger to extreme violence – at least George Godly of the Metropolitan Police wasn't. George, Sidney's first cousin once removed, worked on the most famous case in history. Indeed, Detective Sergeant George Godly's efforts on the 'Jack the Ripper' investigation team enhanced his reputation considerably. They never caught the murderer, of course, the mystery man who butchered eleven women horribly in the East End of London between 1888 and 1891, mutilating them in various indescribable ways. But it was said by a colleague at the time that 'Mr Godly's knowledge of these crimes is perhaps as complete as that of any officer concerned.' The Whitechapel Murders, as they were known back then, still fascinate amateur and professional sleuths today. And George might have become the most celebrated policeman in history had he actually detained the world's most notorious murderer. There was a moment during the investigation that his boss thought George had earned just such a claim to fame. For Inspector Abberline, who led the investigation, declared at one point during the hunt that Godly had managed to arrest the Ripper and the case could be solved at last. Sadly he was mistaken and the culprit never was locked away, which must have caused sleepless nights for Godly and the rest of the team.

It is very doubtful whether Sidney Godley would have been exposed to any of the horrific details of the case as a child. The murders happened just before he was born or while he was still a toddler. Besides, Sidney's immediate family had enough of their own problems to worry about, such as how to make ends meet. Such factors closer to home would deny Sidney the sense of stability all children crave. But it wasn't lost on his grandson Colin that Sidney lived much of his adult life in a general area of the East End which had been notorious for its violent cases – and would be again. 'We've got Jack the Ripper and the Krays all within a mile of here, we're in the middle of it really,' said Colin from the comparative safety of Stepney Green in the twenty-first century. But Sidney's birth certificate shows that he didn't start out in the rough, tough East End:

BIRTH CERTIFICATE:
Birth in the Sub-District of East Grinstead in the Counties of Sussex and Surrey.
Fourteenth August 1889, Northend, East Grinstead, Sussex, U.S.D.
Sidney Frank
Boy
Father: Frank Godly
Mother: Avis Godly formerly Newton.
Father's profession: Painter Journeyman.
Informant Details: A. Godly. Mother. Northend. East Grinstead.
Thirteenth September 1889.
Registrar: W.H. Wood.

The voting list for 1889 gives Sid's father as living in Imberhorne Lane, East Grinstead. He had married Avis Newton and at first life in Sussex looked promising for them, though their happiness was to be short-lived. Frank's family had lived in the East Grinstead and Felbridge area for generations. Sidney's grandfather was William Godly, a pit sawyer. That meant he would saw wood at the mines, to create the framework to bolster the tunnels and prevent fatal collapses of the structures. Much later in Godley's life, he was destined to end up working in a mine too – through no choice of his own. For now William Godly provided the only link to mining, and he lived in the wonderfully named local village of Mount Noddy in 1881.

Sidney's paternal grandmother was Harriet Pattenden, from a large family in nearby Horne, and there was no immediately obvious reason why the young boy shouldn't have been able to benefit from the stability of wider family links and a sense of long family history in the area. Like Sidney's grandfather William, his great-uncle John Godly also worked with wood. But John showed a finer, more artistic touch, and even carved the pews at St Swithun's church in East Grinstead. Sidney's family line can be traced back to a George Godly in 1770 and it is believed the family had been around East Grinstead since the 1500s. But sad circumstances were about to uproot the future hero from an area which had provided so much security and continuity for his forefathers.

The 1891 Census has Frank Godly, aged 24, living with Avis Godly, aged 29, and her mother, Harriet Newton, aged 69. Frank and Avis have two children by then – Kate 'Kit' Godly, aged 3, and 1-year-old Sidney Godly. Harriet would probably have acted as a nanny to the children and have done all she could to earn her keep. But it might not have been easy for Frank Godly to live with his mother-in-law, and there are suggestions that he became unsettled. He may have looked elsewhere for an outlet for his domestic frustrations; and domestic tensions didn't make for the happiest of environments for the earliest years of Sidney's life.

Eileen reflected, 'I think he envied people who had a relationship with their mum and dad. His dad wasn't all a dad should be. I'm sure part of the reason my dad was such a lovely dad was because he didn't have an easy upbringing. He was born and brought up in Sussex for the first part of his childhood. He was the second eldest after his sister Kit, and then there was his younger brother Percy, and another sister, Ella. And that was the first family.'

Poor Sidney wasn't able to enjoy a relationship with his mother for very long because she died in Hailsham, Sussex, in 1896, when he was just 6 years old. 'We're not sure but we think she may have died during childbirth,' said Colin. Eileen said, 'I don't know what his mum died of, I don't know what happened to her. But my dad always said that his father had the next wife waiting in the wings. His father married again, and I don't really know much about that part of his life. If anyone started talking about it, my dad would quickly move onto something else. He would change the subject, you see, I think it was a bit of a sore point for him.'

When Sidney lost his mother, the consequences were far-reaching. Since Frank was a painter and decorator struggling to make a living, there was no way he could work and look after all his children at the same time. So Sidney was sent away from his own home, to live elsewhere with anyone who could be found. Records show he was fostered locally by the Wren family at one stage, though little is known about them. Sidney was then passed between relatives whenever they felt they could help to raise him. Colin explained:

When Sidney's mum died, he lost his family, because his father couldn't look after him and he got moved around. I don't know why Frank

Godly couldn't make a living and find a way to look after him, but it didn't happen that way. So when his mum died when he was only six and his father moved him to relatives and the like, it couldn't have been easy at all. The first lot he went to, he stayed with a police inspector at Redhill for a short while, a distant relation. Then he went to Leigh in south London, and on he went from there.

'He had a rough old time being moved around,' Eileen observed. It must have been a confusing time too, being uprooted just when he was getting used to a new environment and starting to consider it home.

At one point Sidney found that he was right back where he had started – living with his father. To say that conditions had changed was something of an understatement. Some years earlier, it appears, Frank Godly had met an Irish woman called Lizzie, who already had children of her own. They married and moved in together in Sidcup, Kent. The 1901 Census tells an intriguing story. It has Frank Godly, then aged 34, living with his new wife, Lizzie Godly. She was aged 28 and there were more children on the scene. Sidney's younger brother, Percy Henry Godly, was then 10 years old, having been born in East Grinstead. But also listed is William John Godly, who was 11 years old, and had been born in Sidcup. Does this suggest that Sidney's father may have started to have children with Lizzie while still married to Sidney's mother Avis? Linda Godley, married to Colin, put it like this: 'Percy was his real brother and then he had half-brothers. William is a step-brother, Reginald is a step-brother.'

It was certainly a confusing situation. At least Sidney Godly is registered to the same family address in Sidcup, an indication that he may have been welcomed back into his father's family fold by then. At 12 years old, he attended the Sidcup National School and was probably considered old enough to work odd jobs and pay his own way. He developed an affection for Kent County Cricket Club, and this quintessentially English sport would always remain a passion for him.

'He was born in Sussex but Kent was always his team,' Eileen insisted emphatically. 'I think he liked living in Sidcup.' In 1920, after his terrible ordeal in the First World War, Sidney visited his old school in Sidcup and he was presented with an inscribed black marble clock and £150 worth of war bonds. He told the pupils there it felt like coming home, so life must have been tolerable when he was 12, even if the family situation at home was still chaotic. As usual, however, any stability wasn't to last. Pretty soon the pressure of sheer numbers and increasing tensions with his father led to young Sidney being cast out of the family fold again.

He went to live with an uncle and aunt in Willesden, north London. That was where he would eventually meet his future wife, who worked in service for an old lady in the area. For now, the source of Sidney's stability was decent schooling, though even that was short-lived. He attended the Henry Street School in St John's Wood, which today is a highly sought-after area, and was respectable back then too. Sidney was also sent to St John's Sunday School and was confirmed in 1903. Given his growing love for cricket, Eileen considers it 'quite possible' that he was able to sneak into Lord's cricket ground occasionally to watch the matches there. It is hard to imagine that the famous gates, so near yet so far, might have remained closed to him; that would have been almost too sad as an added frustration to an already troubled childhood. Yet he formed no lasting bond with Middlesex County Cricket Club, whose home was Lord's, so we can't discount such torment either. What we know is that Godley supported Kent for the rest of his days. Still, for a teenager in England at the start of the twentieth century, supporting a sports team wasn't the priority; supporting yourself, to make sure you could eat, was what mattered. Compared to many poor souls, Sidney had fallen on his feet. The emotional deprivations which came with having no mother and a distracted father hadn't been accompanied by starvation. In that regard he could count himself lucky, because such a fate befell many in Victorian times, and survival into one's later teens hadn't always been a foregone conclusion.

For Maurice Dease, childhood was so much more straightforward. He had continued to study in London, a world away from Sidney Godley, even though they inhabited the same city. And during holidays he had always returned to the paradise of family and country life in Ireland, a joyful environment offering a quality of life that Sidney would never experience. The short voyages across the Irish Sea would continue, though Maurice was given a new English base in a huge place which was both harsh and impressive.

Just before the summer holidays of 1902, Maurice had passed the Oxford Preliminary Examination, a success which underlined his academic credentials and made him suitable for the next phase of his learning. Maurice was sent to Stonyhurst College in Lancashire, where he would remain from 1903 until 1907. Stonyhurst was where many wealthy Catholic families educated their children. Aidan Liddell had made the same journey north to the prep school. Another of Dease's relatives, Charles Waterton – a noted Victorian naturalist – had studied there.

The college had been founded in 1593 by the Jesuit Fathers of the Society of Jesus, though the first 200 years of its history saw it based abroad to avoid persecution in Britain. Those old boys who returned to Britain to become missionary priests risked their lives in the seventeenth century. Twenty-two of them were publicly executed for their faith, a sacrifice never forgotten by future generations.

The chaos of the French Revolution brought the college home towards the end of the eighteenth century. Stonyhurst Hall in Lancashire was secured. By the mid-Victorian era, school life revolved around the magnificent St Peter's church, which looked as though it had been inspired by King's College Chapel, Cambridge. Though the surroundings were spectacular, the boys were anything but pampered. The suffering and whole-hearted commitment that was such an integral part of the history of Stonyhurst became etched in the steely character of the pupils. Even at the start of the twentieth century, there was still a defiant pride at the way the college had survived and then thrived to become one of the very best of its kind in Britain. Yet the ethos of the school wasn't overwhelmingly restrictive – quite the reverse. The reward for that difficult history was sufficient freedom to follow one's artistic leanings, to explore one's potential in a variety of ways. Still, lashings of rigorous discipline under-pinned the place at the same time, and therefore there was no chance of a pupil going soft or escaping from his responsibilities into the lazy idealism of his own dreamy world. Being educated at Stonyhurst was to know that you had a responsibility to your fellow man, and to be taught that, if called upon to do so, a boy had to summon the necessary character and courage to thrive in adversity.

The school motto was *Quant Je Puis* – as much as I can. Whatever you did at Stonyhurst, you were expected to give everything to it. Maurice Dease had no problem with that. And, although the sheer size of Stonyhurst must have seemed daunting at first to a sensitive young boy, he was also a hearty, adaptable individual and soon found his feet. Maurice French reflected:

I think the impression I've always had is that he was quiet, perhaps rather shy, a very gentle sort of guy and I think very religious. But I don't think he would have found life at school in England all that difficult. It was normal to build a child's character in this way. For example my father had nine brothers, many of whom were killed in the First World War, and they all went to school in England, mostly to Downside and Beaumont and places like that. Coming and going between Ireland and England was no problem.

And, besides, while at Stonyhurst, Maurice had a reminder of the country life he loved and all the glories of nature. For one of Dease's great passions at Stonyhurst was the school aviary. The birds were something he doubtless looked forward to seeing again when he returned from Ireland, because it was a constantly changing, sometimes brutal feathered community. Maurice French explained, 'Uncle Maurice was the "bird man" at Stonyhurst, he was responsible for the aviaries as a boy.'

The aviary had been created in the early 1880s by Friar Eyre SJ (Society of Jesus), who was rector of the college at the time. He had begun by buying some canaries, rumoured to have come from a local lunatic asylum. During the following twenty years the aviary had flourished so well that new, spacious premises had been built. As a boy who had always been at one with nature back home in his native Ireland, Dease was never happier than when he was involved with the aviary and its many, varied inhabitants. And he was so conscientious that he earned new responsibilities in the aviary, first keeping records as 'Clerk of Works', and then as 'Head Aviary Boy'.

Such accolades mirrored his progress in the wider school, where the boys weren't members of different houses, as at most public schools. At Stonyhurst boys were organised into year groups known as Playrooms instead, and each year could relax in its own common room.

Looking back at his time there, *The Stonyhurst Magazine* of October 1914 provides an engaging portrait of Dease during his years at the college:

> Good-natured, amiable yet full of determination, he was Head of the Third Playroom, and later of the Second Playroom. He was Aviary Boy during his time at Stonyhurst, looking after the birds there. He discharged his duties with characteristic thoroughness. One permanent native official of the aviary used his best Lancastrian to describe Dease like this: 'Yo've nobbut to tell yon lad what wants doin', and it's bahn to be done.' He was so dependable that any task given to Dease was 'bahn to be done' – and done well.

As Aviary Boy, Dease wrote articles on local ornithology for *The Stonyhurst Magazine* in 1906 and 1907. In 1906, at the age of 17, Maurice showed an appreciation for words and birds in equal measure as he described some illustrations:

> In the first picture we see the birds in the well known attitude which suggested the lines by Somerville

Lo! At his siege the heron
Upon the bank of some small purling brook
Observant stands to take his scaley prize.

The same bird is shown in the third picture … with his 'scaley prize'
in his beak. Not that he won his prize without a struggle. For at least
twenty minutes the honours were with the tench who 'kept his end up
sturdily til he was badly winded by repeated digs in the ribs …'

In time, Dease would also know what it was like to 'keep his end up sturdily'
against a superior, predatory force, before being overcome by his wounds at
last. And even as a child, Maurice certainly wasn't squeamish about the brutality of nature; that much is clear in his writings:

The death rate has almost reached the vanishing point; the only regret-
table incident being the death of a hen Arctic Knot, who reached us in a
moribund condition from starvation and died the same night. When we
add that the herons refused her plucked corpse next morning, with an
air of pained surprise, her emaciated condition will be obvious.

Yet only someone with a great love for his subject would be so observant and
clearly so fascinated by the nuances and pecking orders he discovered among
the birds under his care: 'The Albino blackbird, who plays second bully to the
quail, has lately found an imitator of his tameness in a thrush, who waits at
the gate of the aviary and vies with him in snapping worms from the fingers
of the aviary keepers …'

Dease was also clever enough to understand an opportunity to speak to
those who might improve the aviary and help it to survive for generations
to come. He was unreservedly grateful for any generous gesture and witty
with it:

While on the subject of benefactors we may conclude by thanking
Fr Rector on behalf of the birds for his generous offer of new shrubs
for the aviary and we may assure him in their name that when the
shrubs arrive,
'The feathered choir …
'Perched on the evening bough shall join your worship.'

Maurice Dease

But ensuring the survival of the aviary was often an uphill struggle for Maurice. The following year, 1907, Dease sounded more frustrated by the disinterest of his fellow human beings than the cruelty of natural selection. He wrote:

> The rage for presenting birds to the aviary has not yet set in. Meanwhile the praiseworthy efforts of some of the birds themselves to increase their own numbers have been frustrated by various causes. The green–finches alone have succeeded in hatching out several broods of healthy young ones. Out of a total of sixty-two eggs laid by the hen Californian Quail, only one chick has reached maturity. At present the White Java Sparrows are sitting on eggs in a small cocoanut. The corpse of their eldest born has just been ejected by the nest …

The dead had to be cast out, if those left behind were to have the chance to live. Seven years later, in the final hours of his life, Maurice would discover that under extreme circumstances, the same behaviour could be observed in humans.

# 2

# Birdman, Ironman, Army

Maurice Dease was much too positive to be left disillusioned by anything for long and the aviary remained a source of joy and surprise. For every unpleasant moment in life, he saw at least twice as many charming and humorous moments to make up for it. Dease was one of those marvellous people who saw value in everyone and everything; he adored people and he adored animals in equal measure.

His enjoyment of Stonyhurst's birds shone through once again as he returned to the subject of those mesmerising herons, and he seemed transfixed by a male's attempt to drop a hint to his prospective mate, amused by the bird's hopeless lack of subtlety when the courtship didn't go his way:

> Moreover this 'fayre byrde' evidently possesses a sense of sly humour. During the vacation he was seen building a nest of twigs round the legs of his shy mate, varying the process occasionally by depositing some sticks on her back. Whenever she tried to move, he gripped her by the neck and held her in position.

Dease saw humour and beauty in almost everything, including the following exchange with a British workman at the school. Although he may teasingly question the man's intelligence, he also shows warmth towards the butt of his joke, and seems to have more respect for the worker, as an enthusiastic if ignorant observer of the birds, than he has for more educated and wealthy visitors, who possess the means to donate or strengthen the aviary's numbers but choose not to do so.

Maurice wrote:

The appreciation of intelligent visitors is always gratifying to an aviary keeper. A few days ago I saw a British workman looking at the Albino blackbird.

'That is a white blackbird,' I ventured.

The BW removed his pipe from his lips. 'Nay, it isn't,' said he.

I stared.

He condescended to explain. ''E's white, ya see, so 'e can't be a black-bird, can 'e?'

Que dire? [What does one say?]

After this all the subsequent information I offered him was received with marked suspicion.

But it is good to encourage visitors, even if only one in a thousand presents a bird to the aviary.

M. Dease

Maurice's attention was captured by all manner of creatures, not just birds. He clearly wasn't alone in his love of animals at Stonyhurst, though school-boy cruelty sometimes appears to have done battle with that love. Since he couldn't change human nature any more than he could change the charac-teristics of his beloved animals, Maurice seems to have celebrated the quirky interactions between animals and children in all their comic glory. To read the following passage, written by Maurice in the early summer of 1907, is to understand just why Dease was so popular and why he remained so loved by his contemporaries when he carried his humour and zest for life into his army days:

At this time of year we may suitably begin our Aviary Notes with a word on the subject of playground pets. Just now the third playground is the special home of the tortoise, the grass snake and the lizard. There, groups of zoologists may be seen stimulating the pace of pairs of racing tortoises decorated with their owners' ribbons. If not fast goers, these Chelonians are at least remarkable weight carriers. One small tortoise certainly lived through the ordeal of supporting the weight of his boy proprietor stand-ing with both feet on his back. Another survived a fall from the top storey of the College to the grass plot below. After this who can doubt the truth of the legend that a certain Greek philosopher was killed by a tortoise dropped on his head by an eagle who had mistaken the sage's bald cranium for a stone?

The many uses to which a tortoise can be put might seem to render the pleasures of snake charming trivial in comparison; but as everyone knows, in hot weather a grass snake makes an excellent cool wrist band or muffler, and the sensation of something wriggling inside one's waistcoat undoubtedly tends to relieve the monotony of class time. Moreover, unless unduly irritated there is no reason to fear that a grass snake will make himself perceptible to any other sense besides that of sight and touch.

Lizards on the other hand have an awkward habit of crawling out of your pocket or sleeve and betraying their presence by jumping from one person to another. However they are more easily fed than snakes, whose mouths have to be prised open to admit a small frog, minnow or plug of raw meat pushed down by a pen-holder. Whereas the lizard readily snaps meal worms off the hand and drinks till he looks like a sausage on legs.

After reptiles come birds, as every evolutionist knows. And of bird pets it is abundantly evident that Jackdaws are the prime favourites. Sleepers in the west wing will soon be awakened at dawn by the music of squalling young Jackdaws. Fifteen of these charming pets have recently been transferred from their nurseries on the college chimneys to care of their noisy foster fathers in the playground. It is hoped that the epidemic of indigestion which carried off so many last year will be an object lesson to the latter of cramming their charges with a surfeit of cold beef, cake and lemonade. We can recommend instead soaked dog biscuit, with, let us say, a dash of Birds custard powder, as a wholesome diet that keeps well.

In the aviary proper the birds have been displaying their usual activity in nest building. As for those busy architects, the Weaver birds, their neat pockets of plaited grass may be seen in every direction. Some of these have been appropriated by other birds as the builders show no disposition to live or lay in them. Besides building nests of their own design the Weavers have been obliging enough to roof in several of the unoccupied nests with domes of woven grass, leaving a small entrance hole in the side. Inside a deserted thrush's nest thus roofed in was found the corpse of the builder ...

M. Dease

June 1907

Before long Maurice Dease would be swapping birds' nests for machine gun nests, and he was probably already starting to lean in that direction. While the fascinating world of nature would continue to demand Maurice's attention, he also experienced the pull of the military at Stonyhurst. The Boer War in South Africa was on every schoolboy's mind, with its endless possibilities for heroism and adventure. Scores of Stonyhurst old boys were serving with a variety of regiments and wrote back to the school magazine with their colourful stories. If Dease hadn't already decided upon joining the army like his Uncle Gerald, the Boer War must have captured his imagination further still. Despite its deeply religious nature, the school embraced the war unquestioningly. It was all about doing one's duty for God, queen and country. You fought the good fight; you didn't question whether it was right or wrong to do so, because someone above you had decided it was right. And, when victories came in the Boer War, Stonyhurst embraced them as though the foundations for such glory had been built right there, as well as at other like-minded places.

Thus the liberation of Ladysmith prompted great rejoicing and running up of flags. The Stonyhurst magazine reported how, 'On the Friday they had a football match and a concert in the evening, which was, of course, largely patriotic. Father Rector said a few words on the greatness of the occasion, and called attention to the prominent part taken in the war by specially Catholic regiments.'

Three months later Mafeking was relieved and Stonyhurst celebrated by playing cricket all day. Britain was one of the great forces in the world, the empire still the envy of other European nations, and it was going to be down to the next generation of would-be soldiers to keep it that way. Even if you didn't join the army, you could still be made ready to fight any invader and given the skills to cope with any crisis. Therefore, as the twentieth century began, the Boer War had another knock-on effect: the formation of a cadet corps at the school. *The Stonyhurst Magazine* couldn't hide its excitement:

At last the Cadet Corps is an actuality. And, as usual, everyone is asking why there was not a Cadet Corps before? The answer might be difficult to find, but it is certain that the South African War has brought it home to us that the civilian soldier, with a good rifle, and a certain amount of drill and skill in firing is a very formidable foe: and our long casualty lists tell only too eloquently, what havoc a volunteer army can work when well handled and led.

The latest generation of boys were spoiling for a fight of their own; and in time they would get one. Dease didn't intend to remain a 'civilian soldier' either. While at Stonyhurst, he served as a cadet in the newly established Officers Training Corps, and it is recorded that he was a below-average shot scoring 121 out of 200 in the annual course of musketry in 1906. Perhaps a healthy number of those partridges he had hunted for as a smaller boy in Ireland had flown away to survive after all. Perhaps, given his love for birds, he hadn't wanted to kill them in the first place. At any rate, the fact that he wasn't a naturally gifted marksman at that stage of his development as a man didn't deter him from the course he had already pretty much decided to take.

On the same page as his aviary notes in *The Stonyhurst Magazine* of 1907, there was a column full of 'Cadet Corps Notes'. Maurice would undoubtedly have taken part in the following:

> May 19th, Whit-Sunday. There was a church parade in the morning before High Mass. The two Corps formed up in the play-ground and went through a few manoeuvres before Col. Irwin and several visitors. As is usual on these occasions the Seniors found some difficulty in accommodating their step to that of the Juniors, but this defect was scarcely noticeable; otherwise the parade was quite satisfactory.

Schoolboys playing at soldiers. But it would all become deadly serious before Maurice had seen very many more summers.

Some twenty-first-century readers might wonder how such a kind, conscientious, deeply religious boy could have set his sights on such a violent life. Yet, as we have seen, religion and war went hand in hand in those unquestioning days. And Maurice Dease was exceptionally kind and truly gentle. His warm personal qualities were recorded in the October 1914 edition of *The Stonyhurst Magazine,* the one which looked back on his short life:

> To see old father Myers, then a man of no small weight, limping steadily along to say Mass, leaning on the arm of his favourite server, Maurice Dease, was an object lesson in the respectful and thoughtful sympathy of the right-minded boy for the vulnerable old age. 'There is something very lovable about that boy,' the old man used to say. 'There is a Lancastrian word which hits off his character – he is jannock.' The English Dialect Dictionary says that 'jannock' means 'fair, straightforward and genuine'.

It was a lovely tribute, and one echoed by so many of the men who counted themselves lucky enough to be his fellow officers once he joined the Royal Fusiliers. Yet Dease was also more than happy to choose a path in life which he knew might end in him killing other people or being killed himself. There was nothing gentle or sensitive about that; but, if Maurice was to remain 'jannock' all his life, he had to be prepared to fight for what he believed in, to protect a certain way of life. If courage was the quality that guaranteed all others, he would show he had it. From what we know of Maurice Dease as a person, it is hard to imagine that he actually wanted to kill people. But he was clearly a chivalrous individual and becoming an army officer would allow him to demonstrate that chivalry. His Uncle Gerald had joined the army and it hadn't done him any harm. Nor had he been forced to kill anyone. Perhaps Maurice felt he owed it to his uncle to choose an identical career path. If he was to receive so much land and property in return, as part of his inheritance, Maurice wanted to please Gerald, the man who still treated him like the son he never had. Maurice was just a teenager, he was impressionable, he wanted to do the right thing, and so he bowed to the strongest influence, the man who seemed to hold his future in his hands. Dease's nephew, Major Maurice French explained:

> He probably decided to become a soldier at Stonyhurst. He thought, 'Well I'll do the same as my uncle. I'll go into the Fusiliers.' I think Maurice always knew he would get the Estate at Turbitston, because Uncle Gerald had no children. So Maurice was the only male heir. And so he thought he would join the army, in due course get married, and go back and run the place at Turbitston.

So much sadness is contained in that last sentence. Plans for a perfect life and total fulfilment; plans that were to be dashed horribly. And, though Maurice Dease was destined to live almost twenty-five years, and therefore more than many, he really hadn't lived very much at all. His nephew added, 'I think I've got photographs of Maurice with various cousins, but he certainly never had a proper girlfriend as far as we know. I think my mother would have told me.'

Destiny had taken hold of Maurice Dease and wouldn't let go now. He left Stonyhurst in June 1907 and entered Army College Wimbledon in September of that same year. He then moved on to Sandhurst, where he struck up a friendship with Francis Steele, with whom he would eventually face the German onslaught at Mons.

After Sandhurst, Dease was commissioned on 25 May 1910 and joined the 4th Battalion, Royal Fusiliers (City of London Regiment). His choice of regiment was predictable: his uncle, Major Gerald Dease, had served with the same regiment. From that moment on, the fate of Maurice Dease was sealed. He was starting out on something new, he was an adult at last, a man; he was excited about the future and he was just as keen to prove himself in the wider world as any young man – perhaps more.

In October of that year he was selected for a two-week course in mountain warfare, which was held in North Wales. There are photographs of him on cold-looking, craggy slopes, listening to instructors, sucking up new knowledge in the kind of rugged surroundings he adored. In stark contrast, there were also ceremonial duties to perform, when he and his fellow officers would don dashing uniforms and wear scarlet tunics with heavy 'bearskin' helmets on their heads. On these occasions, the only enemies were boredom or the heat during summer, when men would faint due to the collision of unnatural uniforms and rising temperatures. But this was still a dashing life, the crowds would cheer and the Royal Fusiliers commanded respect wherever they went. Maurice was loving every moment … but would there come a time when he would have to fight in a war?

The answer was yes – and the same would be true for Sidney Godley.

Eileen remembered sketchy details of what her father Sidney had told her about the remainder of his childhood, before he too joined the army. 'He'd lived a while with his uncle and aunt in Willesden. At one point he had gone back into his father's family, when he was old enough to earn his living – at about fourteen, I should think. They had him back, but it didn't last.' Once again, father and son didn't appear to see eye to eye. Had Sidney worked out that his father, Frank, wasn't all he should have been to his mother, Avis, even when she was alive? You can imagine Sidney trying to find some common ground between them, helping Frank do some painting and decorating, before their relationship soured again. After such a fragmented childhood, the bond between them was fragile, easily frayed at the edges. Sidney had been through too much already to have his confidence destroyed again by his own flesh and blood. He went back to the Willesden and Harlesden area, where an elderly couple offered him the crucial stability every teenager needs as he turns from boy to man – and a job, too. Eileen explained:

> An elderly couple fostered him for his last childhood years. He liked that because this elderly couple had an ironmonger's shop. He got on alright with them. He was at the ironmongers for four or five years. When they weren't working, it was the old gentleman who introduced

my dad to big football matches. He used to take him and his brother Percy in a pony and trap to the football.

The ironmonger's shop was in the Kilburn High Road. Sidney learned a related trade as he sold goods to customers. That apprenticeship enabled him to state on official documents that he was also a plumber. Colin explained, 'After he went to Harlesden and Willesden, he became a plumber's merchant and plumber. I don't know whether they called them ironmongers as such, but he has often been described like that.'

A lot of the time, Godley was stuck in the shop, helping the elderly couple who had done so much to help him to keep his head above the water. Thanks to that sort of kindness, he had survived family tragedy, trauma and rejection to become a kind young man. He poured all his energies into what was fairly mundane work, which nevertheless gave him the chance to pay off of a personal debt of gratitude to the owners. But after a few years, when he became a man in his own right, he was ready to go his own way, to find a girlfriend, and perhaps even have a family of his own eventually.

Although he wasn't tall, Godley was athletic, good-looking and already appeared quite self-assured. A tough upbringing and the knowledge that you had survived everything that life had thrown at you could give a young man a certain confidence, though there would have been an underlying vulnerability too. Sidney lacked any trace of arrogance, partly because he didn't have much to be arrogant about, partly because it wasn't in his nature. He had been swept this way and that through his tender years, but now he had grown up and his feet were firmly on the ground. This blend of qualities made him attractive to the opposite sex, and it was only a matter of time before he met someone he liked too. Eileen explained:

He met my mother, Eliza Norman, at a wedding. It was my mother's cousin, Will Norman, who was getting married. They all lived round a place called Gray's Corner. And guess who Will Norman was marrying? My dad's sister, Kit Godly! Her real name was actually Kate but she was 'Auntie Kit' to us. So my mother and father were related through the marriage but not through blood. They were related through mum's cousin and through dad's sister. Will and Kit's wedding was before the First World War.

Whereas he was known by many as Frank after he joined the army, Godley introduced himself to Eliza 'Nellie' Norman as Sid. They hit it off straight away, and in time Sid and Nellie became an item. Eileen said, 'I don't think there can have been a very long series of meetings, not a long courtship before war broke out. They had probably fallen in love with each other before the war, but they didn't get round to doing anything about it in terms of getting married.' Colin believed they had plenty of time for a pre-war courtship, but decided not to make anything official:

> My Nan was in service, my grandfather was in the plumbers. They met before he joined the army in 1909, so he might even have still been a teenager. She was a bit older, but they were sweethearts before the war. At least they knew each other before the war – how deep it was I don't know.

They seemed smitten and Godley's other grandson, Andy Slade, pointed out, 'The seeds had been sewn for the future they hoped to have together.' It was true. The war was going to place certain stresses and restrictions on Sid and Nellie, but the slow-burning romance was destined to last all through that world war … and then another … and for years beyond that.

Godley couldn't see the future but he knew at the start of 1909 was that he didn't want to remain a plumber or become an ironmonger for life. Although he had enjoyed his time with his foster parents, he never really felt he truly belonged. He hadn't chosen to be an ironmonger; the owners weren't really his parents. He would always remain grateful to them, but it was time to make his own choices and go out into the wider world. They had done more than enough for him.

How did he come to make his next move? It wasn't very difficult to see why the army might have provided him with the answers he was looking for. Colin thinks he knows why Sidney joined up:

> You know why I think he joined the army? I think he wanted to belong. After all he'd been through in his childhood, being moved here and there, I think he wanted to belong and he saw the army as a big family to belong to, something he could always be part of …

In the army, he knew he would belong all right. They owned you. That might not always feel good, but it was going to feel better than being disowned, which is how his childhood must have felt to Sidney at times. He wasn't the sort of person to leave his foster parents in the lurch, though. He probably waited until they had an alternative source of help in the shop, because that was the sort of person he was. Then, at the age of 20, he began life in the battalion, where everyone was indeed part of one big family – whatever the rank and background. He had fulfilled all his responsibilities to his real family and foster family, at least as many as he felt he could fulfil, and now it was time to think of himself for a change. It must have been a relief to have that troubled and dependent period of his life finally negotiated, and reach a place where he felt just the same as everyone else in essence – a soldier. Eileen explained, 'As soon as he could get into the army, he did that. I know that for a fact.'

Godley enlisted in the Royal Fusiliers on 13 December 1909. In the case of almost anyone else, it might seem a strange time to have joined up, with Christmas just approaching. But the timing seems to say much about Sidney's mindset. Christmas was a time when he might have thought about his family, with all its painful complications. Christmas was a time when perhaps he felt a burden to others, when the lack of a genuine family unit could have hurt most. So there really was no better time to join up.

There was no threat of war. He was sent to the same battalion as Maurice Dease, the 4th Royal Fusiliers, though as usual he was at the opposite end of the spectrum. As a private, Sidney belonged to the Royal Fusiliers so completely once he signed up that they even changed his name. He wasn't Godly any more, he was Godley. He didn't mind. What did his name matter anyway? He was a number – 13814. Colin explained:

When he joined, the recruiting officer put the 'e' in. When he queried it, because he did query it, they said, 'Well, we won't do nothing now until your service finishes, so after that has finished, you can revert back.' After the war he didn't bother. His family tree prior to 1909 is without an 'e'. When you look back, you have to look back without an 'e.' He didn't seem to mind too much, having his name changed.

Colin's wife Linda smiled: 'He didn't seem to mind about anything.'

Godley had his new identity now, and a clean break from a troubled past. It is still the reason why thousands of young men join the army today. The fact that personal identity is subsumed into a greater whole doesn't seem to matter. Who cares if you are just a number? You are a number that belongs, part of a greater number. 'Godley, No. 13814, Private Sidney Frank.' He would settle for that. He was in the 4th Battalion, Royal Fusiliers. That was the City branch, full of Londoners. He was perfectly happy to be surrounded by Cockneys, having lived in London for so long. And there was ample opportunity in the army to show what he was good at. He was a noted sportsman, a good cross-country runner. He was also a footballer and a fine cricketer who had already played for a variety of teams around London.

Perhaps he played cricket in the army with Maurice Dease. Maurice's mother, Katherine, used to tell of a time when he carried his bat right through an innings. Maurice's sister, Maud, told her own son, Major French, how Maurice played in a cricket team mostly made up of nine sons in Roscommon. Four died in the First World War and Dease's sister, Maud, eventually married one of the surviving brothers, Leo. Since there are no records of Dease playing cricket at Stonyhurst, perhaps Maurice took his cricketing talents into the army. Did Sidney walk out to bat with Dease as his partner one day, against another battalion or regiment, with the vast difference in their rank and background temporarily forgotten? We'll never know for sure.

Both men seemed to have enough staying power at the cricket crease to make a difference to their team in the trivial world of sport. But it would take a very different kind of resilience to withstand a storm of shells and bullets for long enough to make a difference to their comrades, in a war which wasn't so very far away.

In the meantime, training and the daily hardships of military life would continue to prepare them. But they were human beings, no more, and the risk of basic human error was never far away.

# 3

# Beyond Control

It was 1914 and this was becoming serious. For any of Lieutenant Maurice Dease's machine-gunners to be poor shots, even in peacetime, was worrying enough. Those concerns were magnified tenfold now that war seemed inevitable, the failures even less acceptable – especially to someone as conscientious as Maurice.

Dease had worked his way to this key position of responsibility precisely because he was so conscientious. His nephew, Maurice French explained, 'My uncle must have left Sandhurst in about 1909, he was an ordinary platoon commander first, then he was picked out to be the machine gun officer. His Commanding Officer would have said, "You're doing well!" and then he must have been given the new role.'

In April 1912 Dease had been promoted to lieutenant and became the machine gun officer of the battalion. This was the new deadly weapon of war, so the men of the machine gun detachment had to become masters of their art if they were to give their battalion the upper hand in combat. Knowing Dease, he must have relished the responsibility of knocking his men into shape, and been determined not to let anyone down. He wasn't always restricted to the machine gun range. At different times during this period, Maurice was also acting adjutant. Dease was turning into a good all-round soldier; he was being given the chance to develop his many skills and talents, but right now the machine guns mattered most and he knew it.

Time was running out. Causing most concern was Private Godley, whose inability to judge distance was ruining his marksmanship. Through the first half of 1914 Godley had been consistent only in so far as he had been con-sistently erratic. Dease's machine-gunners' test for judging distances had revealed the problem as far back as 3 April. Private Godley was bottom of the class with an error percentage of 26.7. When an object was 400 yards away, he believed it to be 500 yards. At 1,000 yards, his estimate was 1,200. At 500 yards, Godley believed the enemy to be 600 yards away. Most alarming of all – and the distance that really put him at the bottom of the detachment – was his assessment of an object just 700 yards away. Godley believed it to be 1,000 yards distant, which meant he would be firing bullets over the heads of any on-rushing enemy. In a real battle, the Germans might be upon him before he even had time to realise his mistake.

With typical optimism, Dease decided the best in the class might be able to pull the worst up to their level if they received special training together. Therefore Lieutenant Harvey, whose error percentage was just 6 per cent, and Private Walker, whose 7.7 per cent was almost as impressive, were grouped with the wayward Privates Godley, Russell, Godman and Marshall, who were all at least three times as wasteful. 'I am going to train these men especially as range takers,' Dease recorded in the Machine Gun Section diary. If it might have appeared safer to throw Godley out of the machine gun detachment altogether, he was probably given the benefit of the doubt because he had excelled at 'tactical handling'. 'Godley and Godman were the best,' recorded Dease with no obvious sense of shock. At least they knew where and how to set up their machine gun to give themselves the most effective field of fire, even if what happened next was rather more in the lap of the gods.

You could almost feel Dease trying to coax the best out of his men. It was said of Maurice by his superiors that 'He had a most excellent way with his men, was always kind and thoughtful to them, but at all times dignified'. Even so, Dease's patience had been tested to the limit later that spring. The next distance-judging test, which took place on 17 April, offered little encourage-ment in Godley's case – quite the reverse. His results were even worse than before, and his error percentage had climbed to a worrying 33.2. He esti-mated an object 1,300 yards away to be just 800 yards away, a miscalculation sure to result in more inaccurate shooting if repeated when it mattered. For one of the final distance-judging tests, on 10 June, Godley was conspicuous in the record book through his absence due to sickness. Maybe Frank, as his fellow soldiers knew him by now, really was ill – or perhaps he had decided this wasn't the time to have any more of his shortcomings exposed.

The reprieve was only temporary. As Europe headed towards war during those sunny summer months, even Dease found it hard to be positive about

Godley's performance on the range. It didn't help that one of his fellow under-achievers from previous distance-judging tests had since shot to the top of the class. Monday 20 July was a very fine day on the Isle of Wight, one which offered precious little excuse for poor marksmanship. Yet, after another round of tests, Dease had no choice but to write dejectedly: 'Completed practices. Only one first class machine gunner – Private Godman. There were three classified as inefficient. Privates Godley, Russell and Cook.'

'Inefficient' was no way to be described just a few weeks before the out-break of a war – especially when you were a regular, professional soldier and part of one of the most important band of brothers in any battle – the machine gun detachment. 'Inefficient' was the word the army used to describe men who were fit only to be removed from their current role. You didn't get to play a prominent role in a machine gun section if you were 'inefficient'. They might not even trust you to fire a rifle.

Yet Godley was destined to go to that war and even write his name in history – just like Dease. The way events unfolded on Nimy bridge sug-gested that Dease was correct to overlook Godley's results and persevere. This seemingly illogical decision must have been based on something he liked in Godley's pugnacious character. Of course, there could have been a simpler explanation – he didn't have time to train up a replacement. And it wasn't as though Godley was much worse than any of the others. After giving his damning assessment, Dease hinted at a further comedy of errors. 'We had some trouble with the targets this morning – the markers could not get them to stand in the ground. There should be some slots just in the ground to hold these targets, considering that five battalions fire here annually'. People had muddled along happily enough before, but, now that war was about to break out, the main players needed their props urgently and they weren't working.

How different life had seemed as recently as 12 November of the previous year, a showery Wednesday on which Maurice had been involved in welcom-ing royalty. He had written in his diary, 'Supplied a guard of honour at Ryde today for Princess Henry of Battenberg for which there was a practice this morning ...' With hindsight, this line becomes poignant. Princess Henry of Battenberg had started life as Princess Beatrice, the youngest daughter of Queen Victoria. Maurice could have had no way of knowing that within a year he would win the Cross which proudly carried Victoria's name. As for Beatrice, her title had changed when she had married Prince Henry, who had then died of malaria in 1896. The fact that she was still known as Princess Henry of Battenberg in 1913 said much about that particular moment in his-tory – and even more about how rapidly events unfolded in 1914. During those peaceful pre-war days of 1913, the clear links between the British and German royal families were considered perfectly acceptable. Kaiser Wilhelm II, Germany's war-mongering leader, was the eldest grandson of the late Queen Victoria. There was certainly nothing that should be hidden or downplayed by Queen Victoria's daughter or her British Army guard of honour. So Maurice was happy to protect a 'Battenberg', and she was happy to be one.

Things changed after Britain and Germany found themselves at war. By 1917 Princess Henry of Battenberg had reverted back to HRH The Princess Beatrice. Her surname was also anglicised to 'Mountbatten'. Maurice's simple diary entry raises a complex question: how on earth did two countries with so much in common reach a situation where they were sending their young men into France and Belgium to kill each other? From the perspective of the twenty-first century it seems ridiculous. Indeed, there are still some intellectuals today who argue that the entire gruesome exercise was wholly unnecessary, since Germany didn't want to go to war against Britain in 1914. They argue that Britain should have continued to recognise what it had in common with Germany and held that communality above all else; that Britain should have let the Germans do their worst on the European mainland, recognising that there were too many links and old friendships between them to warrant fighting over less important European nations. If you are prepared to entertain this theory, then such a course of action – or rather inaction – would have saved millions of lives and left Britain no worse off, even though Germany would undoubtedly have been stronger for the change in the European landscape. It was absurd, some argue, for men of the same, essentially Anglo-Saxon race to have engaged in years of senseless slaughter, resulting in the flower of their youth being destroyed and put under the ground, often in unmarked graves.

This argument ignores Britain's promise to Belgium to help to preserve her borders in the event of German aggression, which dated back to the Treaty of London in 1839. However, Kaiser Wilhelm II viewed the importance Britain apparently attached to that old promise with a sense of dismay, reasoning that it wasn't enough to warrant the two nations going to war. The Kaiser had wanted Britain to remain passive, and soon lamented almost mockingly that Britain had 'gone to war over a scrap of paper'.

Yet there are other flaws in the argument presented by those who claim that British involvement in the First World War was unnecessary. It may be true that Britain could have avoided a war against Germany in 1914; but for how long? A Germany left to invade its neighbours and strengthen its resources immeasurably would sooner or later be sure to set its sights on taking over Britain too, or at least placing it in some form of servitude. Britain had realised this years earlier. For decades British governments had been sensitive to the alliances being formed on the European mainland. In 1879 there had been the 'Dual Alliance' between Germany and Austria-Hungary. France and Russia had formed the 'Dual Entente', largely in response to that alliance, in 1892. Although fully mindful of German concerns that it was now threatened from the east and west, Britain had decided to join its former enemies, Russia and France, in 1907 to form the 'Triple Entente'. That historic move wasn't taken lightly.

Britain's long and 'Splendid Isolation' was over, and for good reason. Gone were the days when it could leave the Europeans to their own squabbles and hope they would simply weaken one another while Britain prospered. There was a dangerous change in the air, and it was coming from Germany. Britain had long considered itself to be the greatest European nation, perhaps the greatest in the entire world. With its naval tradition, its vast empire through India and beyond, having begun the Industrial Revolution and continued to enjoy an unrivalled pre-eminence throughout the world, Britain felt it had reason to be proud. Germany under the Kaiser had become jealous and wanted to grow its own economy, broaden its horizons and start an empire of its own. Germany had looked towards North Africa and beyond; but, before it seized an empire, it first had to strengthen its navy, so that the British would no longer be able to claim that they 'ruled the waves'.

Since the turn of the century, the writing had been on the wall – or rather stated blatantly in German naval laws, which gave new powers for a fleet of warships to be built. By way of explanation, these declared unashamedly that 'For Germany, the most dangerous naval enemy at the present time is England … Our fleet must be constructed so that it can unfold its greatest military potential between Heligoland and the Thames.' As early as 1906, the First Lord of The Admiralty, John Arbutnot Fisher, had predicted that Britain and Germany would go to war in August 1914. By then he had responded to the growing threat of German naval power by building HMS *Dreadnought*, the first of the all-big-gun battleships. Fisher knew that Germany would respond by building a similar class of ships, and he believed the necessary widening of the Kiel Canal would have been carried out sufficiently by August 1914 for Germany to attack Britain across the North Sea.

The predicted timing of aggression proved uncanny, though as it turned out events far beyond the Kiel Canal were involved in the outbreak of war. In essence, however, Fisher and Britain generally knew what was coming and knew what was needed. Germany was going to invade her neighbours to the west and try to push all the way to the coast. There simply wasn't going to be room for two giants to co-exist in such close proximity, however pure the German blood of the British royalty. If Germany seized control of French and Belgian ports, how much time would pass before they tried their luck across the Channel? Britain couldn't afford to wait until it was so vulnerable to German attack. It was all very well the Germans trying to convince the British that they meant them no harm. One of these powers would have to be subdued sooner or later, both probably knew it deep down, and ultimately it was a question of which catalyst would send these European tensions spiralling out of control and create the conditions for war.

The shooting of Archduke Franz Ferdinand in Serbia provided just that catalyst; one man's death far away would soon have catastrophic consequences for Dease and Godley. Ferdinand's assassination in Sarajevo had such a quick domino effect because the tensions between powers in the Balkans and beyond were already so high. Ferdinand, heir to the throne of Germany's ally, Austria-Hungary, was assassinated by Serb terrorists. Although they weren't linked to the Serbian government, it didn't seem to matter any more. Serbia had emerged from the recent wars in the Balkans as the strongest country in the region and appeared to pose a threat to Austria-Hungary. Tensions had been rising since 1908, when Bosnia, containing many Serbs, had been taken over by Austria-Hungary, which didn't appear to be intimidated by Serbia having powerful Russia as its ally. Archduke Ferdinand's assassination prompted Austria-Hungary to react in the most extreme way possible, regardless of a Russian backlash.

Austria-Hungary declared war on Serbia, so Russia mobilized its army ready to help the Serbs. If Russia attacked Austria-Hungary, Germany would automatically lend support to Austria-Hungary, while France would have no choice but to support Russia. As the rival alliances prepared for war, the equation placed France squarely against Germany. The Germans planned to sweep down through Belgium into France, hit Paris and take all the Belgian and French ports. Britain's place in the 'Triple Entente' meant it would be expected to support France, while the Treaty of London compelled it to go to Belgium's aid first. Britain was on a collision course with Germany, which made a certain amount of strategic sense anyway, if the Germans were about to edge so close to British shores.

Even then, British diplomats tried to calm the situation, believing that if Germany respected borders to its west, Britain's involvement might not be necessary. Perhaps if war was averted this time, there might be some other significant and positive development somewhere along the line, one which could question the long-term inevitability of a clash with Germany after all, and create conditions whereby the two powers could co-exist comfortably somehow. It was fanciful thinking, as realists already knew. As July turned to August, it became clear these last-ditch diplomatic efforts were all to no avail.

When they joined the army in 1910, Maurice Dease and Sidney Frank Godley could have had no inkling of how swiftly Britain and Germany would sink into enmity, or how rapidly the countdown to war would come when the line was finally drawn in the sand. Godley and Dease might reasonably have expected to be called upon to show their mettle in battle at some point. There had always been some war or other to go and fight – and perhaps there always would be. But the pace of life in the army had seemed slower back then the atmosphere somewhat more relaxed.

In 1911, for example, Maurice had brought his four-month-old fox-terrier – a cheeky, energetic little dog called Dandy – across from Ireland to Aldershot, then base of the Royal Fusiliers. The officers of the 4th Battalion had become so attached to Dandy that he became their unofficial mascot, and even appeared in some regimental photographs. Since then Dandy had gone almost everywhere with the battalion, and was with them on the Isle of Wight as the regiment prepared to go to war. Maurice wasn't going to put him through that ordeal. But what he was going to do with Dandy if mobilisation and war became a reality was something that greatly concerned Maurice, who felt totally responsible for the animal's predicament.

Back in 1911, he hadn't imagined such a sudden dilemma. The biggest dramas came at ceremonial occasions, and the only casualties were through heat exhaustion. Such had been the case when the Royal Fusiliers played their part in the Coronation of King George V at Westminster Abbey on 22 June 1911. Although he had ascended to the throne a year earlier, this was the moment he became more than George Frederick Ernest Albert of the House of Saxe-Coberg and Gotha. His wife was crowned Queen Mary in a smaller ceremony, having decided wisely that her first name, Victoria, should be avoided because of the greatness of the British monarch of the same name, who had passed away only ten years earlier.

*The Times* reported events inside the abbey as 'The impressive service, of which so little has been changed for centuries and of which a part goes back to the days of the Kings of Israel ...' There was the anointing, the presentation to the king of spurs, the orb, a ring and two sceptres, then cries of 'God Save The King' echoed around the abbey as the Archbishop of Canterbury placed St Edward's crown on the king's head. But, outside in the sweltering heat, hours of endurance in full ceremonial uniform had been too much for some of Maurice's men, who had fainted. War would impose far fiercer physical demands on these men before long. It would also create something of an identity crisis in Britain's 'German' monarchy. The First World War was no time for the royal family to be clinging to its German origins, though it took until the summer of 1917 for George V to change the family name from Saxe-Coburg and Gotha to the more English-sounding Windsor.

War was to provide extreme challenges for many people. In the preceding years, Maurice and the Royal Fusiliers had not always operated in a peaceful environment either. Between 1911 and 1914, in a volatile period known as 'The Great Unrest', which was full of industrial strikes and riots, the army was sometimes called in to restore order, and Dease played his part manfully, though this wasn't combat or anything much like it. Deep down, however, Maurice and his men knew they always had to be prepared for the outbreak of war. That was the point of the army; and to face the ultimate personal test was in some ways the point of joining it.

What no one could have contemplated was a war quite as prolonged and horrific as the First World War, with thousands upon thousands of men lined up for inevitable slaughter on such an industrial scale. And it was the machine gun that would prove to be one of the biggest killers of all. The machine gun was capable of mowing down hundreds in a matter of seconds, ending the lives of nameless masses, who would fall in crumpled heaps, to be cleared away, in some cases, months later. The machine gun was going to be a key weapon; some realised it more than others. How to use it to its best effect preoccupied the thoughts of Dease and now, to a lesser extent, Godley.

Would Maurice and Sidney have signed up to be at the forefront of something quite as prolonged and awful in its destruction as the First World War had they possessed a crystal ball? From the perspective of twenty-first-century peacetime, it is difficult to understand how any sensible, sensitive young man could have done so, yet the defence of Britain's integrity, its standing in the world, and perhaps its very borders were on the line in the long run. Many spirited teenagers and men in their early twenties volunteered, even after they had heard stories of the carnage that possibly awaited them. Many more were given no choice as casualties needed replacing and the pressure back home to enlist became intolerable. This was a patriotic age, when courage counted for everything.

Given what they were about to face, it was just as well that Godley and Dease possessed plenty of courage. But, to translate that courage into firm results, marksmanship was the key. And marksmanship was not in plentiful supply in the Machine Gun Detachment of Lieutenant Maurice Dease. Not yet, anyway.

Maurice knew it was nearly time for the men to do what they had been trained for: to fight other men in battle and shoot dead as many as possible. It was ugly work, but clearly it was going to be an advantage if they could judge distance and shoot straight. If such a farce as Maurice had witnessed on the range hadn't come just weeks before the likelihood of a life-or-death battle, it might have been funny. But, even when targets were successfully set up, they still didn't seem to be hit very often by Dease's machine-gunners – which had to make you wonder where the bullets were going.

On Wednesday 22 July, Dease set the scene on the latest mock battlefield. Different-sized targets were set up at various distances in preparation for any German attack they might soon have to face. Maurice admitted:

The results were bad, very few hits being recorded. Then a row of nine heads and shoulders and eight iron plates was put up in front of a sandy patch and two sections fired, however they got no hits … The other targets, 17 heads and shoulders, were put up further away from the sandy patch and fire opened, but no hits were obtained here either.

Perhaps if the Germans attacked in greater numbers than seventeen at a time when the moment of truth arrived, Dease's machine-gunners would have a better chance of hitting a few of them. For now all he could do was continue to work his men hard and hope the training would pay off when the time came to fight for their futures. There wasn't long left, the training was nearly over. The Germans were gathering ominously on Belgium's borders, ready to sweep down into France. By the start of August, it was time to get ready – and fast.

It was a sign of the times and the changing nature of war that Maurice's time was divided between machine guns and horses. Naturally he adored the grace and nobility of the latter far more than a fearsome metal contraption designed to spew out death on a new scale. He had always adored horses, so there was no better man than Dease to assess the local horses, buy those most suitable and ensure they were cared for. Maurice was in his element. And, while he was thinking about animals, he couldn't forget his beloved fox terrier Dandy.

On 4 August, Maurice wrote home from Albany Barracks. Though his duties centred on the purchase of those horses for the army, the happiness and welfare of that other precious animal was never far from his thoughts. Who would look after Dandy while he was gone? What if he never returned?

And while he was reflecting upon his own mortality, he worried about who would settle his debts if he didn't act quickly:

> My Dear Mother,
> We received the order to mobilize tonight at 6 p.m. and subsequently we shall be very busy for the next four days. I have to collect all the horses, about sixty, fit the harnesses and see to everything as regards them; unfortunately, I have an awful old dodderer of a civilian to deal with, he is the purchasing officer.
>
> May I send Dandy home, he could also go by long sea, I hope himself [Maurice's father] won't mind this suggestion but I suppose he would put up with him at a time like this?
>
> Will you also ask Daddy if he would lodge my next quarter's money now, so that I can pay all bills before I go? It is a bad time to have an overdraft.
>
> We have been expecting this order for some time and wondered why it did not come before …
>
> Your loving son,
> Maurice Dease

It was indeed a bad time to have an overdraft, as Maurice had realised and pointed out with typical humour, though necessarily dark in this troubled moment. He had also concluded that his battalion would be sent to Belgium to try to stop the advancing Germans there. Dease wasn't stupid. He knew how dangerous this was going to be; he knew the following weeks could be fatal for him.

On 4 August, Maurice was writing a letter to his sister Maud from Albany Barracks when the historic news came through. Mysteriously, Maurice and Maud nicknamed each other 'Badge', and Maud never told her own son Maurice why. There must have been humour behind it, since humour played such a prominent part in Maurice's life. When brother and sister spoke, for example, their mother was 'herself', their father was 'himself', and their parents together were 'themselves'.

> My Dear Badge,
> … As you will have seen from papers we have started mobilizing today, and so Sunday we shall be dreadfully busy, I don't know what will happen then, but I think we will go to Belgium.

I have to collect all the horses for the regiment and they all have to be branded and every bit of saddling marked.

I sent my valuables to you yesterday by post, all the rest of my kit I will either send home or have stored here. I have written to themselves asking if Dandy can be sent home too. Palm [Dease's horse] is to be sold to the Government. Just heard that war has been declared against Germany.

Best of love
Your loving Badge

Given Maurice's great love for horses, there was much suppressed emotion in that simple sentence, 'Palm is to be sold to the Government.' It meant Palm was going to war too, probably with no better chance of survival than Maurice.

# 4

# Mollie and the Horses

Every soldier had known that peace was coming to an end, though often relationships with the opposite sex remained unresolved. For example, Sidney's girlfriend, Nellie, lived in London and, though it wasn't far away, it might as well have been on the other side of the world. Sidney and Nellie had been together for a few years. Nellie was still in service in Willesden, north London. Even though she was five years older than he was, and her thirtieth birthday wasn't so very far away, Sidney didn't seem to care. Something exciting, something timeless was developing between them. They enjoyed each other's sense of humour, they were both bubbly characters and soon realised their love might last.

For a man who had lost his mother at the age of 6, the love of a good woman was especially valuable. Yet Private Sidney Frank Godley was a soldier in the 4th Royal Fusiliers, and there seemed little point in proposing to Nellie at a time like this. If he survived the war to enjoy peace again one day that might be a better time to propose. For now they would just have to remember how it felt to be in each other's arms, and keep their relationship going through letters until they could see each other again. In that first week of August 1914, Godley's life on the Isle of Wight was a classic case of so near, yet so far.

Maurice Dease seems to have felt a special affection for someone too – but she was on the island, just a few hundred yards away from him each night. The headquarters for the officers in Dease's battalion were located in the village of Wootton. And in 'The Cedars', one of the biggest houses in Wootton, lived Mollie Hewitt, who was four years older than Maurice and the mother of a 3-year-old boy named John Rupert Hunter Hewitt. The situation was complicated. It appears that Mollie's husband, Rupert Paton Hewitt, had left her, either during her pregnancy or soon after the birth of their child. The 1911 Census had Mollie living in The Cedars as the 'wife' of the 'head' of the house. Yet they were effectively separated, because her husband wasn't listed as living at the same property. The only other occupants of the house were a cook called Fanny Jane Faurmier, a housemaid named Octavia Gertrude Murton, and a nurse called Lucy Elizabeth Sheath. So where was her husband in 1911? Rupert Paton Hewitt was renting a room in a boarding house in Headington, Oxford. Rupert and Norfolk-born Mollie had married in the autumn of 1909 but had apparently managed to stay together for only two years before he had returned to the mainland.

Mollie Hewitt and Maurice Dease had known each other since February 1913, when the 4th Royal Fusiliers had moved from Aldershot to the barracks at Parkhurst on the Isle of Wight and the officers had made Wootton their base. Introductions were made at welcoming social events in the village; but even if he had wanted to, it wouldn't have been regarded as acceptable for Lieutenant Dease to start a romance with a lady who was still married – albeit unhappily. For a start, Dease was a Catholic, very religious and very honourable. Then there was the added fact that Rupert Hewitt returned to the Isle of Wight regularly, to see his son and to keep an eye on the houses and horses he still owned there. Those horses became a key factor in the friendship which developed between Mollie and Maurice, for it could only be a friendship.

Dease rode his first race on a horse owned by Rupert Hewitt on 6 March 1913. The event was a point-to-point for heavyweights at Yafford in the south-west of the island. Maurice didn't win, but with his strong good looks and smart appearance he must have seemed to Mollie a dashing, fearless young officer, who shared her love for horses.

Mollie could hardly fail to continue to notice Maurice and his colleagues, who had centred their final military training exercises around their HQ in Wootton in July 1914. The scenario for 13–14 July was as follows:

GENERAL IDEA

A Brownland subsidiary Force based on Wootton is operating in the Isle of Wight (a province of Whiteland) by means of detachments which move from place to place overawing the inhabitants.

Whiteland has a few scattered Companies of Infantry in the principal towns of the Island, but any attempt to concentrate a mobile force against the Brown invaders has hitherto been nipped in the bud.

SPECIAL IDEA (Brown)
Captain Ashburner's Brown detachment of 2 Companies 4th Royal
Fusiliers arrived at Newport at 7.30 p.m. on the 13th July, where he
received the following instructions:

> Field Force HQ WOOTTON, 13th July, 1914
> The enemy is becoming more active ... I want you to prevent
> him from crossing the YAR River similarly between GREAT
> BURBRIDGE and NEWCHURCH, both inclusive ... If the
> enemy effects a crossing fall back towards NEWPORT ... engage
> him vigorously till reinforcement arrives ...

Such war games would become particularly relevant, indeed poignant within
weeks, as we shall see. The exercises were soon over and a real war awaited
them just over the water. There was precious little time for socialising, even
with the attractive Mollie – at least not until Maurice had completed his
preparations and knew his men were ready to go.

Now it wasn't about riding horses for the sheer love of it in glorious surroundings. This was about buying horses for pulling artillery and shifting
supplies. Maurice must have had mixed feelings about this, to say the least.
The poor beasts would probably be robbed of their dignity and pushed to
the limit as he knowingly set about putting creatures he loved in harm's way.
There was no getting away from the truth. Maurice must have suspected
deep down that he was about to take these animals into a hell they would
hate. For a man who had been on horseback since almost before he could
walk, a man who had formed such a close bond with these noble creatures,
this couldn't have been easy. But there was nothing he could do about it; his
duty came first, as did his men. Horses were needed and horses would be
found and requisitioned from British civilians.

For now, at least, this would be done in the right way. Lord Kitchener, fig-
urehead for all British military recruitment, had ordered that no horses under
fifteen hands (60in) should be requisitioned. While he might have doubted
whether smaller horses could do such an effective job in France and Belgium,
it has also been argued that he was mindful of morale back home. For British
children to see their ponies taken away and sent into what was sure to be a
brutal environment abroad would cause families such trauma that it could
have damaged morale in this sensitive early phase of the war.

Mollie must also have feared for her horses and known that by expos-
ing them to the sights and sounds of war, by sending them somewhere

they risked maiming and death, she was betraying them. Yet she also knew she must be patriotic and loyal to the needs of her country. And right now Maurice represented those national needs and she must help him as best she could. At least she knew he was no callous logistics man, that he had a fine understanding of the creatures he was buying. If anyone would look after her horses, Maurice would.

So, seventeen months after riding for Rupert Hewitt, Maurice visited the Hewitt farm once again, probably one of his most important stopping-off points as he tried to buy sixty sturdy horses from the various farms and stables on the island. It is not known whether he found Rupert at home, but Mollie would have needed her husband's permission for any transaction. Meanwhile, as he set about his task, Maurice soon realised that the purchase of the horses themselves would be the least of his difficulties. On 7 August he wrote in his diary about the horses he had already managed to buy:

> We were fitting harness and shoeing all day. We also drew the remainder of the saddles from the mobilization store. The collars are the greatest difficulty in fitting and those supplied for the heavyweight draught horses are too big ... Finished fitting the harness and had a practical at putting it on the horses. The men are not good at this and take a very long time at the work ...

If the men didn't know what they were doing, the horses would suffer in the long run. That was the last thing Maurice wanted, so he would have to teach the men how to respect these animals and handle them properly just as quickly as he could. In the frenzied build-up to war, this was a complication he didn't need; and it must have struck him that there had been a lack of foresight here. The army must have known that, in any war, horses would be needed, and therefore a basic knowledge of all things equine would have been essential for the troops. But the men had received no such training and now they were suddenly expected to know what they were doing in a matter of hours. A crash course in how to harness a horse wasn't what Lieutenant Dease was supposed to be administering at the eleventh hour. His job was to purchase the animals in these final days before they left for war.

He wrote to his mother that evening to explain. 'I have been very busy buying horses the last two days, and fitting harness today; it is all rather a job as there are so few of the men who know anything about it'.

But Mollie knew about horses; she adored them, she understood them. She was a kindred spirit and he must have been relieved to be able to talk to someone who could appreciate his problems. It is easy to imagine them joining forces to persuade Rupert, as legal owner of the Hewitt horses, to sell Maurice several from their stables. Mollie even let Maurice have one of her personal favourites, a horse called Mattie. It may have been the heavyweight Maurice rode in the race at Yafford the previous year. This letting go couldn't have been easy for Mollie. Did the fact that she was prepared to send a special horse into the unknown horrors of modern war – one to which she felt emotionally attached, judging by a subsequent letter – indicate that she felt a special affection for Maurice too? We'll never know. What we do know is that Maurice could relate to the mixed emotions she must have been feeling, because he too was selling a horse that he adored, his own horse, Palm, as we have seen. So he must have known how Mollie was feeling, it would have been his job to reassure her that Mattie would be well cared for, and the fact that he shared a natural concern for her prized mount would have helped.

What wasn't clear to anyone in authority prior to the war was the fact that thoroughbreds were destined to perform less well than crossbreeds in the theatre of war. Thoroughbreds were more sensitive and rebellious when faced with the flashes and explosions of battle, and they suffered more shell-shock as a result. Crossbreeds proved more resilient, even learning to lie down and hide as best they could when they felt they were in extreme physical danger.

Medium-sized horses with good endurance would prove most effective under the extreme physical challenges of war. They were less likely to become bogged down in the mud and collapse from exhaustion, though still vulnerable to suffering the terrible fate of many horses, who found they simply couldn't raise their heads any more and ended up drowning in muddy water or suffocating in the mud itself. Of all war-related equine deaths in the Great War, only a quarter came in the heat of battle, when a horse would be targeted by the enemy as a more valuable kill than a man. The other three-quarters came from disease and exhaustion.

Taller horses also caused more exhaustion in their riders, because they required greater effort during mounting and dismounting. But Maurice needed strong horses to pull his machine guns, carry his supplies of ammunition, and food and water for his men. Sturdy, strong horses of calm character would have caught his eye as he sought to buy his share. So much was unknown in the build-up to the First World War. Much as Maurice knew plenty about horses, he didn't know everything about horses in war. How could he? Like many of his men, he hadn't yet been to war.

Under pressure to meet his quota in time for mobilisation, Dease simply went about his work using instinct and necessity as his driving forces. With problems mounting, he must have greatly appreciated the gesture of solidarity from Mollie when she and Rupert agreed to sell him several horses, especially since the civilian buyer working with the army, Mr J. Jolliffe, had been driving Maurice to distraction ever since they had met.

Part of Maurice's diary entry for Tuesday 4 August read, 'Got the order to mobilize at 6.5 p.m. Went to see J. Jolliffe about the purchase of horses, he has everything in an awful muddle and has lost his cheque book and everything …'

Dease's sense of irritation probably wasn't helped by the fact that Jolliffe's son had won the 'heavyweight' point-to-point that Maurice had entered the previous year. Meanwhile, Maurice's fellow army colleagues and their ignorance of many things equestrian continued to add to his exasperation. If only they could all have been like Mollie, and possess her knowledge, her love of horses, her understanding.

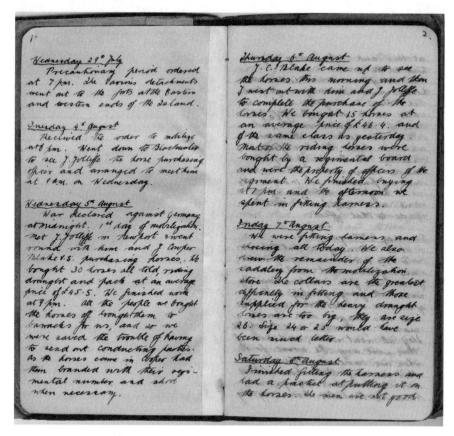

War horses: Maurice Dease's neat diary records the outbreak of war and his immediate purchase of horses for France and Belgium.

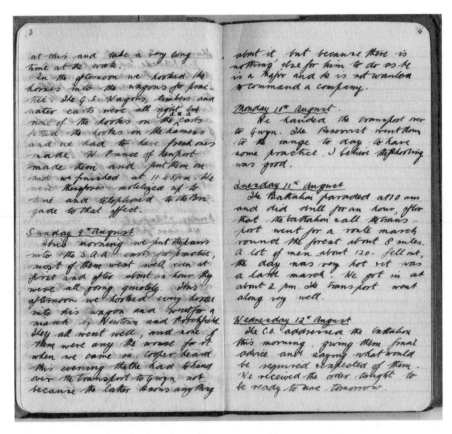

The last entries: horses and men make ready for the dreadful demands of war ... then Dease stops writing.

By ensuring that her young friend would have the horses he wanted from her estranged husband's stable, Mollie had a fresh opportunity to enjoy Maurice's company. He wrote appreciatively in his diary, 'All the people we bought the horses off brought them to the barracks for us, and so we were saved the trouble of having to send out conducting parties.' Did they arrange to meet one last time? Maurice was photographed with a very pretty and charismatic woman when he and two officer friends took tea with unnamed ladies at an impromptu garden party on 11 August. One was Osbert Cundy-Cooper, who wrote in his diary that day, 'Parades in the morning. Lecture by the Colonel to Battalion. After lunch took Maurice and Beazley over to Norton in the car. Stayed to tea. Large number of photos taken'.

This was the last moment of leisure Maurice was able to enjoy before his departure for France, and he seems to have shared a relaxed affection with one lady in particular. Yet, even if this woman was Mollie, the relationship almost certainly hadn't moved beyond flirtation. Mollie was still married to Rupert, and it was unlikely Maurice would compromise his Catholicism. 'Deeply religious, without making a parade of the fact, he gained everyone's respect,' a fellow officer once said of him. The mere thought of committing adultery would have seemed to him a sin, even if Mollie and her husband were no longer man and wife in any meaningful sense. Besides, Dease may have had to deal directly with Rupert over the sale of the horses. Too many factors counted against a love affair between them. His nephew Maurice French observed later, 'I don't think it was in my uncle's interest to have a romantic liaison on the Isle of Wight. It was probably their joint interest in horses that led to a friendship.'

Given their mutual love for horses, there was something very sad about the fact that Maurice and Mollie were almost unwittingly conspiring in what would become one of the great hidden tragedies of the war. Britain sent around 1 million horses to the war, but only 62,000 returned home. The suffering and bravery of those horses was immeasurable. During the war, a total of 725,216 horses were treated by the British Army Veterinary Corps. Amazingly, 529,064 of those horses were successfully healed for further ser-vice. Despite their suffering, these horses showed the strength and inner resolve to regain their health and return to the fray, even though many had been suffering from an equine form of shell-shock. It is a distressing story. Those horses that survived the carnage and saw peace finally break out were in many cases sold to locals in Belgium and France, or else sent straight to abattoirs, to provide meat for the starving. An awful way to treat heroic, sensi-tive animals; yet by then so many men were so desensitised to suffering that only easy logistical solutions dominated their thoughts.

For as long as he lived, as we shall see, Maurice Dease was not one of those cold-hearted types. He kept his eye on the horses he knew, especially Mollie's horse Mattie. No doubt he had promised her he would do so and as usual he was as good as his word. And the significance of Mollie to Maurice Dease is beyond question. By the time he had to leave for war, he had made a note of Mollie's address and told himself that, come what may, he would write. The morality of the day demanded that Maurice and Mollie remain friends and no more; but there was no harm in writing. And he was going to write to her shortly before battle, hoping she would write back, to give him some news from a more peaceful place. There would be just enough time for Maurice to give Mollie news of Mattie, and to encourage a reply by offering her a postal address. Just enough time before all hope of receiving a reply was taken away from him. We can only speculate on what they might or might not have felt for each other. What we know is that, on some level at least, Mollie Hewitt had a significant place in Maurice Dease's heart in those final days of his life. You don't write to someone just before battle unless that is the case. Beyond that fact, the relationship – and what it might have become one day under other circumstances – must remain an intriguing mystery.

Unfulfilled personal relationships – or even ensuring that his men came home alive – were not among the priorities of Lieutenant-Colonel Norman Reginald McMahon, the Commanding Officer of the Royal Fusiliers, when he spoke to his men on the morning of 12 August, just before their departure for war.

Dease wrote in his diary, 'The C.O. addressed the battalion this morning, giving them final advice and saying what would be required and expected of them. We received the order tonight to be ready to move tomorrow.' This was his final entry, and only hinted at the commitment Colonel McMahon had demanded of the battalion.

Colonel McMahon called for the utmost courage – and suggested that anything else would be a humiliation for each and every man. He said, 'A Royal Fusilier does not fear death. He is not afraid of wounds. He only fears disgrace; and I look to you not to disgrace the name of the regiment.' No one could have heard that and not shuddered a little inside, when they realised what McMahon foresaw for them.

But McMahon knew what he was talking about. Like so many officers, he had family history in the regiment. He was the son of General Sir Thomas McMahon, 3rd Battalion. Norman had been commissioned in the Royal Fusiliers in May 1885, and saw active service in what became known as the Burmese Expedition between 1885 and 1887. But it was in the Boer War in South Africa that McMahon's bravery came to prominent attention. He was badly wounded and still won the DSO, proof that a good Royal Fusilier 'is not afraid of wounds'. Unlike many highly ranked First World War officers, McMahon was a soldier's soldier. Not only had he already proved himself on the battlefield, he would be prepared to do so again, despite his advancing years.

Undoubtedly a tough warrior of a man, McMahon was also able to show extraordinary compassion to those he felt were of a similar class, as we shall see. That warmth and humanity apparently didn't stretch to those he considered beneath him, however. Corporal Bill Holbrook was his servant and remembered him like this:

Our Colonel McMahon, he was responsible for improving the fire-power of the British Army. Wonderful man, he was. Before he came to us he was in charge of the School of Musketry in Hythe and he was musketry mad! He started the 15 rounds a minute. When I first joined the army you fired at a bullseye – that was your target. He ended all that. You fired at moving figures – khaki, doubling – so from about 5 rounds a minute you went to about 15. You had to lie on the box, unloaded, with three rounds in clips of five in the pouches. When the whistle went you'd have to load your rifle and fire, tip the case out, fire, fire, fire … and get it all into one minute.

His one craze was musketry. I was his servant, but you had to fire your course whatever job you was on. You had to fire five hundred rounds a year. I got Best Shot in the Battalion, and I was proud as Punch. I felt sure the Colonel would say something because I got the Battalion Orders from the Orderly Sergeant every night, and I used to take them in to him. This night my name was right at the top as marksman – Best Shot! He saw it all right. He sat at that table and he read it while I watched him. He never said a word. I shed tears over that! I couldn't help it! I knew he'd seen it, I knew he'd thought a lot of it – but he wouldn't praise me for it. That wasn't long before I went with him to France. I went as a marksman.

In France or Belgium, everyone would have a chance to show whether they could shoot straight or not, even Godley, who had been giving Dease nightmares on the machine gun target range. For the moment, however, the war was still about logistics. Affairs had to be put in order, loved ones reassured.

Despite all the frantic preparations for war, Dease had still found time to ask one of the battalion's vets, J. Cooper Blake, if he wouldn't mind looking after Dandy. It appears that Blake was due to remain on the Isle of Wight or return to the English mainland. Maurice was delighted with the response and told his father that he wouldn't have to look after Dandy after all:

12/8/14

My Dear Daddy,

We are still here, but expect to be moved tomorrow. This however is secret and must go no further than mother.

I think I have now paid all my bills except tailor's – you might pay this sometime out of the £60. I don't quite know how my accounts stand just at present as I have written some cheques and have packed up my account book.

I enclose my will, they tell me it will save you trouble if I don't return.

Dandy is not now going home. Blake is going to look after him but I have told him that if he is a nuisance to send him home.

Our address when we leave here will be 4th Bn. Royal Fusiliers, 9th Infantry Brigade, 3rd Division.

Goodbye and best of love to you,
your loving son Maurice

Perhaps it was the inclusion of his will in the letter; or it could have been the fact that he was leaving British shores. But the word 'goodbye', written on the page in all its bleak simplicity, is startling to the eye.

# 5

# The Road to Mons

Maurice Dease wasn't the sort of man to disobey orders. As they prepared to leave for war, the men of the 4th Battalion, Royal Fusiliers, were told to discontinue any personal diaries or journals they might have been writing. The reason was simple: any diary that fell into enemy hands could tell the Germans where the battalion had been, which key officers had been lost, what morale was like, any number of things. Notes that might appear relatively trivial could provide the enemy with another small piece in a jigsaw puzzle which, when put together, might gift the Germans a picture that could prove very useful indeed.

Being a conscientious young man, Maurice resolved to follow those instructions. No doubt he felt the same mixture of excitement and trepidation experienced by other officers and their men as they left Parkhurst for the last time. At 9.30 a.m. on 13 August the right half of the battalion, comprising 550 men, left the parade ground and marched to Cowes, where they received a warm welcome from the civilian population. This group included A and B companies, some transport and Maurice with the machine-gunners. A steamer was waiting to take them to Southampton. (At 11 a.m. the rest of the battalion marched to Cowes to board a second steamer.) Some had an inkling of the horrors to come.

Corporal Bill Holbrook, servant to Colonel McMahon, summed up this feeling well after they had taken their less physically demanding drive from Parkhurst to Cowes:

We went to Cowes first and I always remember waiting in the quayside to go across to embark at Southampton. There was a big advertisement on the side of a house for a publication called 'John Bull'. It covered the whole gable end of this house and it said, 'The Dawn of Britain's Greatest Glory' – all down the side of this house. I remember sitting there and saying to myself, 'I wonder'.

Holbrook decided to keep putting his thoughts and feelings on paper for as long as he saw action. Not all of Maurice's officer colleagues obeyed orders either. In fact, many of Maurice's closest friends continued to write personal diaries, knowing that the coming adventure would be historically important. We can see through their eyes what Maurice must have seen, and fairly safely feel through them what Maurice must have felt.

Lieutenant K.F.B. 'Kingy' Tower was a fellow officer in the 4th Battalion and a very good friend of Maurice. Maurice was even pictured resting his hands on Kingy's shoulders in one of the last regimental photographs taken together. Kingy recorded the initial embarkation in his diary:

On 12 August [sic] we moved out of barracks for the last time to Cowes where we embarked in two steam boats for Southampton. Large crowds assembled to see us off. As we moved out to the Solent, the Royal Yacht Squadron ran up a signal: 'Goodbye and good luck'. At Southampton we re-embarked on a P and O transport where we were packed like herrings. About 6 p.m. that evening we set sail, and it must have been a wonderful sight to see the convoy of ships passing down the Solent, past the forts and Spithead. We sat all through the night in darkness with a thousand thoughts of the future crowding through our brains. In order to relieve the monotony I started a bit of a singsong in the dark and we all sang the various musical comedy songs and kept cheery that way.

Since there are many future references to Maurice's cheeriness throughout, we can safely assume he joined in too. Maurice was among friends; bonds had been built through four years of training together, for moments such as these. Like Dease, Lieutenant Frederick Longman was also only ten days away from preparing for the German onslaught on the Mons–Condé Canal at Nimy. Son of the chairman of Longman's Publishers, Freddie was friendly with Maurice and had stood next to him in the last official photo of the 4th Battalion's officers, taken at Parkhurst on 11 August. Longman wrote the following entries in his journal:

August 13th: Off at last! Marched to Cowes and so to Southampton on steamer ... As pleased as anything to get a move on.

August 14th: Arrived at Havre. Some French soldiers on the quay gave us a great reception. Our fellows whistled the Marseillaise for their benefit – 1500 whistling together is a good show – and then sang 'Hold your hand out, naughty boy', whilst the French stood bare-headed thinking it was our National Anthem! ... Very hot march to rest camps at Harfleur – not a great show. Discipline wants improving and feet hardening ... Men recovered spirits as they ate. French very kind and amusing.

The 4th Battalion of the Royal Fusiliers soon began handing out so many souvenirs to French children on a daily basis that it was said to have become a rarity to see a soldier still able to wear his cap badge. And any interaction which reminded the soldiers of their humanity was welcome, because the elements were against them even before they reached the enemy.

Longman continued:

August 15th: Yesterday blazing hot and cloud – today an inch of water and six inches of mud. During the night we had a very severe thunderstorm and all today it poured.

August 16th: Still raining this morning, the camp a sea of mud ... We marched back to Havre and entrained by 12. Train left at 3.30. Every station full of people cheering 'Les Braves Anglais' and loading us with flowers. Many of them expected to be embraced in return for flowers and it would not have been a great hardship in some cases! At Rouen we stopped and the men had some coffee, while we had a hurried meal at L'Hotel Moderne – and so to bed.

August 18th: Bed not a great success. There were six in the carriage, so I slept on the floor and the springs left much to be desired. We arrived at Landrecies on the 17th about 6 a.m. and marched straight on to Noyelles [Cottage in undulating countryside like England] where we went into billets ... Maurice was billeted with Headquarters (i.e. George O'Donel, the Col and Mallock) further up the street ...

Captain George O'Donel Frederick Thomas O'Donel, from County Mayo, Ireland, was Adjutant of the 4th Royal Fusiliers. He was to be mentioned in dispatches after the war's first battle, which was by now less than five days away. Compared with many, O'Donel was lucky, because he still had the best part of a year to live. He was destined to survive long enough to see his thirtieth birthday, before being killed in June 1915 at Bellewarde Ridge. Before the fighting started, Maurice would doubtless have been pleased to hear the warm, familiar tones of a lyrical Irish voice in the house where he was billeted.

By 'the Col', Longman was referring to Lieutenant Colonel Norman Reginald McMahon, DSO. And it was McMahon who must have insisted upon Dease being billeted with the top brass. McMahon had taken a special interest in Dease's machine gun detachment, and with good reason. As Chief Instructor of Musketry, Hythe, from 1905 to 1914, Lieutenant Colonel McMahon urged that each battalion be equipped with six machine guns. He had seen into the future, he had realised what modern warfare would require. The Army Council possessed no such vision. It declined McMahon's request for financial reasons.

Some things never change. Even today, soldiers continue to complain of inadequate equipment and penny-pinching at the administrative level, and point to the catastrophic consequences of such miserly short-sightedness by the pen-pushers and bean-counters. The accountants didn't have to fight the battles; they still don't. It wouldn't be their lives in danger due to inadequate weaponry and equipment. All the administrators had to do was ensure that the bottom line on the figures looked acceptable. Human lives came second.

It is doubtful whether McMahon saw fit to share with Dease his little secret about being denied what he saw as essential firepower, or chose to reveal to Maurice the inadequacy of their machine gun quota for a real battle. As they prepared under the same roof for war, McMahon would have wished to sound more positive in front of his subordinates. He would certainly have seen fit to impress upon Dease the importance of his machine guns, though. He may even have gone as far as expressing his regret that Dease didn't have more than two machine guns under his command. But McMahon would not have considered it a good time to spell out the dreadful truth as he obviously saw it – that Dease only had at his disposal a third of the firepower he considered necessary for a modern battle, that the consequences might well be terminal, that so few machine guns would inevitably provide a magnet for more concentrated, murderous fire.

McMahon had at least done all he could to compensate for this deficiency by training the men in the rapid fire to which Holbrook had alluded. The vital nature of this rapid fire, McMahon's obsession with pushing each man's capability up to firing a round every four seconds and fifteen in sixty, caused this exercise to become known as 'The Mad Minute', with McMahon being known as the 'Musketry Maniac'. But there was method in his madness. If he couldn't have more machine guns, he would train his men to fire their rifles so quickly that the combined effect would sound to the enemy like dozens of machine guns rattling away at them. As for Dease, the young Irishman would have to strike hard and fast and never relent if he was to gain and retain the upper hand at the start of the action.

Major T.R. Mallock, McMahon's second-in-command, was well versed in the battalion commander's views. And Mallock in his own right was a cool and impressive officer, destined to show these qualities both before and during the retreat from Mons, and then subsequent fighting at Le Cateau. There could have been no finer officer for Maurice to be with during the build-up to his own ordeal. Mallock had even met the Dease family socially.

Like O'Donel, both McMahon and Mallock would be mentioned in dispatches after the first battle. As they bedded down in their billet, the company of these fine officers would only have strengthened Maurice's resolve further still – if indeed that were possible for a brave young man already totally dedicated to his cause. Maurice's fellow officers were also brave in the extreme, and must have had an inkling of what was to come. Yet they were ordinary human beings, young in most cases, and even now they exhibited a playful streak and a capacity to enjoy nature.

There is a reference to officers and men innocently catching minnows in the stream at the bottom of this street in Noyelles the following day. Given his love for all country pursuits, Maurice might well have been among their number. Whatever he was up to in Noyelles, these would be the final peaceful moments of his life.

Meanwhile, Maurice's friend Longman, billeted well away from the eyes of superiors who might have caught him with pen in hand, continued to make daily entries in his personal diary, which gives us a flavour of the way Maurice must have enjoyed these precious moments in Noyelles, and the marvellous hospitality of the local people:

August 20th: The men were most amusing in their efforts to talk the lingo … My efforts not much better … I shall never forget Noyelles and the kind old people there. On the whole I think it has been the pleasantest 3 days of soldiering I've ever spent.

August 21st: The march today was the longest we have had, tho' not at all excessive. Men came along A1. We reached Longueville in good time. Good billets and nice people. ... The French papers I see state that we are within 25 miles of the direct line of the main attack of the whole German army.

As they drew closer to what would become the temporary front, Maurice's close colleague Osbert Cundy-Cooper received a letter from home, apparently from a woman called 'Phyli'. She may even have accompanied Mollie Hewitt to that intimate tea party on their last day of peace in England. At any rate, Cundy-Cooper recorded, 'Here I got a letter from Phyli enclosing photographs of Maurice, Beazley and self, which had been taken on August 11th, just before we left to the front. I gave these to Maurice to look at ...'

Was it the visual reminder of that lovely last day, and the enchanting female company they had enjoyed that prompted Maurice to write to Mollie one last time? At any rate, he did so on 21 August, in a short letter that was addressed only to Mollie and not to Rupert, the man who was still legally her husband.

My Dear Mollie,
We are getting on grand out here but cannot let you know where we are or what we are doing on account of censorship.

Mattie is going on all right, she had a bit of a rope gall but it is healing now, all Rupert's horses are doing A1. Write me a line when you have time, address it: Battalion, Brigade, On Active Service.

Best love,
Maurice.

George O'Donel, the Adjutant, who had met Mollie on the Isle of Wight, decided to add his own personal message, 'Hope you are fit'. The letter didn't reach the Isle of Wight and go through Ryde until 4.45 a.m. on 30 August 1914 – by which time Maurice had been dead for almost a week. Indeed, from the moment he put his pen down, perhaps wondering whether he should have written more, there was to be precious little time for personal correspondence. The Germans were coming, and the ferocity of their aggression could not be underestimated.

From the headquarters of the German Army at Aix-la-Chapelle, the Kaiser issued the following order to the officer chosen to carry out his destructive bidding, General von Kluck:

It is my Royal and Imperial Command that you concentrate your energies for the immediate present upon one single purpose, and that is that you address all your skill and all the valour of my soldiers to exterminate the treacherous English and walk over General French's contemptible little army.

There have been claims since that the Kaiser didn't use the word 'contemptible' but something less derogatory, which may have been lost in translation. Even so, the word 'contemptible' stuck, and became a motivating force for those in General French's army for the rest of their lives. They used 'contemptible' like a badge of honour, a source of pride, because they were destined to defy the Kaiser with their stubborn determination to provide more resistance than any German had foreseen.

As leader of the British Expeditionary Force, Sir John French's Order of the Day on 21 August was equally uncompromising. Far from being 'treacherous', as the Kaiser had called them, the British were displaying honour of the highest order. They were proving as good as their word and standing up to an aggressor, as they had promised to do. At the same time, they were making a stand against what they saw as an assault on their own freedom in the long run. Sir John wrote:

Our cause is just. We are called upon to fight beside our gallant allies in France and Belgium in no war of arrogance, but to uphold our national honour, independence and freedom. We have violated no neutrality, nor have we been false to any treaties. We enter upon this conflict with the clearest consciousness that we are fighting for right and honour.

Having then this trust in the righteousness of our cause, pride in the glory of our military traditions, and belief in the efficiency of our army, we go forward together to do or die for GOD – KING – AND COUNTRY.

It was read out to the 4th Fusiliers at the end of the day, when their stragglers had caught up with them. They had crossed the frontier close to Aulnois and halted on the battlefield of Malplaquet at 12 noon. It was on the historic field of Malplaquet that another English commander had once led his army to victory. This was where the Duke of Marlborough had been victorious against the French in 1709.

Dease, Godley and the others set out again at 5 a.m. on 22 August – though Sidney later recalled that they had been on the go since an hour earlier, which was probably when he awoke. 'I was in the 4th Battalion, the Royal Fusiliers. We ... marched into Mons ... starting at four in the morning and arriving at 1 p.m.'

At first, they halted in the town, where it was market day, the battalion having arrived on a Saturday. Cundy-Cooper, one of Maurice's colleagues, described the unexpected challenge all the officers faced in an atmosphere of frenzied celebration:

> A multitude of inhabitants appeared and gave the men all sorts of things
> – eggs, fruit and drinks. We, the officers, had great difficulty in prevent-
> ing the men from getting drunk, which would have been exceedingly
> bad for them, after a long march under the hot sun, with entrenching
> etc before them.

Longman also described the temptations. 'The people of Mons beat every-thing in the way of hospitality – eggs, fruit, baccy, handkerchiefs, in fact everything the men could think of was shoved on them. I don't think there was a man in my platoon who sucked less than six eggs ...'

Eggs, fruit, wine, handkerchiefs and hugs ... you name it, the soldiers were offered it. For Maurice and the other officers, it was all they could do to keep their men in some kind of order and focused on the job in hand. For the citizens of Mons, the British were seen as their saviours, the men who would halt the terrible German advance through their country, with all its dreadful atrocities and needless destruction. These men of the 4th Battalion, Royal Fusiliers looked tired. They needed feeding up and bringing back to life if they were going to push the Germans back.

But Lieutenant Dease and the other officers in the battalion knew that they had to maintain discipline among their men, or else the fine fighting force the people of Mons had welcomed would soon disintegrate into a useless rabble. To this end they were helped by an unexpected source. Cundy-Cooper remembered how the impromptu party was broken up:

> Suddenly there was an alarm amongst the inhabitants that the Germans
> were coming, and within a minute there was not one inhabitant to be
> seen, all the shutters were up ... After waiting about an hour [in Mons]
> we were sent out to take up an outpost position in front [of the canals.]
> I had a picket in the most impossible position, on the edge of a wood.
> I entrenched it and sent out patrols, etc. We were then ordered to retire
> to the canal and put this in a state of defence.

For many, the positions they took up just south of the Mons–Condé Canal would be their last. The fun was over. The Germans were closing in. The violence was only hours away.

# 6

# Intelligence

It is easy to point the finger of blame with the benefit of hindsight. Yet it is equally easy to hide from blame using 'the fog of war' as the eternal excuse.

Maurice Dease and Sidney Frank Godley had signed up as professional soldiers many years earlier. In doing so, they had lain themselves open to the inevitable consequences of inadequate leadership from up on high. When your life depends on the judgement of a few individuals in key positions of command, and that judgement is hopelessly short-sighted, there are always likely to be unfortunate repercussions. Even when Sir John French had men risking their lives many times over to bring him the right information, so that he could make the correct judgement calls on behalf of the thousands under his command, he didn't really listen to anything that he didn't want to hear.

On 22 August 1914, for example, Lieutenant V.H.N. Wadham and Captain Lionel Evelyn Oswald 'Leo' Charlton of the Royal Flying Corps set out on a reconnaissance mission. Because of his superior experience, 'Leo' Charlton was made observer despite outranking the pilot, a common practice in the early days of the RFC. What follows is his own description of the reconnaissance, one that he later submitted for publication in the Lancashire Fusiliers Regimental Journal of 1915:

> I was ordered to make a reconnaissance from Maubeuge, via Charleroi and Louvain, to Brussels, and thence homewards via Mons. All went well as far as Brussels; Charleroi was on fire I remember, and I thought

the sight of it from the air compared with one of Dore's illustrations to Dante's *Inferno*. Every village, farm and building in the countryside was in flames, and from a height of 6,000 feet the picture was one of extraordinary desolation. After arriving over Brussels I was very dissatisfied because I had discovered nothing of sufficient importance to report on my return. I had seen transport and troops here and there on the road, but no great movement of army corps which I knew I was expected to find.

When I turned south from Brussels, our height was about 6,000 feet and we got into a lot of clouds. This caused us to lose our bearings a little and made it difficult to distinguish the actual villages by name as they are very thickly scattered in this part. In two or three places I saw Taube monoplanes on the ground and knowing that these machines were operating in the Uhlans at the time, I thought I must be near the head of the German advance. In order to ascertain this positively and also to collect my exact bearings I decided to land and did so in a large meadow near Grammont. The villagers swooped down on us headed by the mayor, who was of the type 'village gossip'. It did not take long to discover that we had landed absolutely in the midst of a large concentration of German troops, the nearest of which was about a quarter of an hour's walk away.

After collecting some quite good information as to their strength, their nature, their conversation, etc., I very hurriedly switched on the engine and started hoping for the best. When about 500 feet up, I flew plumb over a German brigade halted for the dinner hour. I could see the regiments with piled arms, each in its own formation with the officers messing at the head, and a little beyond in the same field what was evidently the Brigade Headquarters, also at feed. I imagine someone must have said: 'By Jove! There goes an English aeroplane; let's have it.' At any rate, every man jack jumped up to his feet and loosed off at us.

The machine was naturally punctured all over. I got two through my belt, and was rather perturbed to see two of the main spars shot through. What surprised me now is that I very coolly and calmly hove three bombs into the midst of them, two of which took effect, and after that I was able to empty the magazine of my rifle right into the 'Brown'. I attribute my coolness and calmness to the fact that there was nothing else to do but be cool and calm. At any rate we went on.

Five minutes later at 1,200 feet we went over identically the same thing again, with the addition of field guns and machine guns. These had been warned by the noise of firing from away back and were ready for us. The machine was again punctured and through and through, but still both myself and the other fellow were unhurt. Yet again the same thing happened at about 2,000 feet. Thereafter, by dint of climbing hard, which was a little difficult, as the machine was somewhat war worn, we got to 4,000 feet and found ourselves over the lines occupied by the British at Mons. This was the worst time we had of all, because the British let us have it properly. More punctures in the machine, strips out of the wings and the tail plane, about a foot long.

This is the whole thing, except that when we got down safely and found the information we had collected was valuable to our Headquarters, and also the French. Counting up afterwards we discovered between thirty and forty separate holes in the aeroplane, not counting the two through my belt.

During this historic flight, the bombs and rifle fire from Charlton at the Germans are believed to represent the first such aerial attack of the Great War. The German brigades they discovered were part of Von Kluck's II Corps, of vital importance to the British and French. As soon as the Bleriot had landed, Charlton left Wadham inspecting the bullet holes and reported to the Commander and Deputy of the RFC, Sir David Henderson and Lieutenant-Colonel Sykes. The details of the position of the German Corps was immediately forwarded to Sir John French's HQ where Charlton's report was assessed and decisions made for orders to be issued for 23 August, the day the Battle of Mons started.

Charlton had been able to report that a highly aggressive, massive German force marching west from Brussels had wheeled south-west and was now heading in the general direction of Mons, but on a course which might well enable them to outflank the BEF on the left. But powered flight was only ten years old and Sir John French, something of a dinosaur, wasn't going to rely too heavily on intelligence gathered by such a new source. He tended to think that situations could seem exaggerated or distorted from up in the air. So, when another report stated that a large German column had been observed near the town of Nivelles, halfway between Brussels and Mons, and appeared to be heading straight for the British, he was equally unconcerned.

Collateral for these reports was now coming in from the British cavalry, which had observed the Germans from a distance and confirmed that a large German column was approaching Mons from Brussels. Yet Sir John remained upbeat in his assessment of the strength of the enemy, distinctly at odds with the intelligence which had been provided by the airmen and his own cavalry. Sir John seemed to think the British were facing little more than one – at most two – corps with perhaps a single cavalry division. In fact it was three corps, and by the afternoon more like four. At this point Sir John still seemed to believe the British Expeditionary Force would be able to advance after no more than an initial skirmish at Mons. How wrong he was.

The enemy were under the overall command of General von Moltke, but it was the German 1st Army, under the cold and efficient General von Kluck, which was offering the most specific threat and making the most ominous gains. Louvain and then Brussels itself had fallen. Around 200,000 men and 40,000 horses were sweeping southward, with the intention of reaching Paris and destroying anything which stood in their way. Some 50,000 German soldiers of the VII Corps were between Nivelles and Charleroi. Another corps, probably the IX Corps, was south of Soignies, and yet another, the II Corps, was moving on Landeuse, north-west of Condé. This force, plus two cavalry divisions, was closing ominously on the BEF.

Any thoughts Sir John had that the intelligence he was receiving from various brave sources might actually be worth something, seem to have been allayed or dismissed by his Deputy Chief of Staff Henry Wilson. The fact that Sir John listened to Wilson was to prove catastrophic for the most vulnerably positioned troops at Mons. And a clue should have come from the retreat of various French forces after their superiors decided the Germans would be too hot to contain. Sir John later wrote:

At five a.m. on the 22nd I awoke, as I had lain down to sleep, in high hopes. No evil foreboding of coming events had visited me in dreams, but it was not many hours later that the disillusionment began. I started my motor in the very early hours of a beautiful August morning to visit General Lanrezac in his headquarters in the neighbourhood of Philippeville. Soon after entering the area of the 5th French Army I found my motor stopped at successive crossroads by columns of infantry and artillery moving SOUTH ... There is an atmosphere engendered by troops retiring, when they expect to be advancing, which is unmistakable to anyone who has had much experience of war ... My optimistic visions of the night had vanished ... It was evident that the enemy was making some progress in his attempts to bridge and cross the Sambre all along the front of the 5th Army.

With his own morale apparently dented, and resentment against his French allies already starting to simmer, Sir John had a meeting with the commander of their forces, General Lanzerac. Neither of them spoke the other's language with even the slightest degree of competence; and they quickly developed the sort of personal antipathy which is so counterproductive in pressurised situations. It didn't help that Sir John seemed to find Lanzerac's first request nothing short of barmy. Sir John went on:

> General Lanrezac was anxious to know if I would attack the flank of the German columns which were pressing him back from the river. In view of the most probable situation of the German army, as it was known to both of us, and the palpable intention of its commander to effect a great turning movement round my left flank, and having regard to the actual numbers of which I was able to dispose, it is very difficult to realise what was in Lanrezac's mind when he made such a request to me.

And yet, in denying Lanzerac his initial outrageous request, it seems that Sir John French somehow felt compelled to grant Lanzerac another, namely to hold the Mons–Condé Canal, even though he claims he already believed this line could become 'very precarious', since the French were already retiring. Sir John added:

> As the left of the French 5th Army (Reserve Division of the 18th Corps) was drawn back as far as Trélon, and the centre and right of that army were in process of retiring, the forward position I now held on the Condé Canal might quickly become very precarious. I therefore informed Lanrezac in reply that such an operation as he suggested was quite impracticable for me. I agreed to retain my current position for twenty-four hours, but after that time I told him it would be necessary for me to consider whether the weight against my front and outer flank, combined with the retreat of the French 5th Army, would not compel me to go back to the Maubeuge position.

With the benefit of hindsight, this decision to hold at the canal seems incomprehensible. Was he about to sacrifice hundreds of fine men as no more than a conciliatory gesture to the French, a token waste of life to make up for refusing Lanrezac's request to attack the advancing Germans on their flank? What was to be gained by holding the Germans at the canal for a few hours? Was he really going to save thousands of French troops by doing so? Wouldn't they have preserved more men by regrouping together straightaway, at the more defensible Maubeuge line?

It was precisely because the defence of the salient, which was largely the responsibility of General Sir Hubert Hamilton's 3rd Dvision, looked so questionable that an alternative plan had been laid. A second line of defence had been prepared behind Mons itself and roughly on the line St Ghislain–Wasmes–Paturage–Frameries. In theory this would straighten out the line and do away with an exposed salient. But such logic wasn't applied in time to save the men who were about to die on the canal.

On the evening of 22 August, French told the corps commanders that, while there would be no further advance, he had agreed to hold the BEF on the canal for another twenty-four hours until the position became clear. Dease, Godley and their friends were left to prepare defences on the most vulnerable part of the most vulnerable loop in the Mons–Condé Canal. They could expect incoming fire from three separate sides when the going got tough, because their position effectively bulged out into what would inevitably become German territory on the north of the canal. They knew they wouldn't have a clear field of fire to return what the Germans were going to be throwing at them, either. Buildings, slag-heaps and even woods in the distance provided cover for the enemy.

What cover would Dease have to defend that Nimy railway bridge with his two machine guns on its buttresses? A fellow-officer wrote later: 'The machine gunners (under Maurice) were posted on the embankment. I believe (railway) sleepers was [sic] all the machine gunners could get to make the emplacement for their guns.'

In addition to the sleepers, Dease was going to have little more than flour sacks filled with shingle and piled around his positions on the parapet for protection, one machine gun on either side of the tracks. He must have known deep down those 'sandbags' wouldn't be enough; but you couldn't dig effective trenches into the tracks or the area around them – the ground was just too hard and stony. Flour sacks and shingle would have to do, though what use they would be if German artillery got a fix on those British machine gun nests was debatable. The Germans would bring up machine guns of their own to try to knock out the British positions, and whereas British tactics only allowed, absurdly, for two machine guns per detachment, similar Germans units had six machine guns to deploy.

Anyone who had been to Sandhurst must have known how precarious their situation appeared, in theory at least. Assuming the Germans knew what they were doing, it wasn't going to be a question of 'if' the British would need to retreat, but 'when'. How many British soldiers would be able to get away in one piece might depend on whether they could deny the Germans the canal crossings by blowing up the bridges before it was too late. Careful plans had to be laid, along with the explosives. A line of communication would have to be kept open at all costs, with an officer on the ground given all the authority he needed to detonate the explosives sufficiently early to prevent major loss of life on the British side.

The problem was that Sir John French didn't seem to grasp any of this. In his state of indecision, even confusion, he wished to remain flexible. And, in his desire to remain flexible, he appears to have issued no clear orders and laid out no clear strategy whatsoever. Neither did he give his commanders any clear indication of enemy strength.

Sir John called together his Corps and Cavalry Division commanders at 0530 on 23 August at General Smith-Dorrien's HQ in the Chateau de la Haie (otherwise known as Chateau de la Roche) near the village of Sars-la-Bruyère. They were about 12 kilometres south-west of Mons, but they were a world away from their men. And if the lack of clear thinking hadn't soon proved so tragic, it would almost have been comical. According to Smith-Dorrien, Sir John told his commanders to 'be prepared to move forward, or to fight where we were, but to get ready for the latter by strengthening our outposts and by preparing the bridges over the canal for demolition'.

But no one prepared the most important bridges for demolition – and others were wired with no satisfactory level of thoroughness. What was the point, some on the ground may have thought, if there was no clear indication of the circumstances under which they would be allowed to use their own judgement to blow them? If a situation deteriorated rapidly and suddenly became critical, it wasn't as though there would be time to request permission from a remotely positioned commander in the hope he could send a prompt reply back through the thick of battle.

Smith-Dorrien did at least seem to try to make it clear to French that he felt retreat might become necessary sooner rather than later. But Smith-Dorrien was also probably aware that French disliked him too, didn't necessarily approve of his appointment, and wouldn't entertain any hint of insubordination from him. Smith-Dorrien had taken command of II Corps less than forty-eight hours earlier, which hardly added to the weight his words carried. It was unfortunate that Smith-Dorrien had only just assumed command of I Corps, following the death of Lieutenant-General Sir James Grierson on 17 August due to a heart attack. And as Smith-Dorrien wasn't

Sir John French's choice that just made the BEF Commander dislike him even more intensely.

Nevertheless, Smith-Dorrien claimed later that he went so far as to tell Sir John that he did not regard the canal as an ideal defensive line. He had already reconnoitred a shorter line a couple of miles south of it, he advised, a position he considered more suitable for a prolonged defence. Orders were being prepared for his forward troops to retire to this line as and when their positions on the canal became untenable. Smith-Dorrien later insisted that Sir John did not express disapproval of these arrangements.

Sir John French was certainly aware of the salient on the canal and the outward bulge in the line which left it vulnerable on three sides, and effectively impossible to defend for more than a few hours. As he met all his commanders, he mentioned the salient twice, though inevitably his mind was on the bigger picture. Sir John wrote:

> I left my headquarters at 5 a.m. on Sunday, the 23rd, and went to Sars-la-Bruyère [headquarters of the 2nd Corps], and there I met [General Sir Douglas] Haig [commanding 1st Corps], [General Sir Horace] Smith-Dorrien [commanding the 2nd], and [Major-General Sir Edmund] Allenby [the General commanding the Cavalry Division] … The 2nd Corps occupied the line of the Condé Canal, from that place round the salient which the canal makes from to the north of Mons, and extended thence to the east of Obourg, whence that part of the line was drawn back towards Villers-St Ghislain. The 5th division was holding the line from Condé to Mariette, whilst the 3rd Division continued the line thence round the salient to the right of the line occupied by the 2nd Corps. The 1st Corps was echeloned on the right and in the rear of the 2nd.

The following paragraph of Sir John French's account can be summed up in one word: confusion. And, within that confusion, French argued that during their early-morning meeting on the day of the battle, Smith-Dorrien had expressed far more confidence about his ability to defend the canal than he later admitted. Was Sir John trying to rewrite history to make his own decision-making look better? It seems likely, though he still failed to paint himself in a positive light, because he could point to precious little decision-making at all. Sir John went on:

> I told the commanders of the doubts that had arisen in my mind during the previous twenty-four hours, and impressed on them the necessity

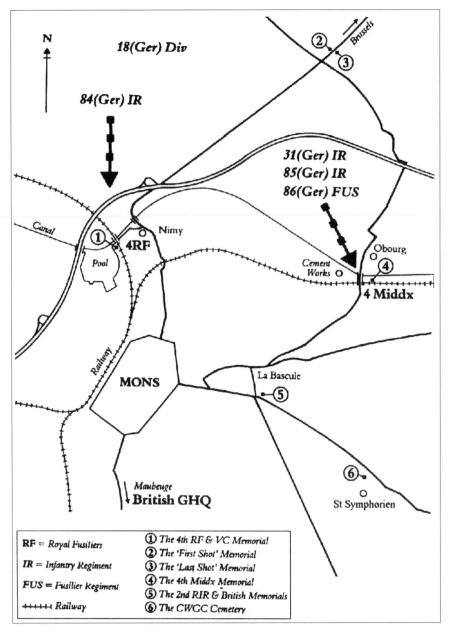

Map of the canal and battle at Mons.

of being prepared for any kind of move, either in advance or in retreat.
I discussed exhaustively the situation on our front. Allenby's bold and
searching reconnaissance had not led me to believe that we were threatened by forces against which we could not make an effective stand.

The 2nd Corps had not yet been seriously engaged, while the 1st was practically still in reserve. Allenby's orders to concentrate towards the left flank when pressed by the advance of the enemy's main columns had been practically carried into effect. I entertained some anxiety as to the salient which the canal makes north of Mons, and enjoined on Smith-Dorrien particular watchfulness and care with regard to it. They all assured me that a quiet night had been passed, and that their line was firmly taken up and held. The air reconnaissance had started at daybreak, and I decided to await aircraft reports from Henderson before making any decided plan ... I left General Smith-Dorrien full of confidence with regard to his position ...

What was he talking about? Of course a quiet night had been spent and the line was held. The Germans weren't attacking yet. As for 'firmly taken up', it was impossible for 'firm' defence of the line, because of the geographical features working against the men there. Any experienced military man must have known there could be no reason for 'full confidence' in their chances of holding the position Dease and Godley had taken up. Was Smith-Dorrien really out to impress his superior by expressing the sort of optimism he knew French wanted to hear? What sort of reassurance was this, if it ignored the facts to the point of sheer irresponsibility?

French could not have been full of confidence with regard to Smith-Dorrien's position, because he added the following: 'I instructed Sir Archibald Murray, my Chief of Staff, to remain for the present at Smith-Dorrien's headquarters at Sars-la-Bruyère, and gave him full instructions as to the arrangements that must be made if a retreat became necessary.' As for his claim to have paid attention to aerial reconnaissance reports, this appears to have been a case of belated, wishful thinking.

Whatever instructions and communications structures he left in place there, they would prove to be wholly inadequate when the time came. As for awaiting the findings of air reconnaissance before making a decision, it seems mystifying that the commanders didn't trust the air reconnaissance reports they already had. French already had enough information from the likes of Charlton the previous day to know that his men were about to be attacked by great numbers of well-organised enemy troops. But there it was. Sir John French didn't know whether to go forward and he didn't know whether to go back. He was full of confidence but he was anxious about the possible need to retreat. He was going to stay where he was but he didn't seem to know why or for how long.

How did this translate itself to the troops at ground level? They didn't even unpack all their ammunition in case they had to move forward. They wired some of the bridges for possible demolition, but not others. The Nimy railway bridge, where Dease and Godley were going to make their last stand, hadn't been prepared for detonation, even though it was by far the most obvious candidate for demolition in case things went wrong. Even at places further along the line where bridges had been wired, there was no firm plan to carry out that demolition.

The men were going to be impossibly vulnerable, but, according to at least one account, there were no ambulances ready at the rear to take the wounded away for treatment. They were where they were; they would just have to do their best. And, since they knew they would be in for an almighty scrap, all they could do was to make ready and fight just as bravely as they knew how. The painful irony was that the officers of the Royal Fusiliers were superb, from McMahon downwards. Yet the fact remained that Dease, Godley and the rest of the 4th Royal Fusiliers didn't just have to contend with the enemy; they were unwittingly caught in the unspoken hostility and confusion which existed between those higher up the chain of command on their own side.

Furthermore, they could expect only limited support from their own artillery. This is how the famous writer Sir Arthur Conan Doyle assessed the situation when he later told of the heroics that followed:

There is a road which runs from Mons due north through the village of Nimy to Jurbise. The defences to the west of this road were in the hands of the 9th Brigade. The 4th Royal Fusiliers, with half the Northumberland Fusiliers, was the particular regiment which held the trenches skirting this part of the peninsular, while the Scots Fusiliers were down the straight canal to the westward. To the east of Nimy there are three road bridges – those of Nimy itself, Lock No 5, and Aubourg Station. All these three bridges were defended by the 4th Middlesex, who had made shallow trenches which commanded them … It has already been said that the line of the 4th Royal Fusiliers extended along the western perimeter up to Nimy road bridge, where Colonel McMahon's section ended and that of Colonel Hull, of the Middlesex Regiment, began. To the west of this point was Nimy railway bridge, defended also by the 4th Royal Fusiliers … The British artillery was unable to help the defence, as the town of Mons in the rear offered no positions for guns.

This last claim was supported by at least one account after the action, which claimed the thin line was supported by 'only half the compliment of gunners'.

While the British were deficient in this area, the Germans were very strong. The enemy artillery had been trained to support infantry attacks, so that the enemy could be softened up from behind. No such carefully coordinated fire had been arranged on the British side.

Dease and Godley couldn't have known about the tensions way above them in the chain of command. Those tensions wouldn't help men like them, who were just tiny expendable cogs in a vast military machine about to find out what modern warfare was all about.

As regular soldiers with common sense, however, they must have realised the strategic difficulties which would arise all around them. They just knew this was going to be the greatest test of their lives. The stage was set and the final countdown to the battle had begun.

# 7

# Nimy Bridge

Maurice Dease was a lieutenant but here he was with his men on the evening of 22 August 1914, shovelling shingle into sacks made for flour, with the inevitable battle sure to come at daybreak. It was typical Maurice. That was why he was so popular with his men. He didn't expect those men to do anything he wouldn't do himself. If there was dirty work to be done, he was quite prepared to do it too, especially if time was short.

He had always been caring and conscientious. He had a natural authority about him too, which wasn't undermined by a wicked sense of humour. All these qualities help to make an officer popular. They were so abundant in Maurice Dease that it is no exaggeration to say that he was loved by everyone in his battalion.

As he helped to fill and stack those sacks, hoping they would absorb German bullets and shrapnel in a few hours' time, Dease must have felt exhausted. It had been a long, tiring march across 20 miles of countryside to Mons. With all the temptations around them in the town, perhaps it was just as well that Mons itself hadn't been their final destination that afternoon. Instead they had carried on to Nimy, a small village to the north of Mons in a salient on the Mons–Condé Canal.

Once the 4th Royal Fusiliers arrived at Nimy they were initially positioned north of the canal salient occupying posts covering Ghlin, just south of the Bois de Ghlin and Bois Brule. There was a very poor field of fire and it was a poor tactical position to withstand a prolonged enemy attack. Even so, they had been told to dig in north of the canal. Late in the afternoon the men were ordered to withdraw back over the canal, having been told that they looked too vulnerable on the north side. So they had been given no choice but to prepare their defences all over again, a gruelling end to an already demanding day.

They were part of a thin, 25-mile front – too long and too thin, as it would turn out. The canal which formed most of this front curved around Mons itself to Nimy and Obourg and passed through mining villages and close to slag heaps. To the north of the canal was a series of woods. Dease, Godley and the others must have re-examined the restricted fields of fire, looked again at the salient and concluded again that it was a natural weak point in the defensive line. Would the new position be significantly easier to defend? The answer had to be no. Those small hamlets and rows of houses, those huge slag-heaps and sprawling factories peppered the approach to the canal from the north. In short, Dease's machine gun detachment had drawn the short straw, as had the 4th Fusiliers in general.

No member of the British Expeditionary Force could feel secure in his defensive position, however. The Mons–Condé Canal itself was only 6 or 7ft deep and rarely more than 60ft wide. There were no fewer than eighteen bridges along its 16 miles. In short, it didn't make much of an obstacle to a determined German advance. Not unless Sir John French was going to ensure those bridges were quickly blown if his BEF found it necessary to fall back. And French didn't want to blow them, not until the last possible moment, if at all, because he still thought he might be able to move forward the following day. Dease and Godley were at the mercy of French's confusion. He still didn't know whether they would have to move forward; he didn't know whether they'd have to move back. He didn't know anything really, and what he did know about the size of the enemy force he chose to ignore. He had no firm plan at all. So the canal remained vulnerable, its bridges intact.

The 4th Royal Fusiliers were dispersed along the western face of the canal bend and they had to cover all the crossings including Nimy rail and road bridges. If the Germans chose to concentrate their attack here, Dease and Godley knew they could expect to face enemy fire from three sides. They weren't alone. To their right was the 4th Middlesex Regiment who were defending the eastern face of the canal salient. They joined at the Bridge des Bragnons. But it was the 4th Royal Fusiliers who were the most vulnerable strategically.

Captain Forster with his two battalions held Nimy road bridge. The other two battalions were entrenched at the railway bridge and on the canal bank on the left. Dease belonged to C Company – also known as Y Company – under Captain Ashburner. Together they must have realised that, if the Germans knew what they were doing, they would be targeted. That meant they were about to see some of the fiercest fighting of all. You can imagine Maurice looking around, taking it all in, and then worrying for his men. D Company, under Captain Byng, held positions to their left, around Lock 6 and the Ghlin–Mons bridges. B Company, under Captain Carey, was positioned around Nimy railway station in support of Battalion HQ. Meanwhile, A Company, with Captain Cole, was held in reserve just north of Mons.

Maurice Dease, 4th Battalion Machine Gun Officer, was in the farcical situation of having just two machine guns at his disposal because only McMahon had worked out what modern warfare might require, but no one had listened to him. Yet, because British artillery would also be limited in its effect, due to those built-up areas around Nimy and Mons behind them, much would still depend on Dease and those two machine guns. He would just have to pick his spot and use his meagre resources as best he could. Major Maurice French explained how short of firepower his uncle had been back in 1914:

> Of course that was a ridiculous time because they should have had far more than two machine guns in each battalion. It would have made quite a difference. They should have had about eight machine guns, I would have thought; a section of two, another section of two, then one with each of the rifle companies. If only they had pictured how the war was going to go, but they didn't. The Germans were far more 'jacked up' than the Brits and had a better idea of what twentieth-century warfare might be like.

On the British side, a machine gun section still consisted of an officer, a sergeant, a corporal, twelve gunners and a limbered wagon carrying the two guns, spare parts and ammunition. The load was pulled by two horses with a driver. Were these horses Mollie Hewitt's Mattie and Maurice's own Palm? Although Mattie had suffered the chafing from ropes and harness mentioned in his letter to her, that kind of discomfort would pale into insignificance compared to the suffering the Germans would soon unleash on them all.

Sergeant Major Pocock of the 4th Royal Fusiliers had witnessed Maurice's arrival on the scene with his detachment, watched him divide his twelve gunners into two sections, with six men to each gun, and oversee the well-drilled unit as they unlimbered the Maxims and moved the horses under cover. Maurice chose the precise spot for his two weapons. There was a parapet flanking the Nimy railway bridge, and it provided the most obvious spot for the deployment. Probably after consulting McMahon, Maurice placed a machine gun on each side of that parapet.

Pocock wrote, 'We took up position on the Railway bridge across the canal at Mons on Saturday evening 22nd August 1914. About 5 p.m. Mr Dease came with his machine gun detachment, consisting of two guns, which he placed on the left and right side of bridge.' Meanwhile the infantry platoons dug in on either side with two platoons in the forward positions and two immediately behind them in reserve.

Near the railway bridge was a mill with an abundance of flour sacks, and plenty of shingle with which to fill them. So that's how Maurice came to muck in with his men on that glorious summer's evening. The Sergeant-Major had quickly gone to work with Dease to do what they could to protect their men. Pocock recalled, 'Immediately he arrived, he took off his coat and set about filling flour sacks with shingle to use as cover for the machine guns, in fact I assisted Mr Dease to hold up the sacks while he himself shovelled in.'

Those sacks would make some kind of defences for the two machine guns. The situation was far from ideal, but the harder they worked now, the more lives might be saved the following morning. These preparations went on into the night and Dease worked hard with his section, filling more sacks and preparing the defences. Ominously, some advance German forces could be heard moving around in the woods north of the canal. A clash of arms the following day was inevitable.

But Deases's men had long been soldiers and they were steely characters who were ready to take whatever was coming their way, and dish out far worse in return if they could. The Royal Fusiliers were regulars but many of them were reservists who had enlisted in the Boer War; most of the 4th Royal Fusiliers (London) were Cockneys. Many of the men in the machine gun section had served under Lieutenant Dease for three years, and they must have appreciated their popular officer rolling up his sleeves to do some of that dirty work with them. When the sacks were finally filled and placed in defence to Maurice's satisfaction, he must have wished his men a peaceful but vigilant night – one man in three would have had to stay awake – before returning to his fellow officers to assess the situation.

These men had trained at Sandhurst and had learned enough about military strategy to realise what a dreadful position they were in. If the Germans had a sustained attack planned for the next day, the British defences would be inadequate. They must have discussed the problems they'd had digging in, and what they had been able to do to rectify the problem.

One of Dease's 4th Battalion friends, Lieutenant Osbert Cundy-Cooper, wrote later about their problems on the canal bridges: 'Longman's platoon were only able to make very inferior defences, it being impossible to dig on the railway line (he had to make use of sleepers with a bit of dirt in front of them). B and C Companies had much the same difficulties.'

But officers in the British Army were not paid to be negative. They were trained to make the best of their situation. The men they commanded, many of whom had been waiting years for this kind of challenge, also shared their excitement. This was what soldiering was all about; and they knew the moment to show what they could do in battle had finally arrived. They also knew these hours of darkness provided one final chance to enjoy each other's company.

Captain 'Kingy' Tower recalled the moments Maurice shared with some of those along his chain of command and later wrote to Maurice's sister, Maud, 'We sat together (Maurice, Ashburner, Steele and I) on the bridge all cheery and happy and drank some awfully good coffee. Old Maurice then lay down and had a real good sleep which must have done him all the good in the world.'

Given the ordeal Dease was to face the following day, this was a heart-breaking line. No doubt Captain Tower meant well. Dease had probably found some kind of peace in that final, earthly sleep, having enjoyed the good company of colleagues. That was what Captain Tower was trying to say. He might even have woken refreshed on the day of battle and therefore been able to perform so heroically partly because of that sleep. But what sleep could possibly do Maurice and his personal health 'all the good in the world', when he only had hours to live? So there was a terrible pathos to Tower's well-meaning account. And it is hard to imagine that it wouldn't have caused Maurice's sister more anguish.

Sergeant Pocock was more basic in his own recollections – and it didn't sound as though he had enjoyed much sleep. 'We laid behind the cover all night … the following morning about 7 a.m. the Germans showed themselves.'

They first showed themselves from the air, an unusual and awesome sight in an age when flight for humans had only just been invented. Private H.C. Barnard was number 3 on Dease's left-hand gun, ready to provide ammunition. He recalled: 'The first I saw of the Germans was one of their aeroplanes flying low over us about 7 a.m. The pilot looked down on us. I remember the plane had wings, shaped like a bird's.'

While the British stood and admired this strange sight, the German plane spotted the canal bridges still intact at the loop, the most vulnerable point. Furthermore, it must have spotted that there was no formidable build-up of British forces there, no special measures to protect the weak point in their defences. There was nothing to deter the Germans from concluding that a concerted effort to take the railway bridge would be the way to go.

Whether or not the plane reported back in time for its intelligence to have any bearing on the German battle plan is open to question. But that huge bird darkening the summer sky above Dease's men was ominous indeed. The villagers of Nimy, young and old, seemed oblivious to the ferocity of the violence which was about to sweep across their village. At least they saw no reason to change their weekend routine. Godley recalled later, 'It was Sunday. People in their best suits were going to church. They didn't know the Germans were so near, of course. No one did ...'

But of course the citizens of Mons itself had known, because there had been a major panic the previous day, when a rumour swirled around the market square that the enemy had been sighted. They knew it was just a matter of time before the Germans turned up to play their part in the battle. Then a girl called through from a station further up the line, warning that the Germans were on their way down the tracks towards Nimy in huge numbers. All the more reason for the locals to pray – especially if it appeared they might soon be caught up in a skirmish between foreigners.

Not long after the plane had come and gone from the skies above the canal, there was a fresh development on the ground – one that said much about the character of Private Godley. As someone who had endured a tough childhood at times, he had always made time for children. And now, just before the dreadful battle, he saw no reason to make any exception. Even as the sense of anticipation hung heavily in the morning air, Godley demonstrated his humanity. He remembered that, 'When I was on the bridge before the action started, a little boy and girl came up on the bridge and brought me some rolls and coffee.' His voice croaked a little on the word 'coffee', perhaps breaking slightly with the recollection of that simple yet extraordinary act of kindness. The rolls became unexpectedly important. Those were the last energy-giving morsels of food Godley was able to consume for some time. How he would need them as the day went on.

It's not clear exactly what Godley's role was at that early point. A newspaper report later claimed, 'At 7 a.m. he mounted his Maxim machine gun on Nimy bridge over the canal at Mons, Belgium, opened his boxes of spare ammunition, and waited for something to happen ...' If Godley did any of these, it was in a supportive role to the principal machine gun teams, of which he was not part. Had he been a starting member of one of those two teams, he would almost certainly never have lived to tell the tale. But he may well have been doing much of the heavy work, bringing boxes of ammunition to the teams, making sure the wire barrier at the far end of the bridge was looking solid, before returning to his own side.

The arrival of the children with refreshments must have seemed like a godsend. He added, 'I was really enjoying the rolls and coffee and talking to the children as best I could, and, er …,' he paused as he remembered how peace was broken, and he knew life would never be the same, before completing his sentence, ' … the Germans started shelling.'

On other bridge, Cundy-Cooper experienced the shelling too. He had been with Maurice for their last pleasurable afternoon of English peace earlier that August; Cundy-Cooper, Dease and Beazley at a small party on the Isle of Wight, in the company of some attractive female friends; they were all a world away from a garden party now. Cundy-Cooper soon wrote, 'This was our first taste of shells. They make a fearful noise and the shrapnel all around is rather alarming …'

Yet the two Belgian children at the railway bridge had stayed; and now they were vulnerable. The picnic they had brought suddenly looked almost as out of place as they were. How on earth had they come to be on the front line in the first place? Had their parents miscalculated and decided they would have time to refresh men such as Godley and then come away again before the fighting started? Those young children surely couldn't have known what they were walking into. Or perhaps they had an idea, but trusted to God that all would be well because they were doing a good deed.

Eileen said that her father never ceased to marvel at their actions, even later in his life. 'My dad always said, "That innocence of a child. That sheer innocence of a child."' Eileen's son Andy agreed: 'They didn't know the danger. Amazing isn't it? But to bring him a drink and some food on the bridge; that's marvellous isn't it, really?'

Perhaps those children's parents underestimated the speed with which the Germans were approaching; or more likely they hadn't considered the possibility of long-range shelling. Godley suddenly felt responsible for them now, in this strange moment at the outbreak of the First World War. You could hear it in his voice all those years later, as he described the firm advice he gave them, which must have been delivered much like an order. ' … So I said to this little boy and girl, "You'd better sling your 'ooks now …,"' Sid says this as if he is talking to the children all over again; he makes the word 'now' last longer than the others, almost as if to convey the mounting concern he felt for them, ' … otherwise you might get "urt!"' Neither the boy nor the girl could possibly have understood the expression 'Sling your hooks', but the worried expression on Sid's face, and a firm gesture for them to move back to the rear, did the trick. 'They packed their basket up and left.' Godley emphasised the word 'left'. He was happy, relieved for them, confident that he had helped them reach a safer place, given them the chance to live a longer, fuller life before it was too late.

Kingy Tower was in an even more vulnerable position than Godley, Dease and the children in those early moments of uncertainty on the morning of 23 August. He wrote later:

I was out visiting my sentries in the woods about a thousand yards in advance of our position about 7 a.m. and was talking to an old Reservist, when we suddenly saw a horseman ride through the wood. He dismounted and tied his horse to a tree and advanced (about 300 yards from us) to the edge of the wood and stood looking at our position on the canal bank.

My old Reservist said to me, 'Is that a German, Sir?'

I said, 'Yes, I expect it is.'

'Whereupon he said, 'Shall I shoot him, Sir?'

And I said 'Yes, have a try.'

He picked up his rifle, took careful aim and fired. The man fell, and we walked over to look at him. He was a trooper of the famous Regiment of the Death's Head Hussars – the first German I had seen. So I took his horse and rode it back to our lines and made my report. I then returned to the sentries in front and before I got there I heard heavy rifle fire from our detachment on the main road. The next moment I saw a German officer with a heavy limp come running in my direction. I ran after him, and he held up his hands and shouted in English, 'I am Count von Arnim.' He was slightly wounded in the leg and was shivering with fright. It appeared he was one of an officers' cavalry patrol that had ridden down the road and had been caught by the fire of our post on the road …

… By this time the sun was getting quite hot. A gorgeous morning. The church bells were ringing and the Belgian peasants could be seen walking quietly to church. What a contrast! It seemed hardly believable that we were at war and that men had just been killed only a few yards away. I was just returning to my sentries when a terrific fire opened on us from the woods to the north and my sentries came running in.

The German cavalry patrol had consisted of one officer and six men. They had suddenly appeared on the Nimy road and galloped towards Nimy road bridge, which had at least been swung back to make the canal temporarily impassable there. Captain Forster's men had opened fire and shot four men dead, wounding the officer to boot. The other two men had escaped unwounded. The captured officer, Lieutenant von Armin, was the son of the Commander of IV German Army Corps, who were soon to be engaged against the British 14th Brigade.

When one of Maurice Dease's men, Private Marshall, wrote to Maurice's sister Maud later, he had his own personal recollection of these surreal moments:

> I was a machine gunner under the command of your brother, Lieutenant Dease … All went well until the morning of the 23rd, when we saw some German Cavalry galloping across our front and C Company opened fire upon them, and, when they ceased fire, a German Cavalry officer came and gave himself up as prisoner.

These minor incidents almost sounded fun for the British, little skirmishes to boost their confidence. Along the canal, Dease's friend Frederick Longman sounded almost apologetic that he hadn't found himself in the thick of the action from the start:

> The only event I had was burning a barge. There were six of them on the canal we were defending and they were supposed to be burnt. Two did not catch so I went along and got them going. It was not under fire, except for an occasional shell and two snipers who popped off as soon as I appeared – I was quite glad when the barges were blazing!

But when he wrote to Maud, Private Marshall hinted at a more worrying threat that was already developing near Maurice's position and the deadly response Dease knew he must prepare. 'Shortly afterwards we saw some Germans dodging about in between some houses and your brother told Private Guines to "Lay the gun on the space between the houses and when we saw the Germans again to open fire"'. As Maurice's friend Cundy-Cooper pointed out, the fact that advanced parties of Germans were able to 'dodge about' in the first place was extremely ominous in terms of how the day would unfold. He wrote, 'The whole line was quite indefensible, houses right up to the bank and no line of fire.'

Many historians still insist that, despite their air and cavalry patrols, the advancing Germans had little idea of the positions they were about to face, in terms of British numbers and firepower. If that was the case, it took them very little time to identify and focus upon the most vulnerable points in the British line. At around 9 a.m. they opened their attack by heading principally towards the railway and road bridges at Nimy. Several British eye-witness accounts claim the Germans first appeared in columns of four, though some German accounts, supported by their official regimental casualty figures, contest this.

Private Godley stuck to the simple facts as he recalled these, the first chaotic moments of a concerted German attack. He explained, 'It was not terribly hot. Our men were strung out along the South Bank of the canal ... Then suddenly the Germans were everywhere ... The attack came in from the north.'

A book by Tim Carew, *The Vanished Army: The British Expeditionary Force, 1914–1915*, gives an account of these opening moments of battle. The reaction of one Royal Fusilier, Private Bert Denner, sounds credible. 'Lumme, there's bloody millions of 'em!' he was reported to have said. Corporal Bill Holbrook of the 4th Royal Fusiliers – Colonel McMahon's servant – described a similarly alarming sight: 'Bloody Hell! You couldn't see the earth for them, there were that many.'

It was now, as the warriors within Maurice Dease and Sid Godley took over, that they had to suppress their humanity. On the rare occasions he recounted what happened, Sid used to grip the table, or the chair he was sitting on, as if bracing himself all over again for the onslaught. In his BBC interview, his tone became very grave again. 'The Germans came over in large formation ... and ... er ...,' again there was a pause, before Sid dropped his voice into an even deeper, sterner tone, '... we opened fire.'

What followed earned Lieutenant Maurice Dease and Private Sidney Frank Godley the Victoria Cross. Two professional soldiers who both had very gentle sides to their nature. Good blokes. But now there was no more time for being gentle. Now was the time to kill or be killed ... perhaps both.

# 8

# Maurice James Dease, VC

Godley pointed his rifle at the enemy and prepared to pull the trigger. At this early stage, he wasn't manning one of the machine guns. After all, as Dease had noted in such detail earlier that summer, Godley wasn't exactly one of the sharp-shooters in the detachment. One colourful account of the war described him like this:

> Frank Godley, five years a soldier, generously moustached, broad and powerful of build – a tireless cross-country runner, a tower of strength at centre-half in the battalion's football team. He had, however, never achieved any distinction as a machine-gunner; in fact, three years before, the sergeant-major had endeavoured to instruct Godley in the rudiments of this complex weapon and told him that as a machine-gunner he'd make a bloody good bus conductor.

To his credit, Godley had stuck at it as a machine-gunner and achieved modest improvements here and there. But, as the detachment prepared for battle, he had been of more use carrying heavy boxes of ammunition or building defences. Now that the machine gun section was as ready as it was ever going to be, Godley had his rifle at the ready. The machine guns had been left to those chosen by Dease, who was overseeing both these vital weapons on Nimy bridge. With their contrasting weaponry and degrees of responsibility, Godley and Dease held their nerve and held their fire as a wave of Germans poured into sight before them.

Exactly what form this first German attack took is a subject of much controversy. There are so many British eye-witness accounts of Germans marching forward in columns of four – as if on a parade ground – that it is hard to discount them. Yet the German historical records apparently dispute this, and the modern claim is that they attacked in open order from the start. Some have concluded, 100 years later, that the Germans sustained far fewer casualties than previously believed.

What we do know for sure is that Dease, Godley and their fellow soldiers didn't flinch as the grey swarm of Germans came into range. Dease and Godley answered that threat in the only way they could. With audible pride, tinged perhaps with a touch of sadness at the human suffering on both sides, Godley recalled later, 'The old order came, "15 rounds, rapid fire!" The lads let 'em have it. Of course the British troops, with this great volume of fire – 15 rounds rapid which we'd been highly trained in  …,' Godley paused, as though he could see the Germans falling before him, '… was very effective.'

Corporal Holbrook remembered that, 'Time after time they gave the order "Rapid fire!" Well, you didn't wait for the order, really. You'd see a lot of them coming in a mass on the other side of the canal and you just let them have it'.

Godley later insisted, 'It stopped 'em dead. They thought we all had machine guns, but we hadn't. It halted the German advance.'

Hauptmann Walter Bloem, a German Infantry Officer attacking to the right of the village of Tertre, further along the line, offered an insight into what it was like on the German side when those first bullets flew:

We had no sooner left the edge of the wood than a volley of bullets whistled past our noses and cracked into the trees behind. Five or six cries near me, five or six of my grey lads collapsed on the grass. Damn it! This was serious. The firing seemed at long range and half-left.

'Forward!' I shouted, taking my place with three of my 'staff' ten paces in front of the section leader, Holder-Egger, and the section in well-extended formation ten paced behind him again. Here we were, advancing as if on a parade ground. Huitt, huitt, srr, srr, srr! About our ears, away in front of a sharp, rapid hammering sound, then a pause, then more hammering – machine guns … A real battle this time!

As Holbrook explained, the British retained the upper hand for a while as the Germans searched for an answer to British marksmanship. 'They kept retreating, and then coming forward, and then retreating again …' Barnard recalled how 'enemy infantry advanced down the railway line, and we and the rifle platoon near us shot them to pieces'.

Having interviewed one of the survivors, the historian MacDonald Hastings (also Old Stonyhurst and father of Sir Max Hastings) made the initial task facing the British sound relatively simple:

> In one of the reserve trenches Corporal Palmerton heard spasmodic rifle fire which became increasingly more frequent and regular. ... Covered by a murderous artillery barrage the German troops, standing shoulder to shoulder in their field grey uniforms, moved forward in mass formation to storm the bridge. To the British riflemen, every one of them a trained shot, it was easy practice.

But the accuracy of the German artillery was already proving a problem. So, even if their leading columns appeared to have been destroyed, causing a cheer among the British as the rest of their foe temporarily retired out of view, the men of the Royal Fusiliers were still up against it. The German artillery began to find its range as it shelled the British positions. The BEF were unable to reply to this barrage in kind, with their artillery depleted and restricted as previously explained. And, while the British were taking their first casualties, the German infantry attacked again – this time in extended order. D Company was not engaged at this point so it felt as though the entire weight of six German battalions was focused on Ashburner's C Company – meaning Dease and Godley.

In his book *The Mons Myth*, Terence Zuber, an American historian with German connections, insists that the Germans had attacked in extended order from the start. He draws on many eye-witness accounts from the German side, men who had been advancing towards the canal and Dease's position, and the relevant German regimental histories. Though that version conflicts sharply with British claims, Zuber comes up with what he describes as a 'plausible synthesis'. He admits that he experienced difficulty in coordinating accounts, and his work appears so pro-German in its overall thrust that he seems perfectly prepared to discredit numerous eye-witness accounts on the British side. Nevertheless, he may be right when he claims that British soldiers believed they had killed more Germans than they actually did. After all, a soldier deliberately dropping down to take cover can look similar to a soldier falling dead or wounded. Zuber is quite mechanical in his description of German movements. But his version is worth reading and certainly adds to the debate, since the battle is seen through the eyes of the German 84th Regiment, or 'IR84', which attacked Dease and Godley at Nimy railway bridge once it had overcome various preliminary hurdles. The overall picture painted by Zuber of the Germans that day is of a highly efficient tactical fighting force prepared to take significant casualties which never became catastrophic, relentless in their achievement of their objectives:

> IR84 deployed II/84 on the right and III/84 on the left, 1/84 held back in reserve. III/84 advanced with 10/84 on the right of the road to Nimy, 11/84 on the left … 10/84 advanced with the 1st Platoon in a well-spaced line of skirmishers, followed at a 300-metre interval by the 2nd and 3rd Platoons. 10/84 quickly drove British security forces out of Maisières, then ascended the reverse slope of a low hill, which gave cover against the British positions on the canal. When they reached the top they began taking heavy MG and rifle fire. The company took cover and, 'just like at a gunnery range at home, returned well-aimed fire' at 700 metres range. The 2nd and 3rd Platoons came on line. The enemy was difficult to see, but 'the squad leaders and troops competed in detecting the enemy position'. Bushes along the canal gave an indication of the likely enemy location. The 10/84 commander was ordered to begin the advance, which he thought was premature, as he had not attained fire superiority and the terrain to his front was open. Nevertheless, he ordered fire and movement by squads. Only at this point did 10/84 begin to take casualties. The company commander was hit in the leg and the lieutenant had been killed, so the first sergeant took over. The company advanced to within 80–100 metres of the enemy, when the first sergeant stopped the forward movement and took up the firefight again.
>
> As 11/84 left the west side of Maisières it took heavy fire from the front and left flank, which caused casualties. The reserve platoon was committed on the left. 11/84 advanced by bounds, took numerous casualties, and had to stop 100 metres from the canal.

There can be no dispute about the result of the Germans' determination to advance under heavy fire, whatever casualties they sustained. By now they were getting far too close for British comfort. Dease continued to urge Privates Marshall and Guines to lay down suppressive fire to keep the Germans at bay.

They did so, with some success, but inevitably they drew fire too. Machine guns do so much damage that they will always attract a fearful backlash if the enemy is able to regroup. After about half an hour Private Guines was hit in the head by an enemy bullet, though the wound wasn't fatal. 'Go and get it bandaged up', ordered Dease, who took over the job of feeding the ammunition to Marshall, as he continued to blast away at the Germans he could see traversing from left to right.

Zuber maintains that the Germans didn't outnumber the British defenders on the canal, even though this imbalance has been claimed for most of the last 100 years:

> II/84 advanced towards the rail bridge with 8/84 on the left and 5/84 on the right, followed by 6/84 and 7/84. At 1200 a standing firefight developed. 8/84 sat tight waiting for artillery support. 6/84 and 7/84 took positions in the houses behind 8/84 and fired on the British from there. 5/84 seems to have had an easy time: houses covered its advance to within 600 metres from the canal. A sergeant from 5/84 said that crossing the 'flower-strewn meadow' up to the canal, covered by British MG fire, was not going to be a pleasure, but the company made it, bounding by half-platoons. Somehow the company had drifted to the left and mixed in with 10/84. IR 84 now had 11/84, 10/84, 8/84 and 5/84 on the firing line: the attacking force was no stronger in infantry than the defenders.

To the British it certainly felt as though there were far more Germans facing them. Osbert Cundy-Cooper later saluted the bravery of Maurice Dease and his colleagues, who were positioned in the most dangerous place of all. 'They held on most splendidly, however, for a long time,' he explained. Dease and his machine guns had done significant damage to the advancing Germans, it seemed; they had already fought manfully against the onslaught. But no amount of bravery from Dease and his section could alter the strategic reality of the situation, which was becoming increasingly apparent.

The German attack continued to concentrate on the bridges. The road bridge was swung back and was covered by houses. This obstacle caused the Germans to redouble their efforts in the vicinity of the railway bridge, where the problem from their point of view was that there was more open ground. The German side of the bridge was also blocked by a wire entanglement. The railway embankment stood high and the trees on both its sides gave some cover to the troops between the road and the rail bridge. The two machine guns were still rattling away from their small emplacements on the buttresses of the railway bridge. The right-hand gun had a decent field of fire and commanded the fields below the bridge. But these guns, though well positioned, were also relatively exposed, and always likely to provide a focal point for German fire.

Holbrook explained how casualties began to mount. 'Of course, we were losing men and a lot of the officers especially when the Germans started the shrapnel shelling and, of course, they had machine guns – masses of them! But we kept flinging them back. I don't know how many times we saw them off'.

At the point where the railway tracks ran off Nimy bridge, the air-splitting storm of incoming bullets was fiercest. Marshall, sustained by Dease, kept blasting away for an hour, aiming at any German who dared show himself. But a terrible pattern was developing. Each machine-gunner only had a certain amount of time on those Maxims before he was picked off. Marshall was wounded but not killed by the bullet. Dease ordered him to withdraw to have his wound looked after. But Marshall had barely staggered away when shrapnel caught him and he fell to the ground. Private Marshall would never forget these moments and later wrote to Maud Dease:

> We fired and, in about half an hour, Private Guines got wounded in the head and your brother told him to go and get it bandaged up and then I saw that the Germans were advancing towards us. I soon got the gun to work on the line of Germans traversing from left to right. I kept it up for about an hour, then I got wounded in the head. On going back to get it bandaged a shrapnel bullet caught me in the leg and I fell to the ground about 12 yards from Lieutenant Dease.

Maurice stood up, presumably to try to help, and suffered the consequences almost immediately. He was hit in the knee or calf and quickly felt the excruciating effects. Lieutenant Francis Steele, his close friend from their Sandhurst days, saw this happen:

> Poor Maurice got shot below the knee (or thereabouts) at about 9 a.m. while he was attending to the machine gun on the left side of the bridge. Ashburner and I begged him to go off and get fixed up at hospital but he refused. He continued to direct the fire of his guns, although obviously in great pain.

In the past, it had always been Dease's knee that attracted trouble. He had first hurt it playing school football at Stonyhurst. Then in the spring of 1913 he had damaged cartilage during a bayonet-fighting competition on the Isle of Wight. He had been forced to spend two weeks in bed and then used walking sticks for some time afterwards. The leg wound inflicted by the German soldiers of IR84 was obviously much more serious. It justified going to a field hospital immediately. There would have been no shame had Dease moved back. As he had already shown, if one of his own men had been similarly hurt, Dease would have been the first to order him to the rear. Had he gone to hospital at that point, he would surely have been saved, and at worst made a prisoner of war. He would probably have lived to see his family and his beloved dog Dandy again; he might have hoped to meet Mollie Hewitt once more on the Isle of Wight, where they could have talked horses to their hearts' content and speculated on the progress of Palm and Mattie. He might have convalesced in Ireland, teasing 'himself' and 'herself', the loving parents who would doubt-less have fussed over him until he had recovered. But Dease didn't think of his own safety. Perhaps the words of Colonel McMahon were ringing in his ears, that 'A Royal Fusilier does not fear death. He is not afraid of his wounds. He only fears disgrace.' Dease must have thought of his men, thought of his duty and his machine guns. Moving back wasn't going to keep the Germans at bay, however much pain he was in. He had to direct his guns, because he knew they represented the only hope for all the men around him. Without his detachment's help, all would be lost to this massive German attack.

Hearing the left-hand machine gun rattling away again – Marshall had been replaced but later had his leg amputated – Dease became concerned that the right-hand gun had fallen silent. 'Machine-gunner!' he yelled through the noise of battle. He knew that both weapons must continue to lay down fire, one wasn't enough. For that to happen, the wounded or dead among his detachment had to be replaced by the next men as quickly as possible. Ignoring his friends' pleas for him to retire, Maurice crawled across in front of Steele, to the right-hand emplacement. But the Germans, who had already killed the previous machine-gunners, were waiting for Maurice too, and they hit him almost immediately in the side. As he fell, Dease screamed 'Gunner!' He knew that he too had to be replaced immediately. Horrified, Steele tried to drag Dease back a few yards so that his wounds could be assessed. Dease didn't want to waste time with any of that. Despite having been hit twice, he just wanted to return to the action and keep his machine guns firing. That was his job; that was his duty. While he could fight, he was determined to do just that.

The historian MacDonald Hastings gave an indication of the sort of casualty rate poor Dease's machine-gunners were up against:

> The battle was still at its height when, at about 10 a.m. on the morning of the 23rd, Sergeant Haylock of the Maxim gun section was carried back together with one of his gunners. Sergeant Haylock had a bullet through each arm and another just above the heart. The gunner had had one of his arms smashed by machine gun fire. Badly wounded though he was, the sergeant calmly told Corporal Palmerton that they were 'getting it hot', that Mr Dease was out of action and that it was now Corporal Palmerton's duty to take command of what was left of the section and its guns.
>
> Grabbing fresh belts of ammunition, Corporal Palmerton, using what cover he could, got to the guns. The left gun was out of action, and all the gunners dead or wounded. The right gun had ceased firing and he was told that four of the section had been hit in the head, one after the other, and dropped into the canal.

Never wanting his men to face anything that he was not willing to face himself, Dease was desperate to get back out there, whatever fate awaited him. Steele tried to keep him down. 'Now then Maurice, you lay still and don't move,' Steele said, trying to assure him that the battle was almost won. 'We are getting it all our own way.' Lieutenant Francis Steele had decided, probably correctly, that the only way to persuade Dease to think of himself for an instant was to reassure him that he wasn't needed urgently, because he had already essentially led his men to victory:

> 'Are you in pain?' Steele asked him.
>
> 'No', Maurice insisted, trying to smile. 'How are the guns getting on?'
>
> 'Don't worry about the guns, I'll look after them', Francis reassured him.
>
> 'I can't hear them', Dease said, more worried about the silence than his own condition.
>
> 'I promise I'll see to them, you just stay down', said Steele, who then braved the storm of bullets and shrapnel to move forward and organise a new machine-gunner to replace the dead man on the left.

Refusing to accept the reality that he was weakening physically, Dease persevered through sheer willpower. Maurice was running on adrenalin and became impatient. 'How are the machine guns getting on?' he demanded – and got up once more to see for himself. In Steele's temporary absence, there was no one to keep him down. The motto of Dease's school, Stonyhurst, was simple old French: *'Quant je puis'* ('as much as I can'). He felt he still had more to give, but he had shown his head and shoulders to the enemy. That's when he was hit again, this time nicked in the neck. Almost as soon as he fell, he was comforted by the noisy confirmation that Steele had succeeded in his mission to the left of him.

The machine guns were rattling angrily again and it made Dease smile. 'That's good. Let them have it,' he said.

Steele returned to the centre and noticed that Maurice seemed 'much more happy', though he also 'seemed to me to have been hit again while I was busy to his left'. Sadly the sense of satisfaction that was helping Dease cope with his own ordeal didn't last. He soon heard the sound he feared more than his own wounds – the sound of fresh silence. The latest brave machine-gunners to do their duty had been shot, just like all those before them.

'Why isn't the gun firing?' demanded Dease with a hint of desperation. Despite Steele's pleas, Dease then began to crawl to the right-hand gun emplacement. By the time he reached it, another man had taken the place of the one who had been shot. He began to serve the latest man with ammunition, but it wasn't long before the new gunner was wounded too. Now he faced an almost impossible task. The machine gun emplacements were so cramped that the bodies of the dead or wounded had to be moved out of the way before the next man could get the guns working again. Despite his own wounds, Dease somehow found the strength to pull clear the previous gunner, who rolled down the canal bank and ultimately survived. Dease's action had effectively saved his life. Now it was his turn to fire a machine gun and he clearly relished the task. It was one thing to direct others or feed them ammunition, but doing the job yourself always carried a special satisfaction; and this was his moment to unleash his controlled fury at the Germans who were causing so much devastation. He knew these could be the final moments of his life; he knew that whoever fired the machine guns always attracted everything the Germans had in return. Still he pumped bullets towards the enemy, keeping them at bay while his superiors worked out what to do. He poured fire over the canal for all he was worth; but a machine-gunner can't keep his head down if he is going to be accurate. And sooner or later Lieutenant Dease was going to be struck in the head by a bullet. When it finally happened, even that wound didn't kill him. His spirit remained unbowed; he refused to leave the machine gun and he continued firing until a replacement came forward. Still he held his ground to feed the new man ammunition, until he collapsed sideways across the railway lines. He remained conscious and saw his own replacement mortally wounded. 'Gunner!' he shouted yet again. As the next man went forward to take over in all the chaos, Dease must have crawled towards the emplacement to try to help once more. A fifth German bullet hit home, this time somewhere in Maurice's chest, and he slumped forward against the sandbags, apparently lifeless. This is believed to have happened at about 11.10 a.m.

Maurice Dease may have died with the photographs of his last happy evening in female company still in his pocket, the shadows lengthening in that Norton garden on the Isle of Wight. His friend Osbert Cundy-Cooper admitted sadly, 'I gave these to Maurice to look at and never saw the poor fellow again to get them back.' Dease's last letter to Mollie Hewitt was already making its slow way back to the island, his request for her to write back now futile.

Zuber's cold account describes how the Germans began to close in:

At 1130 the howitzers of II/FAR 9 entered the fight, taking ineffective shrapnel counter-battery fire. At 1310 a two-gun platoon from 4/FAR 9, another from 6/9 and a battery from FAR 36 were brought forward in close support; the platoon leader from 6/9 directed his guns from the attic of a house, under heavy British rifle fire. This close artillery support allowed the attack to move forward.

Captain Ashburner had called for reinforcements, fearful their position would be outflanked. His runner made it back to battalion headquarters. Colonel McMahon sent up about 100 men under Captain Bowden-Smith and Lieutenant Mead for support, but most of them were killed by shrapnel fire on the way up. It wasn't long before Second Lieutenant Jack Mead arrived with a platoon. Mead, a blond ex-public schoolboy, was full of spirited bravado, even when he was quickly hit in the head by a piece of shrapnel. He got back up, covered in blood, and whistled a tune as he was taken out of the firing line and back to a medical orderly. Mead was bandaged up but insisted on returning to the line where his men were now entrenched and joined in battle. Within seconds of reaching the thick of the action, Mead was shot straight through the forehead. 'Kingy' Tower saw it happen. 'Poor little Jo Mead reached where I was when he was immediately shot in the head and died instantly. Captain Bowden-Smith was hit with shrapnel in the stomach and lay at my feet in fearful agony. One could do nothing for the wounded.'

Bowden-Smith was left dying during the retreat, and passed away in captivity a few days later. But he and Lieutenant Eric Smith were effectively doomed within minutes of each other. Tower added, 'Ashburn [sic] had been wounded in the head, and Steele took over command of the Company, which by now was seriously reduced in numbers and the dead and dying were lying all over the place.' Captain Forster and Captain William from the reinforcements were quickly killed. MacDonald Hastings recounted Corporal Palmerton's last memory of Maurice Dease:

Among the dead and wounded he recognised Lieutenant Dease, who had been hit once again at about the same moment the last of his gunners were killed. He was laying, says Corporal Palmerton, on the parapet, either dead or dying, with his head resting on a sandbag and his body still facing the enemy.

The Corporal struggled to get the right gun into action again. He tells me that once the bullets started to chatter through the barrel he suddenly felt quite safe. The Germans were advancing at distances between 300 and 600 yards on the opposite side of the canal, sitting targets to an experienced gunner. He mowed them down as if he was scything grass. Then Corporal Palmerton, too, was hit in the head. With a feeling of nausea he rolled away from the gun position down the embankment. But, unlike the other gunners who had fallen forward into the canal, he rolled backwards … At the foot of the embankment he saw Private Godley … Dizzy with the effect of the shrapnel wound – Mr Palmerton still carries some of the metal in his head – he remembers telling Godley that it was suicide on top of the embankment, that it wasn't for him to order anyone to go up there; but was there a volunteer to man the gun?

# 9

# Sidney Frank Godley, VC

Dutifully, Godley climbed the embankment, trying to assess the situation under fire. One emplacement had by now been neutralised by enemy shells, the machine gun damaged beyond repair. But the other machine gun could apparently still spew bullets if someone was prepared to brave the hail of murderous fire coming over the canal. In order to cover the retreat of 9th Platoon, a volunteer was needed – someone to sacrifice himself. The problem was that all the machine-gunners who were considered to be decent shots were dead. Indeed, Lieutenant Steele, who was now in charge, wasn't sure there was anyone left at all who could do the job – even if someone was courageous enough to try.

'Who else can fire the machine gun?' asked Steele in some desperation.

Palmerton knew Godley could fire the machine guns, but Steele didn't. The Lieutenant might not even have spotted Godley at this stage. For any ordinary man, this would have been the time to stay silent. This would have been a good moment to pray that someone else would step forward, someone with equal training but a better shot. But Private Godley was no ordinary man. He knew that by stepping forward he was probably giving up his life. 'I can fire the machine gun, sir!' The moment he said it, Sidney knew he could kiss goodbye to Nellie, to England, to life itself, because he could tell what was coming next. 'I was then asked by Lieutenant Steele to remain and hold position while the retirement took place.'

It sounded like a calm, simple task, one last job to do in an organised retreat. Nothing could have been further from the truth. It was practically 'each man for himself' by now – and Godley was brutally honest about the nature of the order he had been given. Palmerton's assessment, given down by the canal, had been correct.

'It was a suicide job,' Godley said later. But he was a tough man who'd had a tough upbringing, and he was made for this moment. As his friends prepared to move back, he was moving in the opposite direction, in among the dead bodies, with Dease not far away, dying or dead too. His grandson, Colin, said, 'I don't think he was ever fazed by anything … He could have stayed silent when they asked who else could work the machine guns. He must have known what he was going into; he must have known he could easily have been killed.'

Just in case he had other ideas, Godley was left in no doubt that he would be required to sacrifice his own life in order to save those who could still get away. His commanding officer would be some distance behind him, though entirely unable to help in a crisis. No one was going to carry Maurice Dease away to safety now either; no one really believed that Dease could survive his wounds. And, if there was any chance at all, the advancing Germans would be the only ones who could bring him back to life. When he talked about it, Godley couldn't see much difference between Dease's tragic situation and his own. It was only a matter of time. Sidney said, 'Then the order came to retire. But Mr Dease and I were to stay. "To the death," they said. When you think of it afterwards, it does seem a bit strong. But at the time it seemed just routine. What we were paid for – carrying on …'

Poor Maurice Dease was in no position to carry on. Meanwhile Godley was running on pure guts and fighting spirit, adrenalin and defiance. As for food and drink, he had been grateful for the coffee and rolls the children had brought him before the battle had started. He recalled, 'All day we fought. I'd no food, but my water bottle was full. There was no time to eat, anyway.' Even reaching the last working machine gun to get it firing again was a dangerous and sickening experience. Steele wrote that evening:

This afternoon Pte Godley of B Coy showed particular heroism in his management of the machine gun: Lieutenant Dease having been severely wounded and each machine-gunner in turn shot. I called Pte Godley to me in the firing line on the bridge and under extremely heavy fire he had to remove three dead bodies and go to a machine gun on the right under a most deadly fire.

Those bodies had been Godley's living friends minutes earlier, men he had lived with round the clock, paraded and drunk with for years. Now they were an unbearable dead weight, to be shifted and discarded because there was no time to respect the dead. The necessity to commence firing as quickly as possible; that's what drove him on. To approach a machine gun and not be able to lay down immediate fire to suppress the enemy meant death within seconds in this worsening bloodbath. So the people who had lived inside those bodies would have to be remembered with more reverence later. To move them out of the way and start spewing bullets was all that mattered if more lives weren't to be lost, beginning with his own.

Godley's daughter Eileen believed his calm temperament would have helped him. 'I wouldn't imagine he was nervous, no! He would have taken himself off to the machine gun and had a look to see what sort of state it was in, and sat down.'

Palmerton observed, 'With glorious courage Godley scrambled towards the emplacement and, under heavy fire, he brought the right gun into action again.' But, once he had done that, Godley couldn't just blast away in the erratic manner which had too often been his trademark during training. 'As a machine-gunner he'd make a bloody good bus conductor,' he had once been told. It would take more than a bus conductor to salvage anything from this situation. Economy and accuracy were required, along with a cool head. Luckily, he had always been unflappable; his poor results on the machine gun range hadn't been down to a poor temperament, only his poor judgement of distance. But the Germans were so close now that judgement of distance was scarcely relevant any more.

'When they're running towards you, and getting that close, I'm not sure you have to worry too much about distance any more,' said his grandson Andrew Slade. With his senses further sharpened by the extreme danger he was in, and an officer bellowing orders from a safer position behind, Gunner Godley began to come good at last. Lieutenant Steele seemed as impressed by his ability to fire to order as he was by his bravery in reaching the gun in the first place. Steele added, 'Not a shot did he fire except as I directed and with utmost coolness ...'

It must have felt strange to Godley to have Steele issuing the orders, not Dease. But the familiar Irish voice that all the men loved had fallen silent forever. Godley said later, 'During the action, we lost Lieutenant Maurice Dease ...,' Godley spoke Dease's name with pride, knowing what he was about to say next, ' ... who also received the VC on that day ... And I came under command of Lieutenant Steele.' Perhaps it was entirely unintended, but there seemed to be just a hint of disdain in the way he said 'Steele', before he added, almost casually, '... who then gave orders to me to fire – small bursts of fire whenever he required it.'

It was an incredible effort and must have felt like one man against the German Army. There were one or two other British riflemen dotted along the canal, perhaps too wounded to move. But Godley and his machine gun was keeping the enemy at bay almost single-handedly at the bridge. Zuber's dispassionate account barely hints at the heroism:

> After a long firefight the Germans gained the upper hand. 10/84 reached the edge of the canal and could see the British sandbag positions on the other side, which led to a murderous gunfight at point-blank range. The 10/84 first sergeant organised systematic fire on the British riflemen and MGs and the British fire weakened. In the 11/84 sector, German artillery was effective in suppressing some of the British fire.

No one knows how many Germans fell to Godley's well-disciplined machine gun bursts. Eileen said wryly:

> If I know my dad, if he heard you saying he wasn't much of a shot, he'd say 'Well, I certainly remember hitting that bloke!' His sense of humour was beautiful. I imagine he let rip with that gun. He didn't talk much about it but I can imagine he did his job. He did his job well.

Godley's grandson, Andy Slade, echoed her, saying, 'It might not have been the job he was employed to do by then, but someone had to do it at the end and he did do it.'

As before, it was hard to tell whether an enemy soldier went down voluntarily to dodge the bullets or because he had been hit. And, as before, the devastating metal flew in both directions. But Godley refused to give up. 'Whatever he did, his whole heart was in it,' Eileen added almost a century later. He had to give everything, because there was no one to take his place. There wasn't even anyone to pass him a fresh box of ammunition. He may have suffered a bullet in the thigh as he tried to grab another box. He was also soon bleeding from a wound to the shoulder. Still he poured fire at the advancing Germans. Without question, Sidney's fire kept the men of IR84 from crossing the bridge, as precious minutes turned into hours, enabling countless lives to be saved. His previously questionable performance with a Maxim was forgotten now that his targets had turned into a very real, swarming enemy who were threatening his survival.

Early direction from Steele could only have helped, though soon Steele thought of himself and knew he had to move back. Ahead of him, Godley fought on through the pain, just as Dease had done before him. Though apparently lifeless, Maurice's presence, still slumped nearby, could only have reminded Godley of the standards already set that day. He stayed where he was, though his account suggests he had lost all track of time.

Godley recalled later, 'And at the end of the day, we carried on towards evening, when the order was given for the line to retire.' The matter-of-fact way in which he delivered his recollection of the order masked the fact that for him it would mean almost certain death. He had been asked by Lieutenant Steele to remain and hold the position while the retirement took place, 'which I did do …'. Sidney spoke those four words with pride, though he added painfully, '… although I was very badly wounded several times.' For most, to be very badly wounded once is trauma enough to end a man's contribution to a battle. But, just as Dease had done, Godley refused to give in. 'I managed to carry on,' he said. His intonation suddenly rose; the helplessness of an abandoned child somewhere deep within, as he added the words:

> … on my own … I was on my own at the latter end of the action. Of course, Lieutenant Dease lay dead by the side of me, and Lieutenant Steele retired with his platoon. I was there for a couple of hours or more on my own. I remained on the bridge and held the position.

Though his heroics that day were over, Dease's fellow officers weren't as sure as Godley that he was dead. There was no time to pick up those wounded who couldn't walk. There was no time to feel for a pulse when someone didn't respond. Lieutenant Steele explained in the immediate aftermath, 'When we retired, Maurice had to be left there. So, to say whether Maurice is still alive or not is impossible …'

Later Maurice's family would be given a glimmer of hope for the future. Colonel McMahon wrote to Maurice's father, 'We have some faint hopes that he may have survived. If so, it is certain that he would have been well cared for.' In truth McMahon and his men had no idea, because McMahon, who ordered the retreat, had to save the battalion from being wiped out completely.

Steele had been forced to leave Godley to almost certain death too. The gun was becoming so hot that it was almost impossible to handle by now. Godley ignored the burns on his hands and kept pumping away. But one man with one weapon can't hold off an army forever. Sooner or later even the bravest of stands is likely to be ended by overwhelming odds. The German artillery had already caused massive casualties among the British troops almost from the start. And then a shell landed just behind Godley, with devastating consequences. The flesh on his back was torn off in strips, and what was left had been peppered with burning shrapnel.

He tried to ignore his fresh wounds, and used his painful hands to attempt to fire the Maxim once more. It wouldn't work. He thought it was a question of clearing a jam; then he even tried to thread a fresh belt of ammunition into the gun. But his Maxim had fallen silent, because the German bombardment of his emplacement had left the water-bags riddled with holes and probably torn pieces off the machine gun too, just as it had torn pieces out of his back. Whatever the cause of that silence, Godley couldn't break it. With every passing second, it acted like an invitation to the German units across the water. They had been delayed for so long by this one heroic man, but now they could finally finish him off. They could take aim, carefully and unhindered, and shoot at Godley's head. One German rifleman didn't miss. The bullet flew in and embedded itself in the top of his skull. Miraculously, the brain remained untouched, but he was stunned and concussed. Colin said, 'There was a bullet in the head but I don't know if there were any other bullets in him. They didn't have steel helmets until 1915, so he was wearing a peak cap if any. It went in right on the top.'

As Steele was retreating, he must have seen Godley being hit and barked orders, telling him to retire while he still could. Steele had to oversee the others' escape to safety, and felt he couldn't go back to help the wounded man. Steele recalled later that same day how Godley continued to fire the Maxim 'until it was irretrievably damaged and he was shot in the head. He then left the firing line under orders to go to the rear.'

It is doubtful whether Godley heard Steele. As far as he was concerned, he was alone. 'Then I was wounded in the head and back, and the gun was almost red-hot. I smashed it up and threw it in the canal.' In the recorded interview Godley again claimed, 'When it was time for me to get away, I smashed the machine gun up, threw it in the canal, and then crawled back …' Suddenly he sounds quite detached from his misery, even chirpy. He doesn't quite seem to be living this part like the rest of the account. It may even be that on this particular point, he wasn't telling the whole truth, though no one will ever know for sure.

Any pieces of machine gun he saw flying towards the canal were more likely to have been propelled there by a German shell, rather than by Godley himself. It is hard to believe that he was in any condition to 'smash up' his machine gun and deposit all the pieces in the water in front of him. He was still under murderous fire from just 100 yards away on the other side of that canal. It would have been truly suicidal to hang around trying to deprive the enemy of key machine gun components. Even Colin admitted:

> In my own mind I find it hard to believe that he broke up the machine gun before he crawled away. He would have had to pick up the gun, which was a Maxim, remember, and it must have been red hot – he'd been firing for two hours. He'd have had to carry that forwards to the river and throw it in. I don't think he'd crawl forward with the gun and then crawl back. He was out of ammunition. Whether the gun had been damaged by gunfire, I don't know.

This was surely the case, since a survivor of the action claimed later of Dease's machine gun section:

> The machine guns were a special mark to the German machine guns, rifle and artillery fire, and, in spite of this tremendous fusillade and the fact that their emplacement was hardly bullet proof, they stuck to it as long as any of them could keep their places at the guns. The fact that the guns were practically knocked to pieces testifies to the appalling nature of the fire.

The Germans later claimed they captured both machine guns on Nimy bridge, though they didn't specify what damage had been done to either gun – and they could have been lying. Godley had no need to embellish his own story, he had been heroic enough. He may have picked up what he considered to be a vital piece of the smashed gun and tried to hurl it towards the canal in one last act of defiance. However, on this day of suicidal hero-ism, when the logic of self-preservation and the limits of human endurance had been bypassed so many times, he may have done even more to deny the Germans his weapon. Perhaps he really did pick up pieces of the smashed Maxim and throw them in the canal before retiring. No crazy act could be ruled out entirely in all that chaos.

One account even had Lieutenant Steele carrying his good friend Maurice Dease away on his back under heavy fire. If only he had felt able to do so.

Had there been clear instructions about blowing all the bridges over the canal before the British Expeditionary Force retreated, such a scene might even have become reality. As it was, Steele himself admitted later that Dease had been left on the bridge by the canal during the retreat, much like the other wounded, 'who became prisoners of war or were killed by the Germans'. It is possible that poor Maurice was finished off by a German bayonet, because there are accounts of Germans crossing other bridges over the canal and putting a bayonet through the first British officer they saw. But it remains far more likely that Godley had it right and Dease was already dead before the enemy finally charged across the railway bridge. Godley just had time to make his own escape on all fours before that happened, as he explained, 'I crawled back on to the main road, where I was picked up by two Belgian civilians, and was then taken to 'ospital in Mons.'

Poor Godley was probably hardly recognisable as the cheerful man who had chatted away to the local children a few hours earlier. His life had changed forever – if indeed he was going to be allowed to live at all. Zuber's account sounds merciless as it tries to remove any shred of credit from Britain's heroes and focuses instead on the bravery of the advancing Germans:

> Two platoons from 8/84 manoeuvred to the left of 10/84. A patrol from 8/84 led by Sergeant Rover reached the Nimy bridge. Musketeer Niemeyer swam through heavy fire to the other side and brought back a boat so that the patrol could cross the canal. The patrol occupied a house from which it could engage the British. Niemeyer then turned the [road] bridge back over the canal, but was killed immediately afterwards. A squad succeeded in rushing across the bridge and enfiladed the British position. 10/84 and 11/84 swarmed across the bridge and the fighting became hand-to-hand. The first sergeant of 10/84 says that he bayoneted a British officer in the chest. There was no mention of IR 84 being held up by the MG of Dease and Godley, and as for this MG successfully covering the battalion's retreat, about sixty men from 4/ Fusiliers surrendered here and both MGs were captured.

Although some of the 4th Fusiliers were indeed captured, there can be no doubt that Godley's heroics gave others their chance to live to fight another day. Colin puts it best:

> By all accounts there was army corps that couldn't get across the bridge and I've been told by someone in the Fusiliers that they estimated there

were seven thousand Germans who couldn't get across the bridge. He held them up for two hours. He gave all his British colleagues two hours to get away. His two hours of glory gave them all two hours to move back. When he left there he was on his own. When he crawled away there was no one to help him. No British servicemen or soldiers, only Belgians. It was suicide.

Maurice Dease's friend Kingy Tower only withdrew once Godley and his defiant machine gun had been put out of action:

> The enemy had now got right round our right flank, driving in the Middlesex Regt. We were now being shot at from all sides and the position was hopeless. Dease and all his machine gun crew and both guns had been knocked out. We darted off under a hail of fire and I don't know how on earth we got away.

Twenty-six officers and 983 other ranks made up the 4th Royal Fusiliers at Nimy. Of those, four officers were killed at Nimy bridge and another 150 of their number died in defence of the Mons–Condé Canal. As Zuber described the last of the action from the German point of view, he probably didn't realise how poignant his description was:

> The 10/84 first sergeant said: 'Once on the other side of the canal, we could see what excellent work the company had done. Almost three-quarters of the British in our sector were dead or wounded, and the British sandbags had been completely shot full of holes.' 8/84 charged across the bridge and into the factory complex where it took thirty prisoners. A young German soldier, who was in civilian life a travelling salesman from Hamburg, took charge of the prisoners with the command in English, 'Gentlemen please, four and four', and the British formed up in march column

Around Dease's machine guns, the British 'sandbags' were full of holes and so was poor Dease. Those who escaped and left his body behind them probably held out no more hope for Godley's survival than they did for Dease.

Not that Zuber believed their losses were very heavy. He states that IR84 had lost only one officer and twenty-three enlisted men killed in action. Six of their officers and fifty-five enlisted men had been wounded in action. He says their total casualties were ninety-four, though the total of the casualties he specifies is only eighty-five. His source is the official regimental records, though even official accounts didn't always tell the full story, and that was true of both sides.

The claims that IR84 had lost so few men don't seem to sit comfortably with the total German casualties by the end of the battle, which were said to have exceeded 5,000 according to many accounts. British casualties would eventually number 1,638 from the Battle of Mons. Although the British Expeditionary Force had lost the battle, the greater overall casualties on the German side, and the determination with which the British had fought, sowed seeds of doubt in the German ranks about their own supposed superiority.

The British continued to suffer though, especially when it was realised too late that the bridges needed to be blown. This further highlighted the shambolic nature of Sir John French's leadership that day. There are those who will tell you that this was a new type of war, that it is wrong to criticise with the benefit of hindsight, that no one could have known how the battle would unfold. They have a point, and yet … the ignored intelligence, the lack of coherent plan, the willingness to sacrifice lives with no realistic hope of territorial reward … all these would become depressingly familiar as the First World War discovered its bloody rhythm.

After this first day of battle, Maurice Dease, a fine and pleasant young Irishman, lay dead. Sidney Godley, a warm-hearted Englishmen hovered somewhere between life and death. And the only consolation was that neither man would suffer any more horrific violence or witness further hell on earth in this so-called 'Great' War.

Not that the pain was over for Godley, or the relatives of either man. As for the people of Mons, the violence wasn't over that day either. Not while there were still scores to be settled.

# 10

# Aftermath

There is evidence that the Royal Fusiliers kept in their minds the image of Maurice Dease and his heroic defiance of the Germans, which gave them strength under the most terrible conditions during their retreat.

Among the British, the need to maintain good order fought the natural impulse to panic. Ashburner's C (Y) Company, of which Dease's machine gun section had formed part, had lost about seventy-five men, and by now the Germans were within 20 yards of their position. The 4th Battalion had lost not just some of their key officers, but also 150 men from other ranks. For the most part, they slipped safely back to Mons, the retreat covered by W Company, acting as rearguard with Major Mallock in charge. The bravery of Maurice Dease's friend prevented more casualties. Mallock's rearguard then joined the rest of the battalion in the market square, where they drew breath.

The previous day, the men of the 4th Royal Fusiliers had marched into this square as the feted saviours of the city, showered with all manner of gifts. But the battle hadn't gone their way, and now it was all they could do to hold their nerve as they took in their losses. In his excellent book, *The Royal Fusiliers in the Great War*, H.C. O'Neill, OBE, revealed:

> There were many remarkable escapes. Lieutenant ('Kingy') Tower, of Y Company, had his hat shot off, his rifle hit and two bullets through his puttees. Private Denners, of the same company, had three shots through

his hat, one on the end of his rifle, and one through the sole of his boot, but he was unhurt.

The Germans might have tried to press home their advantage and turn their victory into a complete rout of the British forces. But O'Neill explained, 'They had learned a new respect for the British fire, and no small part in the inculcation of this lesson was played by the 4th Battalion.'

In other words, the heroics of men such as Dease and Godley, and the fire they had lain down for so long, had created such an impression that the Germans preferred to regroup in the final daylight hours, rather than seek a fresh contact with the enemy.

Part of the Royal Fusiliers and the Middlesex Regiment gathered in an open field at the hospital in Mons. Ashburner's company was probably among them, not knowing that Godley was inside that hospital, hovering somewhere between life and death. Even if they had known he was there, he was so badly wounded that it would have been foolish to try to take him out of medical care and haul him back into the traumas of the next phase of the retreat.

So Sidney lay where he was – not knowing what would happen to him next. Initially, at least, German revenge for their own losses seems to have been taken out on the local population. With the British dead, wounded or resting out of the way after their initial retreat, the poor citizens of Mons knew there would be a backlash. They had fed, watered and championed the British Expeditionary Force. Some had even taken up arms of their own against the Germans.

Given some of the atrocities they had already perpetrated elsewhere in Belgium, it is perhaps surprising that the people of Mons didn't suffer in even greater numbers once the Germans overran their town. However, the citizens of Nimy, whom Dease, Godley and their comrades had tried so hard to defend, paid an early price for their allegiance. As Don Farr highlighted in his excellent *Mons: 1914–1918*, an unnamed nun who helped keep the diary for the Congrégation des Filles du Sacré Coeur de Jésus, whose convent was situated just off the direct route from Nimy to Mons, wrote of the repercussions for the local population:

At Nimy, we have learned since, civilians had fired on the enemy; horrible reprisals followed. A number of inhabitants were shot and killed or so badly wounded that they died shortly afterwards. Several houses were torched but the flames stopped before reaching our Maison du

Sacre-Coeur. We poor Sisters fled and took refuge in the cellar of a neighbouring house.

O'Neill explained what the Royal Fusiliers did in the dead of night. 'At 2 a.m., after about four hours' sleep, the battalion left Mons hospital and took up a position south of Mons, covering Framières. An attempt was made to put an extended line into a state of defence.'

That line of defence couldn't help the man who had bought his colleagues so much time. When the Germans caught up with Godley, his chances of survival still looked bleak. Godley recalled the moment when he realised that he hadn't escaped after all:

I realised then that the Mons had been taken, and the Germans were occupying the best part of the town. I was being attended to by the doctors in hospital, having my wounds dressed, when the Germans came in and took the hospital. I was asked a good many questions. What regiment did I belong to? Who was my Commanding Officer? But I 'knew nothing'.

Apart from the probability that Sidney would die of his wounds anyway, there was no reason to believe he would be shown any mercy by the enemy, who had themselves sustained hundreds of casualties in the advance. Godley's life hung in the balance and every time he refused to answer a question he must have infuriated the enemy a little bit more.

The doctors had counted the wounds on Godley's body – mostly on his back, where the force of the explosion had ripped away so much of his skin. His grandson Colin said, 'He had 27 wounds. The Germans were the ones who counted. Then they noted it down.'

Was there any point in trying to piece back together a stubborn British soldier, who was already making it abundantly clear that he was going to be of no use to the Germans whatsoever? There was an easy solution, one often applied to wounded enemy in the heat of battle – and its immediate aftermath too. Put another bullet in his head, penetrate his thick skull this time, and end his irritating resistance once and for all; that would solve the problem. On a day as violent as this, one more bullet wouldn't be any trouble at all.

With his refusal to cooperate, Sidney was still testing the Germans to the limit. He was also risking his life all over again, yet there was something in the nature of Sidney Frank Godley which simply wouldn't give in. Even forty years later, Godley loved the fact that he had told the Germans nothing. As Colin pointed out, with a smile, 'He always was a bit stubborn. He was stubborn doing his job at the bridge in Mons.'

And his battalion, despite its heavy losses, was regrouping on the Framières line south of the city, with some of Dease's friends at the forefront of the action. O'Neill added:

> The battalion was in support to the 7th Brigade at this time beyond the brow of a hill. On the crest was a small house with Lieutenant Longman's platoon loopholes, and it was later used to cover the retreat of the firing line. The officers of the battalion were receiving verbal instructions as to the way the supports would have to go when the Germans attacked, opening with an artillery bombardment to which the British guns replied. Dawn had just broken when Byng's company was sent to reinforce the left flank of the position which the Germans were trying to turn. This part of the line had not been entrenched and the half company lying on the extreme left suffered very heavily. The rest of the line had fallen back when Byng retired with a loss of about 40 per cent, covered by Longman's platoon. About 2,000 yards further back the battalion stood in an entrenched position, and waited for the Germans to appear over the crest of the hill. The British guns were bursting over the reverse slope and the heavy rifle fire which met the enemy as they reached the crest line caused them to fall back. The battalion remained on this position a little longer and then retired through Genly. Byng's section of this company alone had lost 43 men.
>
> Then followed a long and tiring march as rearguard across the French frontier to Bermeries, which the battalion reached at 10.30 p.m. Despite the weariness of the men they marched very steadily, and on the following day covered about thirty-five miles to Inchy. They had left Bermeries at 5 a.m. and arrived at Inchy about 6.15 p.m. It began to pour with rain as the battalion reached the northern side of Inchy. This was the worst day of the retreat. The men were all deadbeat and suffering badly from sore feet. Two of the companies, X and Y, were put on outpost duty. The French maps had been handed in on the 22nd, when only Belgian ones were retained; and, consequently, the men were compelled to operate in an unknown country. The night, in a spiteful mood, sent alternate downpours and high wind. Not far to the north the sky was lit by the flames of burning houses. The cavalry could be heard exchanging shots with the enemy.

For the families of soldiers who had been left behind in the battle, presumed dead, there was an agonising uncertainty with which to contend during these chaotic days. Even when the dust finally settled for a while, claim and counter-claim, hope and despair impacted with equal force on those who had loved Maurice Dease.

His family was unluckier than most, because it suffered one torment after another. There was no word of Maurice at first, because no one seemed to want to be the one to declare him dead officially. In fact, for a long time the Dease family didn't even know that Maurice had been harmed. Maud Dease left the following heartbreaking account of those grim weeks:

After the departure of the Royal Fusiliers for France we received a post card from Maurice, dated 19.8.14 merely saying they were getting on well and telling where to address letters, and on 21.8.14 he wrote a short letter – the last we ever had from him. It ran:

My dear Mother,
We can let you know no news on account of censorship. So far we have got on well and the weather has been good though somewhat hot. Palm is with the Regiment still and is looking well.

In case you did not get my last letter, you should address letters: Battalion, Regiment and Brigade, and On Active Service.

If Maud has not got home, you might let her know the address. It is not worth writing to her as there is no news.

Best of love,
your loving son, Maurice.

After receiving this letter we heard no more news of Maurice – and it was not until 15th September that we heard the first alarming rumours.

This was a letter from Major Dease saying he had heard from Captain Walter Hill saying the 4th Battalion had suffered heavy casualties at Mons and that Maurice's name was given as seriously wounded and left behind. Captain Hill's letter also mentioned that some of the returned men gave Maurice's name as amongst the killed, but this we did not know till later.

Major Gerald Dease, Maurice's uncle and the man who had most influenced him in his decision to join the army, and indeed the regiment, had received a letter from Captain Walter Hill of the Royal Fusiliers. Hill had been adjutant to the 4th Battalion of the Royal Fusiliers, and was currently stuck back in Britain as an instructor at Sandhurst. Hill mentioned a Lieutenant Harding of the Royal Fusiliers, who had witnessed what had happened at Nimy. Hill's letter went like this:

> I have been wondering if I should write or not to tell you that I have visited a number of our men in Hospital at Aldershot who were present at the fight at Mons on August 23rd and they all gave me the following list of casualties in the 4th Battalion.
>
> Captains Forster, Bowden-Smith. Lieutenants Dease, Mead. Killed – others wounded.
>
> This morning Harding who has returned invalided gives me the list as Mead killed, Forster, Dease, Sampson, etc., badly wounded and left behind.
>
> As you may imagine I collected all the facts I could about Maurice and the men were certain that he with the whole of the machine gun detachment (but 2) were killed.
>
> Apparently they behaved with great gallantry covering the bridge over the canal but were decimated by artillery fire … I am too sad for words. I was deeply attached to the boy, as was everyone.
>
> He was one of the most conscientious and thorough soldiers that we had, a straighter and better fellow never stepped …

It appears that Gerald Dease simply couldn't bring himself to give Maurice's closest family the worst of the news, and chose to convey only the part of Hill's letter that said Maurice had been 'badly wounded and left behind'.

Major T.R. Mallock had planned to write to the Dease family at the earliest possible opportunity to break the terrible news, but had been too busy trying to protect the lives of the rest of his men during the retreat. Mallock was Second-in-Command of the Battalion and had been billeted with Maurice at 'HQ' in Noyelles on the way up to what became the front. He was fond of the genial young Irishman and knew his family too. It may even be that Maurice and Mallock had agreed to write to each other's mother at the earliest opportunity in the event that anything terminal happened to either of them. But first Mallock had been required to play a key role in keeping order during the temporary panic which grew among the 4th Royal Fusiliers in a place called Le Cateau. O'Neill's history of the regiment describes what happened:

About 6 a.m. the battalion fell back through Inchy. The cavalry had ridden through about two hours before. The battalion had now reached the battlefield of Le Cateau. Trenches had been dug the preceding day south of Inchy by civilian labour, but as they faced the wrong way the battalion had to begin digging feverishly. They had only been engaged between half and three-quarters of an hour when the battle began. The Northumberland Fusiliers took over the trenches and the Royal Fusiliers moved back into support. A little distance behind the firing line, and roughly parallel to it, was a sunken lane. The battalion was moving into it when a sudden burst of shrapnel caught them. Second Lieutenant Sampson was wounded, one man was killed, and about 20–25 were wounded. A slight panic resulted, but the cool and firm handling of Mallock brought the men speedily under control. For the remainder of the battle the men had a comparatively good time. The cookers were in Troiville and a hot meal was obtained. About 250 yards in the rear of the lane were two batteries of artillery and, as a result, shells from both sides continually crossed overhead, but without doing any damage.

About 1 p.m. there was a short lull, and then came a sudden burst of firing about half a mile to the right. It was about 2 p.m., and the Germans could be seen passing through the British lines. Shortly after this the order was given to retire. The Royal Fusiliers had had a good rest and Colonel McMahon, whose coolness, clearness and decision had meant so much to the battalion, was now ordered to command the rearguard to the 3rd Division with the 4th Battalion; and half the Scots Fusiliers were placed under his orders. The roads leading south were packed with the retreating troops in considerable confusion.

Maurice's friend Kingy Tower witnessed this chaos but struggled to find the words to describe it in his diary:

The scene on the road baffles any description I can give of it. It was a veritable rout – men, horses, guns, refugees and wagons struggling along in disorder to get away at all costs. Progress was naturally slow and all roads seemed to be blocked in the same way.

Had the Germans only taken advantage of this, the Expeditionary Force must have surrendered. However, the enemy did nothing. He did not shell the roads and his cavalry did nothing. So, after continual blocks and fearful disorder, we managed to get away unmolested and unharmed.

O'Neill added:

> The rearguard formed up in front of the junction of two converging
> roads until the confused mass had streamed past, and then fell back in
> perfect order in a series of extended lines. The Germans had learned a
> new caution and when pursuit would have been perhaps decisive, none
> was made. The attempt had been made to separate the two corps; but
> when it was virtually achieved there followed the inexplicable failure to
> exploit the success.

Tower wrote:

> And so the great retreat continued, all through the next two days and
> nights. No rest, no food and no excitement. We walked as if in a dream,
> seeing only the backs of the men in front and only longing for the end
> of it all. It was difficult to cheer up the men. We had obviously suffered
> two serious reverses and were in full retreat, our losses had been heavy
> and we were losing men daily on the road from exhaustion.
>
> Nothing could have been finer than the bearing of the men through
> all this long tedious march, largely over cobblestones, over mile after
> mile of road, through endless flat country, past hundreds after hundreds
> of poplar trees acting as sentinels along our line of retreat.

At times the discipline of the men was impressive, given what they had been
through. O'Neill explained:

> The 4th Battalion marched through a village at attention, arms sloped
> and fours dressed. They were seen about this time by General Hamilton,
> the Commander of the 3rd Division, who, no doubt, contrasting the
> disorderly retreat of the garrison of the firing line, could not resist
> exclaiming, 'Well done Fusiliers!'

At other times, discipline slackened but there was still solidarity among the
men. Kingy tried to improve their spirits by joining in any efforts to make
music. 'We sang, we played mouth organs and penny whistles, we made endless fun of anybody we could, in fact anything to make us think of something
else except the dull monotonous tramp of tired feet getting more and more
sore as we went on.'

The battalion marched on until about 2 a.m. on the 27th, rested by the roadside for ninety minutes, then carried on retreating. They reached Haricourt at 10 a.m., snatched another half an hour's rest and marched on again to Vermand, still acting as rearguard all the way. They arrived at 6.30 p.m. and the fact that they arrived at all was a considerable feat of endurance. Two and a half hour's rest was all they had been able to take in twenty-eight hours of otherwise-continuous marching. It was far from over. Soon after midnight they were back on the move and reached Ham at 9.30 a.m. There was hardly time to pause for breath before the battalion fell further back to Crisolles. Finally, they were given the opportunity to feel like human beings again. The Germans were not in hot pursuit and so, after their arrival in Crisolles at 6.30 p.m., the British soldiers were billeted and given hot food. Sleep must have come quickly.

The fact that Dease's superiors and his friends were still retreating on a daily basis, and their very lives now depended on their stamina and resilience, meant there was little time to lend any true clarity to a desperate situation at the Dease family home over in Ireland.

There was so much confusion. There was still confusion back home and there were still moments of confusion during the BEF retreat. O'Neill described what had happened:

On the next day, Saturday, the battalion moved out again as rearguard to the division. Here the country is well wooded and the Fusiliers could see several Uhlan patrols. In front of a large forest they were even able to shoot two Uhlans who proved over-venturesome. At dusk the battalion fell back through the wood and marched all night via Noyons and Cuts, and, after a short halt, to Montois. On arrival at Montois at 7 a.m., on Sunday the 30th, the battalion rested and did not leave the village until 24 hours later. Leaving Montois at 7 a.m. the battalion arrived after a hot march through woods at Vauciennes, midway between Villers-Cotterets and Crepy on the national road to Paris. They were billeted in a sugar factory, which did not have very comfortable recollections behind it. The battalion was once more rearguard when it marched south at dawn on September 1st to Bouillancy. Starting at 4.30 a.m. on the following day they arrived at Penchard, on the main road to Meaux, at 2 p.m. and placed outposts for the brigade.

The 4th Battalion of the Royal Fusiliers were retreating but still in good spirits, partly because they were representing those like Dease who had been braver still. Sooner or later that retreating would stop. In fact, it was nearly over. On 3 September the battalion passed through Meaux and found Le Mans farm, where good food was supplied to replenish their dwindling supplies of energy. At 1 p.m. the following day the Fusiliers were ordered to take up a defensive position south of La Haute Maison. Ten hours later they began to march once more, refreshed to some extent at least by the break in their gruelling routine. They reached Châtres at 7 a.m. on 5 September. It was the furthest south the Fusiliers would have to go. The feeling of defeat was soon to be shrugged off. They were going to turn and face the Germans once more. The prospect felt much more appetising to soldiers than running away. O'Neill claimed that the Royal Fusiliers 'had suffered comparatively little', despite their ordeal at Mons, and that:

> the fatigue and hardships of the long retreat had not weakened their spirit. And when on Sunday morning the order came to advance once more, it was certainly received with a sigh of relief. It was exactly a fortnight since the men had first found contact with the German troops and they were anxious to resume that inconclusive encounter. They had been rearguard during the retreat. Now they marched as advance guard.

For the British, it was a turning point, though for Maurice Dease's close friends the situation was no less dangerous. They were about to endure the Battle of the Marne, and those who were able went on to fight in the Battle of the Aisne. For all that Maurice's parents and sister knew, he might even still be with them – and the rumours a terrible mistake.

# 11

# Not Knowing

Officially, there was no news at all, much to Maud's exasperation. She explained:

It was now three weeks since that action and, though many columns of casualties had already been published in the papers, we had heard nothing … We still hoped that the men's account might have been inaccurate, but next day, September 16th, the following letter [came] from a Sergeant [Gerrard] of the Royal Fusiliers whose name had been given in the lists of wounded men admitted to the London Hospital, and to whom we had written for information:

Dear Miss Dease,
In reply to your letter I must tell you that I do belong to the 4th Battalion and I was at Nimy a place about 1½ miles the other side of Mons in Belgium when the 4th Battalion got into action.

The fighting started at about 11 a.m. on Sunday 23rd August. Lieutenant Dease was our machine gun officer and I am awfully sorry to have to state that the machine guns got put out of action by the enemy and I am sorry to say that Lieut Dease was, as far as we know, killed in this action. The officers, NCOs and men of 4th Battalion were greatly grieved at the loss of Lieut Dease as he was very popular with everyone in the Battalion.

'As far as we know'. There it was again – another clause that allowed the most painful of emotions under such grave circumstances – hope. Maud continued the family's story: 'Next day, Thursday 17th September, we received a telegram from a Mrs Hartes (whose son James was in the 4th Battalion) saying she had heard from James that Maurice had been killed at Mons.' That letter, which had been sent on 2 September, went like this:

> We have had ten days of hell starting August 23rd at Mons in Belgium where the four divisions were strung out over twelve miles of front and with no ambulance and only half the compliment of gunners.
>
> We were attacked by a large force of Germans and forced to retreat – we took up another position at Le Cateau and since then have been fighting rearguard, men tired out and fed up with this continual retirement with heavy guns behind you all the time.
>
> Poor Maurice Dease was killed at Mons and real well he died, we hope to get a special mention in despatches for him. He and all the machine gunners were killed. Bowden-Smith, Fred Forster and Smith were all badly wounded and left in Mons which was afterwards shelled very heavily and poor Mead had his head blown off.
>
> At the Le Cateau position Sampson was hit in the stomach and I caught it in the side and hand but luckily grazes. Poor Stevens a bullet through the stomach ... The regiment is doing wonderfully they defended Mons for six hours against six Battalions and have marched very well indeed. We're all proud of them, especially Maurice Dease.

There can be little doubt, judging by this letter, that the sight and memory of Dease refusing time and again to succumb to his wounds, showing a totally selfless bravery right to the death, continued to inspire his regiment through the next ten days, when morale was sorely tested.

But the Dease family didn't believe that the writer of this letter had been close enough to Maurice at Nimy to know what had happened to him with any certainty. Maud reasoned:

> As this was not official information, we hoped there might have been a mistake in the report – specially James Hartes not having been with the regiment – he was then on the Staff.
>
> Telegrams to the War Office and personal enquiries then by several influential people were of no avail – the reply being always the same. 'Nothing has been reported about Lieutenant Dease.'

Still, we thought that, as the authorities at the War Office knew nothing of these reported casualties, there was some ground for hope and that if the rumours had been facts surely it would be known by now – nearly a month since 23rd August.

Meanwhile, a second letter from Captain Hill to Gerald Dease could have left Maurice's uncle in no doubt about what had happened. It mentioned a diary that Lieutenant Harding wasn't supposed to have written while on active service. That diary contained grim yet inspiring news. Hill's letter read:

My Dear Major,
I have received Lieut Harding's diary of Mons and the next two days. He speaks of dear old Maurice's end as follows: 'Lt Dease, the M.G. officer behaved magnificently taking his place at the guns he was wounded five times before he was mortally wounded.'

The men confirmed this and one and all had heard of the glorious way he died. The last remaining man of his M.G. Section, says Captain Ashburner, removed his dead colleagues from the gun emplacement and operated one gun himself until shot through the head – but he is still living.

I tell you all this as I do not know if you have yet broken the news to his parents. If you have done so and will let me know I should much like to write to his mother. It was the gallant end of an officer and gentleman and he had no enemy and knew no fear. The Royal Fusiliers will be ever proud of his connection with the Regiment.

I am heartbroken, all my dearest friends leaving us and I am cooped up here.

Ever yours,
Walter Hill

Precisely what made Hill think that Godley, the 'last remaining man' of the machine gun section, was still alive is something of a mystery, since the British had long since left Mons, where Godley's life had been hanging in the balance. But if there was flimsy evidence for Godley's survival, there was also less than conclusive proof of Dease's death. The men of the 4th might all be convinced that he was dead, but they couldn't be totally sure. There hadn't been time to check for a pulse before they retreated, even if the rough and ready Cockneys of the City of London Regiment had been trained how to do so in the heat of battle. Gerald Dease could break such news as he had been told to his brother, sister-in-law and niece. He could tell them he was 99 per cent sure that Maurice was dead. But it was only human nature that Maurice's loved ones would cling to the 1 per cent. Then they received a letter from someone they knew and trusted. It changed everything, as Maud explained:

But next day – 18th September – our worst fears were realised, and the news was alas true. Major Mallock, 2nd in command and a great friend of ours, wrote as follows:

You will I expect have heard by now of your son Maurice having been killed at the Battle of Mons. He died as a gallant soldier should defending the passage of a bridge with his machine guns most heroically. Nearly all the machine gun detachment were killed and the guns continued firing until they were put out of action by the enemy's rifle fire and shells. Maurice set the men a splendid example, although wounded quite early in the arm, he refused to leave the guns. It is with the deepest regret and sorrow of all ranks that I acquaint you of his death. We all loved him, one of the best officers in the regiment. May God rest his soul in peace and comfort you his parents in your great loss.

Yours affectionately,
T.R. Mallock

It was a lovely, heartfelt letter; though there is just a hint that Mallock may have had second thoughts during the writing of it, wondering whether or not the Dease family had actually been told that poor Maurice was dead.

He had been right to worry about that, because official confirmation didn't arrive until four days later, almost a month after Maurice had lost his life, at his family's home in Calmullen, Drumsee. Maud confirmed:

It was not until 22nd September that we received any official information – this was a telegram as follows:

War Office London Sept. 22nd.
To E.J. Dease Esq.
Regret to inform you that Lieut. M.J. Dease Royal Fusiliers has been dangerously wounded further information when received will be telegraphed immediately. Secretary, War Office.

The infant Maurice and his sister Maud.

Ready to ride: Maurice, aged 4.

The horse of his dreams: Maurice aged 8 on his magnificent grey pony, Kitty.

Padded up and ready to go. The young Sidney Godley (right) adored cricket and all sport.

Maurice Dease during his
Stonyhurst days.

A portrait of Maurice Dease in
all his military finery.

Pride and joy: A happy
Maurice in bearskin,
smiling with his parents
after a parade.

Friends. Maurice Dease (back row, second from left) puts his hands on the shoulders of his
close friend Kingy Tower. Meanwhile, Dease's dog Dandy, the unofficial battalion mascot,
steals the show (front row, second from right).

Dease, Cundy-Cooper and Beazley at their final garden party together.

Beazley, Dease (front) and Cundy-Cooper with two mystery women. Is Maurice's friend Mollie all smiles on the left?

The last photo.
Maurice Dease ready
for action.

Bleak end. The Nimy
railway bridge over
the canal, where
Maurice Dease
and Sidney Godley
braved a hail of
bullets.

A subjective representation of the fighting at Nimy railway bridge. Artist unknown.

Maurice Dease's Victoria Cross.

One of these is thought to be Maurice Dease's first burial site, close to the bridge he died defending.

Private Godley VC, in captivity but comfortable for the moment.

Final resting place: The graves of Dease and Mead in St Symphorien Cemetery outside Mons.

Alive and well, Nellie! Sidney Godley (centre-front with hair carefully combed) sent this group POW photo of himself with various soldiers and sailors to his sweetheart, while he was in captivity in 1916.

Celebrated. Sidney Godley VC with two rugby-playing friends and minders.

'Love from your Nellie.' The photo she sent Sidney while he was in captivity.

A wonderful wedding. Sid and Nellie (centre-right) are almost lost in the crowd among extended family. Missing is Sidney's mother, who died when he was only 6.

Gloriously contemptible. Sidney Godley (centre, middle row) sits proudly with some of his 'chums' in the newly formed Old Contemptibles Association.

Beach golfer. Sidney was a fine all-round sportsman and would try his hand at anything.

Sidney Godley and friend,
cooking on the beach in the
sunshine.

Sidney and Nellie Godley,
happy on the beach with their
grandson, Colin.

Sidney Godley (centre) with Nellie and their son Stanley.

Proud grandfather. Three generations of Godleys smile for the camera: Sidney (centre), his son Stanley (right) and his grandson Colin (left).

An ageing Sidney Godley wears his medals with pride at yet another function.

Always a soldier. Sidney Godley marches proudly through London with the Old Contemptibles in the 1950s, remembering their fallen comrades.

The last visit. Sidney Godley remembering the fallen in Mons, 1954.

Sidney Frank Godley VC, laid to rest at last by 'The Old Contemptibles'.

Lovingly tended by his descendants, the grave of Sidney Godley – always remembered.

Godley and family in Ypres, Easter 1939. Sidney squats, centre front. To the right (next to the man in the light suit) stand Godley's wife Nellie, his daughter Eileen and son Stanley.

On the face of it, the telegram might have given the Dease family a glimmer of hope. 'Dangerously wounded'. That wasn't the same as 'killed': far from it. The parents Maurice amusingly called 'himself' and 'herself' might have felt they had reason to pray for his survival after all. It must have been tempting for Maud to cling to that faint hope of a miracle. Clearly his wounds must have been life-threatening, otherwise they wouldn't have talked of danger. But Maurice was a strong young man and perhaps he had been able to defy those wounds and live through the sheer force of will he'd always had? But, no, Maud and her parents refused to hope any more. T.R. Mallock was their friend, and he would never have written them that letter if he hadn't been totally sure of his information.

It was inevitable that a more accurate telegram from the War Office would arrive sooner or later. Maud recalled:

And only on 26th September were we officially acquainted with the news which had been known by so many of the Regiment for more than a month. The wording of the telegram was:

Deeply regret to inform you that Lieutenant M.J. Dease Royal Fusiliers is now reported killed in action Lord Kitchener expresses his sympathy. Secretary, War Office.

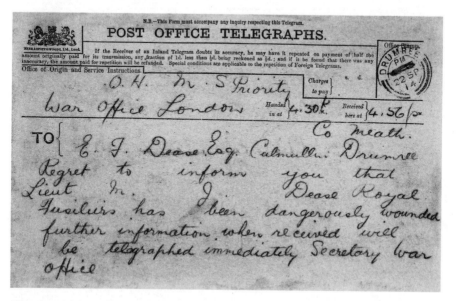

'Dangerously wounded.' The Dease family is cruelly misled about Maurice's fate by War Office telegram.

We also received a telegram from their Majestys – the same as that sent to the next of kin of all those who gave their lives for their country:

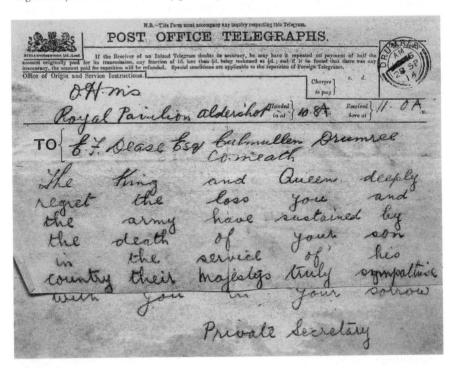

Tragic reality. The War Office finally gets it right.

Royal sympathy for the Dease family's loss.

28th September Royal Pavilion in Aldershot.
The King and Queen deeply regret the loss you and the army have sustained by the death of your son in the service of his country their majestys [sic] truly sympathetic with you in your sorrow. Private Secretary.

Then, absurdly, even more heartbreakingly, the War Office belatedly decided to keep their options open again over Maurice's fate. In a telegram sent on 30 September, 'Secretary War Office' stated:

Beg to inform you that Lieut. M.J. Dease Royal Fusiliers reported killed Sept 5th is now Sept 12th reported to be wounded and missing. Both reports from O.C [Officer Commanding] Battalion.

Maud insisted:

To this, however, we could attach no importance – besides the dates not coinciding with previous information – all that we had now heard from so many other sources showed that indeed that Sunday 23rd August had been the fatal day, and our dear Maurice had been called on to make the Great Sacrifice.

Yet Colonel McMahon had also written to Maurice's father at a time when it might have given them cruel hope of Maurice's survival:

Although for some reason which I cannot explain, your son's name has not appeared in any of the published casualty lists, you will have heard that he was very badly if not fatally wounded in the heavy fighting at NIMY just North of Mons on the 23rd August.
    He was in command of the Battalion machine guns placed to protect the crossing over the Canal at the Railway Bridge which the Germans attacked strongly and seemed to make their principal objective.
    Maurice was wounded and man after man of his detachment was hit. He appears to have received a second wound after neglecting a first wound in the leg. Taking a little time to recover, I understand too that he managed to return to the fire after this second serious wound and kept it in action. He was then incapacitated by a third wound.
    Thus his conduct was heroic indeed and of the greatest service in delaying the crossing of the enemy, which it was our object, in accordance with orders, to effect.

We have some faint hopes that he may have survived. If so it is certain that he would have been well cared for.

I have brought his conspicuous gallantry to notice. Please accept sincere sympathy of us all.

Yours sincerely
N.R. McMahon

These doubts at the highest regimental level had surely been reflected in the official War Office correspondence, which must have arrived at the Dease family home at roughly the same time. We can only assume that McMahon had explained to someone at the War Office that he couldn't confirm Dease's death with total certainty. And therefore the latest telegram had been sent, just in case Maurice was alive, because the War Office was covering itself in the unlikely event that Dease returned home very much alive at the end of the war.

McMahon's compassion, his refusal to accept the inevitable, might have brought fresh suffering to the family, a torment he had never intended. So many soldiers had written to the Dease family, even though some were destined to die or be badly wounded before long. It was an astonishing show of compassion for the bereaved relatives of the much-loved Maurice.

Yet the emotions of the Dease family had been pulled this way and that as a result of this compassion, until they could hardly take any more. At last they had accepted the overwhelming reality of the evidence before them, and shut out the desperate optimism that had been allowed to invade and almost destroy them for weeks.

'They didn't believe the last telegram,' said Maurice French. 'They dismissed the contents because they had already come to their own conclusion that my Uncle Maurice must be dead.'

They finally entered into a less complicated though no less painful kind of mourning. Maurice's parents and sister Maud did not allow themselves to hope against hope any more. The seductive fantasy that Maurice had somehow survived and been patched up to become a prisoner of war was kept at bay by a brave family who realised that they must continue to face facts and let nothing else sway them.

No one was braver than Maurice's sister Maud, who decided to get more detail from the only men who could know the story of what had happened – the men of the 4th Battalion, Royal Fusiliers.

She said that, 'It only remained for us now to ascertain what details we could about his end, [and they] tell all the same story of his glorious death and extraordinary bravery against such terrible odds.'

One by one those who watched Maurice get shot time and again volunteered more facts – or at least as many of the facts as they thought poor Maud could stand. Most of their accounts have been used to build the picture presented in the chapters relating to the Battle of Mons. Some reflected Maurice's personality as much as his heroics. One superior officer said this:

So strong was Maurice Dease's sense of duty that from when he joined the regiment I never once remember having to find fault with his work. He had a most excellent way with his men, was always kind and thoughtful to them, but at all times dignified. Deeply religious, without making a parade of the fact, he gained everyone's respect. His gallant death is only what I should have expected; his duty was always first, and he had a complete mastery over himself. Maurice leaves a blank space in the regiment which will not be filled as long as his friends serve in the Royal Fusiliers. We have lost a gallant comrade, and a cheery and steadfast friend.

A week after the fatal battle, Mollie Hewitt had received a letter from a living man (see Chapter 5, p. 68). He sounded happy, excited, yet full of compassion for the horses they knew, and full of understanding that she would be worried for her favourite. He asked her to care about him too, at least enough to write him a letter. There was no one else to ask, other than family.

By the time Mollie Hewitt received Maurice's letter, she may already have suspected he was dead. News travelled quite swiftly back to the Isle of Wight, where the 4th had been based. Perhaps scraps of information reached Mollie's house ahead of this letter, which had to go through the slower military postal system, unlike the urgent telegrams. The tragic events around Nimy bridge were becoming painfully apparent to many. Since she had no official connection or relationship with Maurice, however, we'll never know whether Mollie had any early information.

If Mollie wasn't party to this terrible knowledge, she must have opened the letter happily, perhaps pleasantly surprised that Maurice had thought to write to her so soon before he was due to fight the Germans. She must have read about the reasonable health of the horses with considerable relief, though worried that Mattie had suffered slightly while pulling along those machine guns. She probably wondered how soon she should reply, assuming she felt it appropriate for a 'married' woman to write to a bachelor-officer while he was on active service.

But if she already realised that this was, in all probability, the final letter of a man now dead, at least the last to anyone outside his immediate family, she would have opened the letter in a state of shock. The fact that Maurice had chosen to write to her just before battle would have moved her, even upset her. There was nothing inappropriate about the communication. His jaunty, reassuring note was hardly a love letter, after all. But he had considered her to be important to him, and there was an underlying sadness to that. As they both knew, her marital situation didn't really allow for such importance, which was probably why Maurice had kept the tone of the letter so casual in the first place. One thing was for certain. They would never be more than friends now; perhaps they never really had been. Did Mollie Hewitt already know her dashing friend was dead, or was she innocently pleased and relieved to hear he was 'getting on grand'?

Calmullen, scene of so many joyous days in Maurice's childhood and beyond, was in mourning. His family accepted he must be dead. For so many other families, the agonising uncertainty continued. Kinglake Tower and another of Maurice's close friends, Lieutenant John Roland Beazley, who had been at the garden party on the Isle of Wight just before they all left for France, fought on. Not knowing what fresh horrors they might meet in this bloody war, they summoned fresh courage. With the advance well and truly under way, the lives of Maurice's friends were in even more danger.

" O Lord ! Thou gavest him to us to be our joy. Thou hast taken him away from us; we give him back to Thee without a murmur, but our hearts are wrung with sorrow."—ST. EPHRAIM.

## Pray for the Repose of the Soul

of

# Maurice Dease, V.C.

*(Lieutenant, Royal Fusiliers)*

Killed in action at Mons

## August 23rd, 1914,

## Aged 24 Years.

ABSOLVE, we beseech Thee, O Lord, the soul of Thy servant, MAURICE, that, being dead to this world, he may live to Thee; and whatever sins he has committed in this life, through human frailty, do Thou, of Thy merciful goodness, forgive; through Jesus Christ our Lord.—Amen.

## May he rest in Peace.

Prayers for the soul of Maurice Dease – a good Catholic.

# 12

# Wounds, Death and Decorations

On 9 September the Royal Fusiliers crossed the Marne unopposed, took up outpost duty for the night and lay in their trenches. Feeling exhausted the following day they were under a cold rain when they reached Veuilly. There the cavalry tipped them off that the German rearguard was having breakfast just 2 miles ahead. The Royal Fusiliers decided to seize their chance, using the element of surprise. Once again Lieutenant Steele's men were in the thick of it from the beginning, but a German machine-gunner reacted quickly to the sudden attack as the Germans fought back in a desperate attempt to preserve their freedom.

Lieutenant Longman was sent up to reinforce Steele and they soon found themselves in the middle of an intense fire-fight. The men Dease had known and loved paid a heavy price for their eagerness, as they ran into the hail of bullets spewed out by that rogue machine gun. Five were killed and twenty-nine were wounded. Lieutenant Tower and Lieutenant Beazley, Maurice's great friends, were badly wounded. Lieutenant Longman was another casualty, though his case was not so severe. But their bravery carried the day and the German rearguard was overcome. Along with the Scots Fusiliers, the Royal Fusiliers captured 600 prisoners and the machine gun which had inflicted so many of the terrible wounds on C (Y) Company.

Tower and Beazley had shown great bravery and had begun to redress the balance for what had happened at Nimy. They showed the same courage as they fought successfully for their lives over the days to come, and began a long recovery back in England. Just as soon as he felt able, on 25 September 1914, Tower forgot his own pain, picked up a pen to the Dease family and tried to summarise his feelings about the inspirational Maurice:

> I must write a line to tell you about poor Maurice, he was one of my greatest friends. I am afraid he is dead having been shot at Mons just close to me.
>
> He died really gallantly and certainly deserved a V.C. I am trying to see that he is mentioned in dispatches.
>
> The whole regiment were really proud of him and the way he worked his machine guns on the bridge at Mons and everyone mourns the loss of one of the most popular and best officers of the regiment. I hope some day to be able to see you and tell you about it as far as I know, but at present I am in bed but hope to be back very shortly in France.
>
> With the greatest sympathy in your great loss,
> Your servant
> Kinglake Tower

The following month Lieutenant Longman was having tea on a farm at Le Petit Riez with Osbert Cundy-Cooper, an even closer friend of Maurice, who had been present at the garden party with Beazley. They were just behind a line which ran from Le Petit Riez to the southern outskirts of Herlies, where houses had been searched and a few Germans captured. The opposing forces were locked in a temporary stalemate, more prolonged versions of which would characterise almost the entire war. The Germans began to bombard British positions with field guns and heavy guns and the BEF hit back. Realising they were likely to take more punishment if they stayed where they were, the regiments on the right and left of the Royal Fusiliers, the Scots Fusiliers and the Royal Irish, attacked after a preliminary bombardment. The Germans sent even more shells in the opposite direction. Lieutenants Cundy-Cooper and Longman were with a Captain Waller and a Lieutenant Gorst, who were also part of Z Company. The peace of their tea on the farm at Petit Riez had been shattered. They weren't that far from the trenches and three men ran out to see what damage was being done. Longman stayed behind alone, though no one quite knows why. Perhaps he had begun to take tea after the others and hadn't quite finished, perhaps he intended to answer the call of nature. Maybe he just wanted to sit still a while and treat all the madness with the disdain it probably deserved. At any rate, the decision cost him his life. He hadn't left the room for the war, but the war came to the room. A shell not only landed on the farm but burst in the very place where Longman was having a moment to himself. He was killed still sitting at the table. Poor Longman, who had stood next to Maurice in that photograph of the officers of the 4th back on the Isle of Wight the previous month, was gone in an instant. Another charming young man, whose diary had revealed a love of life and a marvellous sense of humour, was silenced forever. To the few in that photograph who had survived thus far, the day they posed together so proudly and happily must have seemed like a lifetime ago. By Christmas, barely a man among them would have come through unscathed, with the vast majority killed or badly wounded.

At least in losing his life in that terrible second half of 1914, Maurice had met a more inspirational end than his friend Longman, for the manner of Dease's death seems to have helped drive his company on through the fresh hardships and losses they continued to suffer. Maurice had set the standard, and his colleagues knew that, if they fought anything like him, they had done their duty and then some.

Private Marshall, who himself had suffered so badly that he had to have his leg amputated after the action, wrote to Maud to tell her how the fighting broke out and became desperate as they battled to hold the railway bridge at Nimy:

> Shortly afterwards, your brother got wounded in the body. After that he called for a machine gunner and, about half an hour after that he was wounded again and died in a few minutes, still asking for gunners.

That was the story in a nut-shell, though not the full story, as we have seen. Pocock gave Maud some more detail:

> It was not long after the firing commenced when Mr Dease was hit in the neck and laid down. Lieutenant Steele … encouraged Mr Dease by saying 'now then Maurice you lay still and don't move we are getting it all our own way,' but Mr Dease was so brave that he kept on saying 'how's the machine gun getting on,' he got up and was shot down again, and then sometime afterwards he heard the machine guns rattling off again. He said, 'that's good, let them have it.' Mr Dease got up again to handle the machine gun himself – this time he got the fatal hit, which we were all very sorry for.

Corporal G.C.O. Stokes, one of the luckiest machine-gunners because he survived, wrote the following:

> Mr Dease was serving the machine gun with ammunition. This job got too tedious for him and he dragged No 1 away and began firing the gun himself. The man he pulled away rolled down a railway bank and saved his life by doing so.
>
> Now Mr Dease, in firing the gun was very much exposed to a murderous rifle and machine gun fire, especially his head where eventually he got hit. He would not leave the gun even then – another bullet came and hit him and he fell across the railway lines. He died near enough at 3.30 p.m. on Sunday 23rd August.

This doesn't correspond with most accounts, though in truth there are so many conflicting versions that all we know for sure is this: poor Maurice was hit many times, returned to the machine guns several times despite his pain, eventually slumped motionless and sooner or later died there at the bridge.

Back in Wootton on the Isle of Wight, Mollie must have felt distraught for her friend Maurice. There was no longer any doubt about what had happened now. And she didn't seem to feel worthy of being the recipient of this kind young man's last letter. After much reflection, Mollie made the decision to contact Maurice's family and let them have the letter, since, along with the one to his mother, it was the last he wrote. She obtained the address in Ireland through her contacts in the regiment and forwarded the letter to 'himself' and 'herself' forthwith, though she addressed them more formally than Maurice might have done. It was a generous, thoughtful thing for Mollie Hewitt to have done. She knew how precious it would be to his mother, father and sister. And yet it was also a slightly sad thing to have done, since she didn't feel that the letter was precious enough to her personally to warrant keeping, or else she didn't feel comfortable holding onto it. Why not? Everyone loved Maurice Dease. Didn't Mollie? Sure, she was married, albeit unhappily, but should that have come into the equation? Did it? 'Best love, Maurice.' That's how he had signed off. The letter was addressed to her. Not his parents, not to her husband Rupert. Just to her. And it is hard to escape the feeling that Maurice would have wanted her to keep it.

Mollie did what she felt was right and was then left to reflect further on the contents of the short letter. From beyond the grave, Maurice had delivered news of Mollie's horse Mattie. His consideration for her concerns about the welfare of the horses, at such an intense time for him and his men, said so much about Maurice Dease and must have touched her deeply. Yet even that kind piece of reassurance was now clearly out of date, rendered almost meaningless in terms of the information it contained. If the source of that reassurance was now definitely dead, there seemed little reason to remain optimistic on behalf of the horses. Had Mattie suffered the same brutal fate as Maurice, or had the horses been taken to the rear when the shelling started? Those required to pull the machine guns would have had to stay close by much of the time, because they would have been needed in the case of a swift, orderly retreat. Had they survived the hail of bullets and shells? Had there been a point at which the surviving men had recognised that the machine guns were lost and therefore the horses were the next most valuable commodity, to be ridden or guided to safety while still possible?

Mollie couldn't know, just as the fate of Palm, Maurice's horse, remained unknown. What about the rest of her husband's horses? It was hard to see how they could all still be 'A1' as Maurice had reported in the final hours of his life. Poor Mollie Hewitt must have felt awful on so many levels. She had lost a good friend in Maurice, and it was so cruel to receive his warm little letter after he had been killed. And the animals which she loved so dearly and could always provide such comfort were clearly suffering too in this hideous war, which had only just started but was already proving so destructive.

Sooner or later, unless they were among the lucky 62,000 horses which came back to Britain from the million eventually sent out, Mattie, Palm and the Hewitt horses were destined to become part of a grim statistic for animal lovers. On all sides, 8 million horses eventually died in the war. Unlike Maurice Dease – or Sidney Godley, for that matter – these horses were entirely innocent and could have no influence over their fate. It wasn't their decision to join the army, as it had been Dease and Godley's. Yet they were brought into Britain from America, Canada, Australia and Argentina, before they were transported into the hell of battle. As the war progressed, and the demand for horses became more desperate, it wasn't always the decision of British horse owners to release them for military service, either. Just like the naval press gangs of old, 'military impressments squads' were formed to march into villages and round up all the horses which looked fit and healthy enough for action in France and Belgium.

At least Maurice Dease had asked Mollie nicely, and had received the answer he and the country had required. Not that Mollie would have taken much consolation from that, not after the people and animals which had captured her affection were starting to be removed from her life, almost as though they had never been there. But Mollie wasn't alone in feeling that sense of helplessness. However much she grieved for Maurice, that grief was probably dwarfed by the sorrow felt by the thousands of British women in fully fledged relationships, who had their men taken from them.

The woman in Godley's life, Nellie Norman, must have been far more distraught by the news that he was missing in action after Mons. She and her Sid had a firm romantic relationship together, they were going steady; they may even have talked about their plans for the future. Now he was missing in action. He had been seen getting hit, she had reason to fear he had been shot or blown to pieces. Like Dease's family, Nellie must have clung onto hope. She must have prayed that he had survived somehow to become a prisoner of war. It was a faint hope, given that he had last been seen covering the retreat with bullets zipping and shells exploding all around him. He hadn't made it back to join the retreat, she knew that much. Otherwise he would have been with the regiment once more, instead of the subject of official, heartbreaking telegrams. Those official communications haven't survived, though there was no reason for them to have been any more optimistic than those sent to Dease's father.

Whether those telegrams hurt all of Godley's family quite as much as they did Dease's is open to question. For a start, Maurice was his parents' only son. He had been loved and cherished since the day he was born. Sidney's father had other sons and, besides, he had sent Sidney away from the family home during his childhood. That's not to suggest he wasn't deeply saddened when he heard that his eldest son had probably been killed. But it's hard to believe that the grief could have been quite the same. Had Sidney's mother still been alive it might have been different. At least she was long gone, and therefore unable to feel the force of the loss. And Sidney's father must have been proud when he heard how heroically his son had performed. He may even have basked a little in the reflected glory, and put it down to the tough upbringing the boy had been given.

Perhaps unbeknown to the Dease and Godley families at this stage, first Steele and then McMahon had already written simple letters of great historical significance. To his great credit, Lieutenant Steele had done so just a few hours after the battle, to hail Maurice and Sidney as heroes.

Apart from some shrapnel bruising to his face, Steele had been one of the few unwounded officers of his company, and it is significant that he took the time to write these reports on the very day the action occurred. He knew that many who had witnessed their gallantry were either dead, wounded or in enemy hands; and in the event of getting killed himself he hoped the reports would survive and receive the attention of those in authority. Steele wrote:

On 23rd of August, Dease was in command of the machine-guns with No. 9 platoon who were defending the bridge at Nimy.

On the attack developing on the bridge, he was one of the first to be hit – somewhere about the knee. He continued to direct the fire of his guns, although obviously in great pain, until he was hit again, this time somewhere in the body, after which he remained, for a short time, under cover.

Shortly afterwards, the machine gunners having been shot, Dease asked me why the gun was not firing and insisted on crawling to the gun emplacement in order to control the fire, another man having taken the place of the man who was shot. He then received a third wound which incapacitated him and I am of the opinion that he received other wounds but on this point I cannot speak definitely.

F.W.A.S.

Lieutenant Steele didn't forget Private Godley either. His heroics had been no less personal to Steele, who had himself escaped and helped others to escape precisely because of the sacrifices Godley had made, following his orders. Steele's recommendation for Godley read as follows:

In the defence of the railway bridge near NIMY 23rd Aug 1914. This afternoon Pte Godley of B Coy showed particular heroism in his management of the machine gun: Lieutenant Dease having been severely wounded and each machine gunner having been in turn shot; I called Pte Godley to me in the firing line on the bridge and under extremely heavy fire he had to remove three dead bodies and go to a machine gun on the right under a most deadly fire: this he did and not a shot did he fire except as I directed with the utmost coolness until it was irretrievably damaged and he was shot in the head. He then left the firing line under orders to go to the rear.

23-8-14 F.W.A. Steele Lt C. Coy R. Fus.

These reports reached his commanding officer, Lieutenant-Colonel McMahon, who decided to act promptly and give them the greatest recognition possible. His report on Dease read:

Lieut. Dease was wounded and man after man in his detachment was shot. He appears to have received a second wound after neglecting a first wound in the leg: taking a little time to recover, he managed to return to his gun and kept it in action. He was then incapacitated by the third wound. Thus his action was heroic indeed, and of the greatest service in delaying the crossing of the enemy, which it was our objective, in accordance with orders, to effect ... I have brought his conspicuous gallantry to notice.

On the basis of the account written by Lieutenant F.W.A. Steele of Dease's role in the action at Nimy bridge, it is almost certain that the Officer Commanding of the 4th Battalion, Royal Fusiliers, at Mons, Lieutenant Colonel N.R. McMahon, DSO, recommended the award of the Victoria Cross. He did the same for Godley, who was missing and also presumed dead by many at this point.

As the officer and technically the first to win the VC, Dease was celebrated most of all. The news became official quite quickly, given the slow workings of the War Office. Maurice's parents received confirmation of the award with the following certificate.

'FOR VALOUR'

WAR OFFICE,
NOVEMBER 16, 1914.
HIS MAJESTY THE KING has been graciously pleased to approve of the grant of the Victoria Cross to the under-mentioned Officer for conspicuous bravery whilst serving with the Expeditionary force:

LIEUTENANT MAURICE JAMES DEASE,
4TH BATTALION THE ROYAL FUSILIERS.
Though two or three times wounded, he continued to control the fire of his machine guns at Mons on 23rd August until all his men were shot. He died of his wounds.

Sidney Frank Godley's VC award was announced little more than a week later. It was first made public in the Supplement to the *London Gazette* of Tuesday, 24 November 1914, just over three months since the action on Nimy railway bridge. It was 'Published by Authority' on Wednesday, 25 November 1914 and read:

His MAJESTY THE KING has been graciously pleased to approve of the grant of the Victoria Cross to the under mentioned Officers,

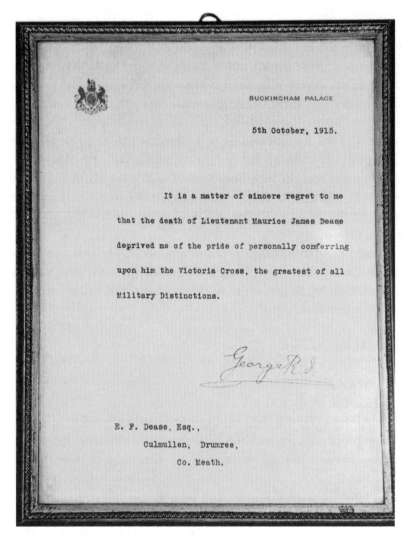

BUCKINGHAM PALACE

5th October, 1915.

It is a matter of sincere regret to me
that the death of Lieutenant Maurice James Dease
deprived me of the pride of personally conferring
upon him the Victoria Cross, the greatest of all
Military Distinctions.

*George R.I*

E. F. Dease, Esq.,
Culmullen, Drumree,
Co. Meath.

Deprived of the personal honour: the king laments not being able to meet Maurice Dease, VC.

Non-Commissioned officers and Men for conspicuous bravery whilst serving with the Expeditionary Force:

Rank: 13814 Private
Name: Sidney Frank Godley
Corps, etc: 4th Battalion The Royal Fusiliers, City of London Regiment.
Action for which commended: For coolness and gallantry in fighting his machine gun under a hot fire for two hours after he had been wounded at Mons on 23rd August.

It is doubtful whether Godley had managed to fight for two hours after he had received the worst of his wounds, though it seems churlish to question the wording of the citation when the act which prompted it was so extraordinarily deserving of the highest accolade. And it is worth considering carefully precisely what it was that Dease and Godley had won.

It is impossible to understate the importance of the Victoria Cross, or its place in British military history. During the Crimean War against the Russians, Queen Victoria had instructed the War Office to strike a new decoration that would not recognise birth or class. Influenced by Prince Albert, Queen Victoria turned down the name 'The Military Order of Victoria' and suggested it should be called 'The Victoria Cross' instead. The name, like the design, was all about simplicity, the true value being in the act itself, for which the decoration was to be awarded. The recipient would have shown 'Most conspicuous bravery, or some daring or pre-eminent act of valour or self-sacrifice, or extreme devotion to duty in the presence of the enemy'.

The work of producing the Victoria Cross was entrusted to a firm of London jewellers, Hancocks of Bruton Street. The idea was to make the medal out of bronze, though one of the first specimens produced was made of copper. Queen Victoria didn't like what she saw, and her comments show what a keen interest she took in the end product:

> The Cross looks very well in form, but the metal is ugly; it is copper and not bronze, and will look very heavy on a red coat with a crimson ribbon. Copper would wear very ill and soon look like an old penny.

Bronze it had to be, and an engineer was dispatched to Woolwich Barracks to take bronze from cannon captured from the Russians in the Crimea. To leave the cannon more or less intact, he sawed off the knobs at the breech end, known as 'cascabels', and brought back the bronze for the first medals.

On 26 June 1857, Queen Victoria presented the first sixty-two VCs personally to heroes of the Crimean War. Later that year, on 16 November, some eighteen VCs, the most ever on a single day, were won during the Second Relief of Lucknow during the Indian Mutiny. The focal point for that historic haul of VCs was the assault and capture of Sikandar Bagh. Overall, twenty-eight VCs were awarded during the Second Relief of Lucknow.

Perhaps the most famous day of all for the winning of VCs came at Rorke's Drift, South Africa, during the Zulu War. In the two-day period 22–23 January 1879, seven men from the same unit – the 2/24th Foot – won VCs, another record. The fight was made into a movie, and wasn't entirely dissimilar in its bloody, defensive nature from the way Dease and Godley later won their medals.

So Maurice and Sidney joined a fine band of men when they became part of Victoria Cross history. They were the first of 628 men to win VCs in the First World War. No other conflict has spawned so many VC heroes. It is an indication of the desperate, near-suicidal nature of so much of the fighting over many years. Both inspirational and grim, the story of the First World War VCs almost beggars belief. And Godley could rightly claim that he and Dease had begun that story, and set the standard for those who were to follow.

For all that, Maurice Dease's VC was destined to be sent to his family by registered post, when the powers that be finally got round to doing so. It would take a while before the next of kin were treated more decently.

# 13

# The Heavy Price of Glory

Norman Reginald McMahon, whose speech to the battalion had set the standard for Maurice and the others in the first place, didn't live to see the official announcement of the Victoria Cross awards he had recommended. Not long after Mons, McMahon had been promoted to the rank of Brigadier-General. But before he could take command of the 10th Infantry Brigade, military necessity meant he was left in place with the 4th Fusiliers a little longer, to lead them into the First Battle of Ypres. On 11 November, they were facing the ferocity of an enemy advance, just as they had done at the Mons–Condé Canal, little more than ten weeks earlier. Again they faced the worst of the attack, on the Menin road. Corporal W. Holbrook gave this frenzied account of what happened next:

> They do silly things! We were on the right of the Menin road, and the Menin road itself was held by French Zouaves – the worst possible troops to stand shellfire. We had no trenches of course. The shelling was so near to you that you could feel the heat of these bursting shrapnel shells on your body as you were lying there, it was so close.
>
> On the way up I'd seen a guards NCO. We were resting on the side of the road, so I said, 'What's it like up there, Sarge?'
>
> 'Boy,' he said, 'a dog couldn't live in it!' He was damn right about that.
>
> We'd had a draft from England, two hundred men. We were about five hundred strong then. By 9 a.m. on 11th November we had thirty-four

men left. Not a single officer. Well, the Colonel got killed there; Colonel McMahon – he'd just been made a general then. We lost all our officers, except one, a fellow named O'Donell. I don't know where they'd gone. You see the few who were left occupied a front of four or five hundred yards and it's all thickets and bits of wood. I knew where I was facing but there wasn't a soul near me. They'd been killed and wounded and we were driven back.

It appears that McMahon had been blown to pieces by a German shell; at least his body was never found. He had no known grave, but he is commemorated at the Ploegstreet Memorial.

For Osbert Cundy-Cooper, life changed at Ypres that day, because he was badly shot in his right foot and had to leave his unit. There were complications and Cundy-Cooper was sent to various hospitals before setting sail from Boulogne to Southampton, where he arrived on 18 December.

Meanwhile, Major T.R. Mallock had been seriously wounded at Neuve Chapelle, two months after the Nimy action. The officers of the 4th Battalion, Royal Fusiliers, paid a heavy collective price for their commitment to the cause. Mercifully, Mallock was destined to survive the war, and the achievement of the 4th Royal Fusiliers, and the British Expeditionary Force in general, must have made him proud for the rest of his days.

Though the British had been forced to retreat before they turned to face the enemy once more, the men of the BEF in that vital first phase of the First World War had achieved their most important objective, and that was to defy the Kaiser's demand to have this 'contemptible little army' forced back into the sea. Paris had been saved. The ports, the loss of which might have threatened England, had also been saved.

And the part Maurice Dease and Sidney Godley played on that first day of fighting should not be underestimated. Had Dease not ensured that his machine guns continued their fire for as long as they did, the British line could have been breached quite early at Nimy bridge. Had Godley not bought the retreating troops more time, then that retreat could have turned into a bloody rout by the Germans. Even after their heroics were over and their machine guns had fallen silent, the future of the BEF hung in the balance. There were those who believed that, had the Germans pressed home their advantage at Mons and Le Cateau, the British might have been forced to capitulate. With the French also on the back foot, the Germans might even have been able to sweep on to Paris and the ports, leaving Britain threatened.

That didn't happen. And one of the reasons why it didn't happen was that the Germans had learned to their own cost how stubborn the British could be in battle. They had laughed at the British prior to battle. They weren't laughing any more. The German unit IR84 may have claimed later that their casualties remained below a hundred, but that didn't reflect the wider picture and the thousands of casualties their army had suffered. Besides, to lose scores of close-knit friends in the space of a few hours was enough to make any advancing unit think twice about doing something unnecessary which would guarantee the loss of many more. And the effect on the German mindset of British bravery at Mons shouldn't be underestimated. They knew Maurice and his machine-gunners had refused to give in when the battle was at its fiercest. They knew one soldier had held them up single-handedly towards the end on the railway bridge. So what would other British soldiers do with their backs well and truly against the wall? And how many Germans would die before this contemptible army finally folded?

Dease, Godley and men like them had taught the Germans some respect for the BEF. And that respect allowed the British enough breathing space to regroup and take the fight back to the enemy. True, there would be a terrible, bloody stalemate for years before the war was finally over and Britain and its allies would emerge victorious. But Dease, Godley and their colleagues in the BEF had helped to save their country from the threat of German invasion. It would be for others to claim the ultimate victory.

At this stage, Godley's fate was unknown, and he would not taste the fruits of his sacrifice for some time. By rights Godley should have met his Maker along with most of his superiors, but he had been spared and decorated. How proud Nellie must have felt. And how sad she must have been at the price he had paid for those heroics. It is not known how much sympathy she received, how many consoling letters from Sid's comrades, because any such letters didn't survive.

Similar letters to Maurice's sister Maud have fared better, including one from Private Pocock, who wrote:

I was so pleased to hear his [Dease's] name appear in the papers for the V.C. as he deserved every fraction of it and knowing Mr Dease so well, as he was an officer in my company before leaving for the front, that I cannot speak too highly of him.

Yours faithfully,
H. Pocock

Meanwhile, Maurice's Uncle Gerald, who had first inspired him to join the army, received a letter from a friend called 'Nick' Nicholson, a vicar in Lymington and family friend. On 27 December 1914, he wrote:

> My dear Gerald,
> I have been meaning to write to you for weeks past about your magnificent young nephew … he was a grand boy, and I am glad to think I made his acquaintance when I went over to see the regiment twice this summer at Parkhurst. How very proud you must all feel of him, and I can only hope that is some consolation in his loss. Anyhow in this war of, I believe endless, heroic deeds, you can feel no one of them had a more splendid end. I know you will feel it very deeply and can only offer you my sincerest sympathy … The 4th Btn has been awfully cut up: I believe now only two of the original officers are left, and very few men.

'A splendid end.' Such was the thinking of the day, even among the well-educated – especially among the well-educated. Maurice's own sister persuaded herself to look at the tragedy in the same way. But all the time there was an underlying sadness too, felt by so many and expressed in this poem, which soon appeared in *The Stonyhurst Magazine* under a pseudonym.

Maurice Dease, VC

The Spring of his life had scarce gone by,
There was promise of fruit to be:
Summer was still in the Belgian sky,
But the Autumn-harvester Death came nigh,
Gathering flowers for glee.

He gave his best and he gave his all,
When he put his youth at stake;
He dared what he might at duty's call,
Eager to live but ready to fall
If it were for his country's sake.

The Spring of his life no Summer knows –
Farewell to the fields of Meath!

In his Irish home is a budding rose
Shall live perchance to the early snows,
Til the winds of Winter breathe.

He held the bridge and he worked his gun –
It was what he was set to do;
For cowardly fear in his heart was none,
The thing to do he had always done,
And now he would fight this through.

He fought and he bled; he fought and he fell;
He did what a brave man could
He faced the terrors of shot and shell.
Is it well with him? Oh indeed it is well,
For he died as a brave man should.

Honour to whom there is honour due,
To the soldiers that strove and died:
And here, for honour, dear Maurice to you,
Is a posy of flowers we come to strew
With our sorrow and lasting pride.

Q.Z.

It was still mid-winter and early 1915 when the Victoria Cross won by their brave son and brother arrived at the Dease house in Ireland. There was no great personal touch in that delivery, far from it. Indeed, someone somewhere decided that something should be done about that kind of insensitivity, if many more young men were to die so heroically only for their loved ones to be treated poorly. With their sense of loss still so raw, it was some consolation to the Dease family that letters continued to arrive, full of love and respect for Maurice.

Officers from the 4th Battalion, Royal Fusiliers, kept writing, even as they still recovered from their own wounds back in England towards the Easter of 1915.

Kingy Tower wrote to Maude Dease from the 'Duke of York's School, Guston, Dover', replying to a letter she had sent, requesting more information about her brother's death. She knew that Maurice and Kingy had been friends, along with John Beazley and Osbert Cundy-Cooper. Indeed, it is believed that Maud had been sent copies of the photographs of Maurice and his officer friends Beazley and Cundy-Cooper, as they had enjoyed that final day of peace in an English garden on the Isle of Wight, before their ordeal had begun. At any rate, Tower added a further note at the top of his own letter to tell Maud that 'Beazley is getting on very slowly and is at Metropole Folkestone now. Cooper also doing well.'

But Osbert Cundy-Cooper wasn't doing well, not really. Although his original period of leave had been granted from 22 December 1914 to 21 March 1915, this had been extended further because his right foot hadn't healed. Worse was to come. Indeed, the following letter was later sent to the War Office from Cundy-Cooper himself:

Sir,

In view of my having had part of my foot amputated (Syme Amputation), I have the honour to request that I may be assessed a Permanent Wound Pension. I am now in receipt of a temporary wound pension of £50.00 per annum.

Though he could count himself lucky to be alive, Cundy-Cooper was never going to be able to fight again. As for Kingy Tower, he still had other ideas. Tower was typically warm in his letter to Maud during that Easter of 1915:

Dear Miss Dease,

Thanks so very much for your letter. I'm afraid I've been very under not writing but have been so very busy lately. I enclose a photo of Maurice that I got hold of. It may interest you if you haven't seen it before. I am getting the enlarged group and will send it along.

I hope you are having glorious weather over there. It's too priceless here but still very cold on top of these cliffs.

I am trying to get out with 11th Division of K's 1st Army but it is very difficult as the doctors won't pass me yet. They want to make me adjutant here, which would be too awful as I should never get out again.

I have been made a captain in today's paper. Poor old Maurice would be one too if he was here. I do miss him so frightfully. You've no idea what awful subalterns we've got here now. They simply aren't fit to 'push a perambulator about', let alone run a platoon or company.

You really ought to hear the men back from 4th Battalion talk of Maurice. It would do your heart good. They simply adore him and it's quite funny to see so many of them have bought photographs of him taken in the old groups of the battalion and cut him out.

They have found out about poor Fred Forster from the Americans. He is buried in the cemetery at Mons and the American Gaston by name brought back his cigarette case etc to Miss Forster his sister.

I'm wondering if I can get hold of anything of Maurice for you in this way? I think this American Gaston is rather a rogue and charges fabulous sums of money to get information.

F. Forster's things were found in the Hotel de Ville at Mons and I expect Maurice's are there too. I have great hopes that the German line will withdraw soon back to Liege and if so I am going to try and get straight off to Mons and see what I can recover.

Hope you are all well. I will write and tell you if I can do anything. Am sick to death of soldiering in England and would really like to get back to have another 'go', although it is not very amusing.

Every good wish for Easter.

I was so glad to hear from you.

Yours sincerely,
Kinglake Tower.

P.S. Sir A. Conan Doyle, the writer is lecturing on 'The Great Battles of the War' in several places now and he talks at some length about Maurice and his VC at Mons. I sent him my diary on the subject. If you get a chance it would interest you.

Maud was given a clearer idea of what the renowned author Sir Arthur Conan Doyle – also Old Stonyhurst – was up to by another well-wisher. Suddenly men such as Dease and Harry Ranken, of the Royal Army Medical Corps, were being hailed as heroes not just by their military superiors but by the British public too. Ranken had won his VC tending to the wounded in the trenches at Hautevesnes in September, even after his thigh and lower leg had been shattered. So Maurice Dease was in good company.

Maud was proud of the acknowledgement her brother was getting:

The following was sent to us by the brother of the writer, who was present at the great Patriotic Meeting at the Royal Albert Hall, which was crowded.

Young Maurice Dease, VC, and Captain Ranken, VC, were both shown on the screen and the thousands present rose to their feet and cheered enthusiastically.

It was a wonderful tribute from Great Britain and if the mothers of those two boys who gave their lives for their country could have seen it, it might comfort their sad lonely hearts.

The bravery of Lieutenant Dease had been breathtaking, as Conan Doyle was quick to point out as he hailed the heroes:

Lieutenant Maurice Dease, five times wounded before he was killed, worked his machine gun to the end, and every man of his detachment was hit. Lieutenant Dease and Private Godley of his party both received the Victoria Cross. The occupants of one trench, including Lieutenant Smith, were cut off by the rush ... Altogether the Royal Fusiliers lost five officers and about two hundred men in the defence of the bridge, Lieutenant Tower having seven survivors in his platoon of sixty.

As the infantry retired a small party of engineers under Captain Theodore Wright endeavoured to destroy this and other bridges. Lieutenant Day was twice wounded on the main Nimy bridge. Lieutenant P.L. Boulnois succeeded in blowing a smaller one up. Captain Jarvis received a VC for his exertions in preparing the Jemappes bridge for destruction to the west of Nimy. Captain Wright, with Sergeant Smith, made an heroic endeavour under terrific fire to detonate the charge, but was wounded and fell into the canal. Lieutenant Holt, a brave young officer of reserve engineers, also lost his life in these operations. Having held on as long as possible, the front line of the 9th Brigade fell back upon the prepared position on high ground between Mons and Frameries, where the 107th RFA was entrenched. The 4th Royal Fusiliers passed through Mons and reached the new line in good order and without further loss.

But perhaps it was Kingy Tower, among all Maurice's friends and complimentary celebrities, who put most passion into his words, during one of his many attempts to make Maud feel better:

I feel too proud for words that Maurice was a friend of mine. He was a gallant gentleman and one we shall look up to in the regiment for centuries ...

Poor old Maurice was awfully cheery and well the whole time and did us all good the way he worked away at his job. Never in my life have I seen a more conscientious fellow. He always did whatever he was told thoroughly.

I simply can't describe to you how gallantly he fought. My God, he <u>was</u> a gallant gentleman in every sense of the word and no man on earth has ever died a more glorious and honourable death.

Poor Maurice, he <u>is</u> a loss to us but I'm <u>certain</u> he is gloriously happy now.

'He always did whatever he was told thoroughly.' It had been the same since his days as Aviary Boy at Stonyhurst, where the local bird expert had recalled: 'Yo've nobbut to tell yon lad what wants doin' and it's bahn to be done.'

The aviary continued to thrive, as Maurice would have hoped it might in his absence. Birds continued to fight for survival, cast rivals out with bloody brutality, do all the things that men had done since the outbreak of the war. The Aviary Boy was gone, having fought bravely for his machine gun nests and for his country.

The Dease family were glad of the outpouring of love for Maurice, which went on for years. They also wanted to do something for other bereaved families of VC recipients. They had a friend called Charlie, who was more formally known as Captain The Honourable Sir Charles Fitzwilliam, KCVO. Charlie was also friends with Lord Stamfordham, Private Secretary to King George V. Behind the scenes, an idea was born. The bereaved relatives of recipients of the Victoria Cross would receive something from Buckingham Palace. Wasn't it the least the king could do for the families of the poor men who had given their lives while showing the highest bravery? Just over a year after Maurice died, the Palace and Charlie came up with the answer:

25th September, 1915.
My dear Charlie [Captain The Hon. Sir C. Fitzwilliam, KCVO],
It has now been arranged with the War Office that a Message signed by the King shall be sent to the Next of Kin of those who have been awarded the Victoria Cross, but have been prevented by death from receiving it from the hands of His Majesty.

This message will therefore be despatched to Mr Dease in due course.

I return his letter to you, together with the War Office enclosure.
Yours ever,
Stamfordham

Sure enough, on 5 October 1915 a letter was sent from Buckingham Palace to E.F. Dease Esq. of Culmullen, Drumbeg, County Meath. It was from His Majesty George V and read:

It is a matter of sincere regret to me that the death of Lieutenant Maurice James Dease deprived me of the pride of personally conferring upon him the Victoria Cross, the greatest of all Military Distinctions.

George R. I.

While his heroism continued to be celebrated and acknowledged at all levels of British society, the body of Maurice James Dease hadn't yet been permanently laid to rest.

After the Battle of Mons many civilians hurriedly buried the dead near where they had fallen. Soon after that, however, the Germans decided to collect all the war dead, both British and Germans, and bury them in a new military cemetery they created at St Symphorien, 2 miles south-east of Mons.

There was an artificial mound on the already existing site. At the top of this the Germans erected a grey granite obelisk, some 23 metres high, with the German inscription 'In memory of the German and English soldiers who fell in the actions near Mons on 23 and 24 August 1914'. They originally buried 245 German and 188 British soldiers here.

However, Monsieur Maigret, Bourgmestre of St Symphorien obtained permission to place the bodies of Dease and another fallen soldier called Lieutenant L. Richmond in a more private spot. A Mme Bouilliart, near whose house Lieutenant Richmond of the Gordon Highlanders had originally been buried, offered Monsieur Maigret, who was her cousin, a more respectful resting place for the two British soldiers. Maigret obtained permission from the Germans to bury Dease and Richmond in the Bouilliart family vault at the village cemetery at St Symphorien.

After the war Mme Bouilliart contacted the War Office with the information and the Dease family decided to have Maurice reinterred in the nearby military cemetery. They chose a location alongside that of Second-Lieutenant F.J. Mead and the body was reinterred in early 1924, almost ten years after his death. Dease rests in Grave 2, Row 13, Plot V. Twenty-seven British graves were brought into the cemetery after the Armistice, as many families came to the conclusion that those who had been buried elsewhere would prefer to be laid to rest with their fallen comrades and fellow warriors.

Maurice's headstone, as well as having his name and rank, date of death and an engraving of the regimental crest of the Royal Fusiliers, bears a sculpted replica of the Victoria Cross.

At last, Maurice James Dease, brave soldier and lover of birds, horses and people, could rest in peace.

# 14

# Survivor

It was 2 August 1919. Sidney, the man waiting for 34-year-old Nellie Norman to walk down the aisle, had a thick moustache, he was stocky and handsome, and looked for all the world like any other groom – nervous and excited about what was to happen in the next few moments. His body's strangest features were well hidden. A hard little bump on his head was barely noticeable; you almost had to feel around for it and know what you were looking for. As for the strange-looking skin patterns on his back, only Nellie and a few others knew they were there. It was probably just as well that this 30-year-old plumber, the centre of attention for now, was well covered up as he stood with his back to the congregation in the parish church of St Mark, Harlesden. Not for any sense of shame about what had happened to him; it was just that the guests might have remained more fascinated by what they saw on his back than the intricate detail of the bride's wedding dress. No less craft, no fewer hours of patient stitching had gone into what lay beneath the man's tunic; quite the reverse.

That is no slight on Nellie's wedding dress, which was a beautiful work of art. No expense had been spared on that extravagant white dress or the wedding in general, because she had struck lucky and received a reward for her own kindness. The elderly woman who employed the 34-year-old Nellie in a big house in Willesden liked her very much, so much so that, when she heard that Nellie was to be married, she didn't merely lament the inconvenience it would cause her, or curse the need to try to find someone just as conscientious to do her daily bidding. She was sorry to be letting Nellie go, of course, but happy for her that she was starting a new life. She could have a family of her own and not before time. It was something to celebrate, so she had offered to pay for the wedding herself. How could Nellie not have the best, when the man she was going to marry was the courageous winner of the Victoria Cross, and had fast become a kind of national celebrity?

No tiny wedding for a VC and his bride, who had waited the entire war to be together again. It seemed impossible, but he had survived. How did he manage to live? Colin thinks he has the answer:

> He'd played cricket and football. We have a photo of him prior to the First World War in a cricket team. He was very sporty and, after he joined the army, he was a cross-country running champion for the regiment. He was very fit. That's quite possibly why he survived despite the injuries he had.

The happiest person on the planet was Ellen Eliza Norman. She was about to enjoy the wedding of her dreams after all. At long last. It was going to be worth waiting for. Nellie's father George couldn't have afforded a wedding as big as this one, because he was only a farm labourer. Sidney and Nellie's daughter Eileen said later, 'It may be that my mother worked for a woman who really liked her and that's why she had a nice wedding. It was a big wedding.'

The joy and relief Nellie must have felt is easy enough to imagine. It was one thing to be 29 and unmarried, as she had been at the outbreak of hostilities. That was unusual enough, when most women were married almost as soon as they were old enough to find a man. But to be in her mid-thirties by the time the wedding day came around? That was a considerable feat of patience, when the couple had had so little to sustain them through troubled times. There had been letters between Nellie and her man, of course. That they had got through their separation was something of a miracle when you consider the chaos of the prisoner of war camps and the increasingly bitter hatred between nations that were destroying each other's youth in their millions.

At first it had been hard to communicate because the British prisoners had been moved about. One, Alf Bastin, revealed how hard it was in late 1914:

> After a while we set off again and it took us two days to get to a place called Doberitz, north of Berlin. We stayed there right through the

winter of 1914. It happened to be a bad winter and the conditions were pretty grim. Eventually in March, another camp was built for us in a place called Delotz, which wasn't far from Doberitz.

But after that terrible first winter, in the early spring of 1915, the Germans learned that another of their prisoners, Sidney Frank Godley, had been awarded the highest British accolade for bravery. Bastin recalled the moment this became public knowledge:

> On Sunday the whole British section was turned out for a special parade, we were told it was special news from the American Ambassador. We thought what the hell was this going to be, the Americans weren't in the war.
>
> It transpired that he had been requested to inform Private Godley of the Royal Fusiliers that he had been awarded the Victoria Cross for his courageous efforts in the early weeks of the war when the 'Contemptibles' (as we were called 'a contemptible little army', according to the Kaiser) were being hounded out by the Germans.
>
> Apparently what happened was that Private Godley was a machine gunner, in position on a bridge. He prevented the Germans from advancing on to the bridge by continuous firing. He eventually got captured and landed in our camp. He was quite an unassuming sort of chap and for some unknown reason he was called 'Mug' Godley.
>
> He was congratulated by all the British of course and we all cheered when the announcement was made. Incidentally the German Commandant of our camp shook Godley's hand after he had been presented with the Victoria Cross.

Furthermore, Frank was toasted at a dinner held in his honour by a group of German officers. Men who had already lost comrades in their hundreds of thousands openly saluted the bravery of the enemy.

When it heard the news, Godley's local newspaper, the *East Grinstead Observer*, commented on 26 February 1916 that, 'Private Godley, who won the VC but is now a prisoner of war in Germany, had the "honour" of being invited to dine with German officers on Christmas Day, because they understood the VC in England was equal to the Iron Cross in Germany …'

It was an honour indeed, though part of Godley would still probably have preferred to see them at the other end of a machine gun. 'He played along with things like that dinner,' Eileen said:

He knew he had to if he wanted to stay alive, so he played along with the Germans. I think they looked up to him, looked upon him as a hero. Because he was awarded the Victoria Cross, the Germans looked upon him as a hero. I didn't know the American ambassador came to the prison camp and told him he'd won the Victoria Cross. But I did know that the German officers thought it was brilliant that he'd won the Victoria Cross and they looked up to him. He told me about being invited to the officers mess to mark the award. I think he accepted the Germans. Put it that way. That's what dad did. He knew that if he started doing anything that wasn't quite the ticket, they wouldn't put up with that. So he played along with them. He accepted it and if he wanted to live he'd play along.

His fellow prisoners of war looked up to him too, though Godley wasn't the sort to brag about what he had done. As Eileen explained, 'He was just doing something he had to do. "I done my job," that's what he'd say. "That was my job and I did my job." That would be my dad's answer.'

Nevertheless, his new-found fame meant he was photographed with two top rugby players from the north of England, who had also become prisoners. They acted as Frank's minders if he received too much attention. Colin observed, 'These two English professional rugby players were in the camp with him. What they decided was that they would be his "minder". Played for England, that's what I was told. So he was in good company when you think about it.' Eileen found this revelation amusing. 'If my dad talked about anything, it would have been football, not rugby,' she smiled.

For a while peace and quiet was hard to come by for Godley, but there were also advantages. His new status with his captors couldn't have done his chances of sending and receiving letters successfully any harm at all. The trouble was, there was only so much that Sidney and Nellie could write to tell each other – for he turned back into Sidney when he wrote to her. They missed each other, they would be together one day, they loved each other, the war had to finish some time.

Eileen said, 'He talked about his days and what he'd done and things. He was very much a sportsman. He probably taught the Germans how to play cricket, if I know him!' Had Maurice Dease survived to become a prisoner of war, you suspect he would have enjoyed doing that too. Colin explained the respect the Germans showed as they sent Sidney's letters on their way: 'The Germans stamped the cards, "From Private Godley, VC, – British Prisoner of War". And my grandmother sent him a photograph of herself.'

It is a lovely, sensitive portrait from a woman who wasn't going to let her man forget her face, no matter how many years it took him to come back to her. Sidney had probably requested such a photograph himself, determined to have that face to focus on when times got tough; determined to get home one day and be with that woman forever.

The letters passed back and forth, their only variation coming in bits of news about what they had done that week or day. Sidney would talk about some football match he had played in captivity, or joke about how he had tried to teach the Germans cricket, the game he had loved before the war almost as much as football. He could talk about a dog that had turned up in the camp and become a pet to the British prisoners there, though some had been tempted to eat it. He wouldn't have stood for that. Eileen explained, 'He mentioned he'd done something for a dog. He did like animals.'

Nellie would send him news of his family, since she knew his sister 'Kit' and her husband, Will Norman, Nellie's cousin. But that Victoria Cross helped to keep spirits high too. Nellie knew her man was now to be regarded as having a place among the very bravest of the brave. He was a war hero, and if he could prevent his stubborn nature from upsetting the Germans too much while he remained in captivity, he could come home. That was more than most of the poor young men of his generation had been able to do. The 4th Royal Fusiliers had been decimated and even the Commanding Officer, Colonel McMahon – the man who had told them not to fear wounds or death, only disgrace – hadn't survived to see the end of 1914. The boys in the machine gun section of the 4th battalion had been wiped out back in Nimy. So Nellie's Sidney – it remained Sidney to women and family, though Frank to army and male friends – was one of the lucky ones. And that made her one of the lucky ones too. He might be far away from her, but at least he was alive.

Inevitably Godley's celebrity status subsided gradually in the camp, at least enough to allow him to reflect upon the most basic question of all: how had he survived? Who was responsible? That question must have made him feel uncomfortable, because the answer demanded something he didn't probably didn't want to feel – gratitude to the Germans who had saved his life. Sure, they had been medical men and not soldiers as such – but he couldn't get away from which side they were on. The whole thing must have been hard to fathom.

He must have played the immediate aftermath of his last stand at Nimy over and again in his mind. The kindness of the Mons citizens who took him to their hospital, the shock of the local doctors as they examined him and wondered how it was that he was still alive. The defiance he felt when the Germans arrived to take over the hospital and interrogate any British soldier receiving treatment there. He had insisted that he wasn't going to tell the Germans anything at all; he had lain there conscious, though as much of a physical wreck as any man could be yet still speak. Why hadn't they just finished him off? You didn't have to look hard to find examples of German atrocities in the First World War, and not just on British soldiers. If the civilian population of Belgium didn't bow sufficiently quickly to the will of the invader, they were murdered in their thousands. So what was the point in keeping alive this belligerent little man, who would be nothing more than a drain on the time and energy of German medical staff when taken into captivity, a distraction for doctors who would be far better employed trying to save the lives of thousands of their own wounded? If the Germans had known how many of their compatriots had been shot by Godley and his machine gun, would they have been so merciful? He must have had some success, despite his woeful record in Dease's pre-war tests – otherwise the Germans would have just poured over the bridge before the retreat could be carried out.

We can only put this outstanding example of German mercy down to two possible factors: either their humanity hadn't yet been eroded in the immediate aftermath of this first battle of the war, or someone did indeed realise that the battered British private must be the machine-gunner who had stood his ground until he was shot and blown up – and they admired him for his bravery. The more likely scenario, in those first hours after the Germans crossed the bridge at Nimy, was the former. Souls had not yet been numbed or corrupted entirely by the monotonous horror of war. On this first day the horror was fresh, yet decent fighting men were somehow reluctant to walk into a hospital and finish a man off. So the bullet stuck in Godley's skull was not followed by another, more penetrative bullet to end the debate. Colin Godley said:

> I think he was grateful to the Germans in the respect that they saved his life, because the German surgeon who took over (from the Belgian doctors) didn't try to remove the bullet from his head. They said, 'It will kill you if we do.' They did his back up, they put all his bones in the right place, they wired him up with silver wire and stitched him back up with 150 stitches. The silver wire never came out. It was very fine wire, just to hold the bones while they knitted. He felt gratitude towards the German doctors, because they saved his life. The one who didn't remove the bullet from his head saved his life.

To refuse to kill a man is still a far cry from pulling out all the stops to help a man recover. It is one thing to leave a bullet in a man's skull – the correct decision, for any other would have killed him. It is quite another to authorise the use of 150 stitches to sew up a man's back when it has been blown apart so thoroughly. But the most extraordinary development came in the follow-ing weeks and months, before the Germans could possibly have known that this irritating, feisty individual had won their enemy's highest bravery award. Private Godley was sent to Berlin to be subjected to a technique which was still in its infancy – skin grafting. 'They patched him up and then they sent him to Berlin for skin grafts,' Colin confirmed. 'In 1914 that was quite new. He didn't talk about it.' Sidney's other grandson, Andy Slade, who works in a hospital, still marvels at what the Germans did:

> When you think of skin grafts in that day and age! Nowadays it is a fairly common occurrence, but in those days it must have been quite an operation, and I'm not sure they had too much anaesthetic going on either. It must have been fairly crude, don't you think? In 1914 it couldn't have been as good as it is now.

Eileen said, 'I think he was well treated in the German hospital. You could see what they had done. And you know he had a piece of shrapnel or a bullet left in his head. He never had any scars on his face, but how it entered I don't know.' The main thing is that it never exited, either of its own accord or by the surgeon's hand. Andy explained, 'It could have killed him. I think that's why they left it.'

As for those skin grafts, they would surely have had to act quickly, while the wounds were still relatively fresh. Did they use Sidney precisely because he was an enemy soldier, and therefore if the surgery went wrong it didn't matter? Surely with resources and expertise so limited back in 1914, they would have preferred to 'practise' on a soldier of their own, having at least some faith in the techniques they were going to attempt to use? Besides, Godley had to undergo several skin grafts; the repairs couldn't just be done in one fell swoop. So, if the first surgery looked promising, it didn't make sense to continue with an 'enemy guinea-pig'. It would have made more sense to switch at that point to one of their own men, if they were encouraged by their initial experiment. So we are left with a rather surprising conclusion. The Germans didn't care what nationality the patient was. Right there in the middle of the mass slaughter, they wanted to help someone. It didn't matter if he was British or German or from another continent entirely. They just wanted to make him better. So they took him to Berlin and used all their skill and science to do just that. Even 100 years later this is a highly delicate, complex process which produces mixed results. So what the Germans achieved for Godley was truly remarkable. Eileen and her son Andy think they probably took the skin from somewhere else on his body – though it wasn't unheard of to use skin from dead bodies in the early, primitive stages of skin graft history.

'We used to chuckle about it,' said Eileen. 'He had a wonderful sense of humour, my dad, and, if I know him as well as I think I know him, I have a good idea about where that skin came from. He used to think that having two different skin colours on his back was comical.' Eileen remembers her innocent confusion fondly. 'I can't help laughing when I think of it. I used to say to him, "I don't understand why you have those brown patches on your back but I don't have them?" After he had those skin grafts, there were brown patches left.'

Godley was thick-skinned and his hide was tough as old boots, but that didn't count against him. Crucially, his body didn't reject the new skin which covered the raw flesh and first stages of scar tissue. That skin was accepted and helped make him whole again. His immune system was strong enough to avoid infection; and, as he recovered, he knew deep down that the Germans had done him a massive favour. That didn't make him love them, because you didn't feel any great affection for a people who had shot and shelled you, killed your friends and then taken away your liberty, whatever they had done more recently to make amends. Godley wasn't going to change for anyone. He was British and that was where his loyalties always lay. 'The stubborn streak came out in the prison camp because he wasn't going to give in, even though he was stuck there,' Colin explained.

One of the reasons why Godley was still simmering with resentment against his captors was that they had killed his brother, Percy Henry Godly. Percy had enlisted in the Royal Sussex Regiment as number 967 and then followed in his brother's footsteps by joining the Royal Fusiliers, though he was known to his superiors as L/14736, 32nd Battalion. He had been born in East Grinstead not so long after Sidney, and died at the age of just 23. Percy was killed in action on 4 October 1916. He was buried in Belgium and is remembered with honour at AIF Burial Ground, Flers.

'I don't know when Sid found out,' Colin said. But when he did, it is hard to imagine that his grief wasn't tinged with raw anger towards the Germans who continued to deny him his freedom. There was one person he could still turn to for solace, albeit by letter. Godley had no love for the Germans but there was someone back home he still loved, and that was Nellie. He enjoyed her letters, though he wasn't a prolific letter-writer himself. Besides, writing became more difficult during the final years of the war. Colin said:

> He sent her a letter where she was living for a while at Maida Hill from the Prison Camp. They kept in touch but not a lot. I've seen some people who wrote all the time, but he didn't seem to write too much from the Prison Camp. He was at Doberitz, then Deloit.

Eileen believed it was dangerous to assume that her mother had any real understanding of what he had been through in order to earn his decoration. 'I don't know whether that's right. She knew he had the Victoria Cross and that was something that made her feel good.'

The realisation that her boyfriend was something of a national treasure would certainly have sustained Nellie during the periods when communication between them broke down. And there were further reasons why they didn't get to hear from each other for months at a time.

Godley wasn't always as compliant with the Germans as they might have expected. That meant they didn't always give him a quiet life in return. Colin explained:

> I think what happened was that he didn't take too kindly to being kept in a camp, so I don't think he was very cooperative with them. That's why he won the medal, because he was very stubborn. And that's also why he got taken out of the camps and lumbered with jobs elsewhere. He was forced to work in a munitions plant. He worked for a while in Silesia in the Salt Mines. A lot of them did from Deloit. Doberitz was in North Germany anyway.

During such periods, Nellie's letters to the camp were met only by silence, and she must have feared something terrible had happened. In a way she was right because, as the war became more desperate, the tasks allocated to the POWs had become more brutal in their physicality. The shifts in the munitions factories lengthened, and those terrible months in the Silesian salt mines were no picnic either. The Germans had invested a lot of time and energy in Godley's body – so they probably thought they could do what they wanted with it when they became short of labour and work it as hard as they liked.

Finally, when it became clear that the war was about to end, the treatment of the prisoners improved a little, and there were no more spells of hard labour in Silesia. Camp life returned to normal, though the strength of resentment among Germans who had suffered for so long only to lose the war was incalculable. Would this bitter frustration be taken out on British prisoners of war or on the German authorities who had put them through such hell? There was a revolution in Berlin and anarchy spread. A terrible, petty revenge could have been exacted on the British prisoners, but it didn't happen that way, at least not at Delotz. Camp guards decided they didn't want any atrocity on their conscience, nor did they want to feel the wrath of their prisoners when peace broke out. So one day Godley and the rest of the inmates woke up to find that the Germans were gone. They had walked out of the camp in the dead of night and headed for home, before they could be captured to become prisoners themselves. What would happen if the prisoners just followed suit, and walked out too? Godley decided to find out, though he had no intention of staying in Germany a second longer than he had to. He didn't want to risk the chaos of France and Belgium either, because he couldn't even be entirely sure the war was over. So he headed for Denmark, which he hoped would be friendly enough to help him return home. He found a ship preparing to cross the North Sea and climbed aboard. When he saw the shores of England, he knew his long nightmare was over – not that anyone knew he was coming back. There had been no time to let anyone know by letter and, besides, he had been used to sending mail out from the camp via the Germans – a postal system which didn't exist any more.

Imagine Godley's sister Kit's surprise when she went out shopping one day in Lee, on the Kent side of London. She must have gone there to try to learn the latest on Sidney and when he might be home. And she received her answer when she bumped into him, by chance, on the street. There he was, the man whose safe return she had prayed for over so many troubled years.

'Sidney!' she cried.

'Hello Kit,' he replied casually, before giving her a big hug. 'Seen Nellie recently?'

Eileen loved that story. 'That was typical him! That was typical him! He was just sort of "Well that's me, that's who I am."'

'That's marvellous,' echoed Andy.

# 15

# A Hero's Wedding

Before Sid and Nellie could be together again at last, there were rules to observe. Like the professional soldier he was, Sidney Frank Godley, VC, had reported straight back to his battalion, the 4th Royal Fusiliers. They were based in the appropriately named Battlefield Street in Lee, which is why he had bumped into Kit on her afternoon off. The battalion welcomed back their Victoria Cross hero, and decided he was due his freedom. His demobilisation notice read:

> Number 13814 Pte S. Godley V.C.
> Royal Fusiliers Corps

> On the occasion of his demobilization, the General Commanding Eastern Command desires to place on record the Army Council's appreciation of the services rendered by him during the present War, and to wish him all success and prosperity on his return to civil life. He trusts that Pte S. Godley V.C. will retain the kindliest feelings towards his old comrades of all ranks and towards the unit or units in which he has served ...

The British Army had still put an 'e' in his surname; the German Army had put a bullet in his head. By then Godley had become accustomed to both. As for showing the 'kindliest feelings towards his old comrades', Godley would

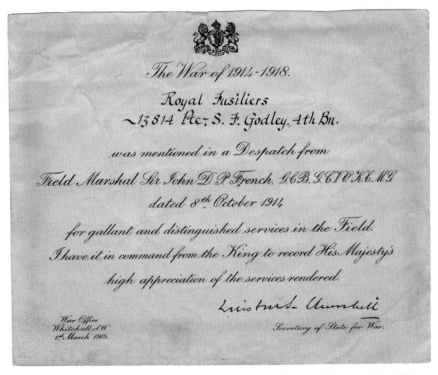

The War of 1914-1918.

Royal Fusiliers
13814 Pte: S. F. Godley, 4th Bn.

...was mentioned in a Despatch from

Field Marshal Sir John D P French, G.C.B, G.C.V.O.K.C.M.G
dated 8th October 1914,

for gallant and distinguished services in the Field.
I have it in command from the King to record His Majesty's
high appreciation of the services rendered.

Winston Churchill

War Office
Whitehall, S.W.
1st March 1919.                                    Secretary of State for War.

Mentioned in Dispatches: Godley receives approval from the king and Winston Churchill,
Secretary of State for War.

show in time that he intended to fulfil this duty with as much commitment
as he had defended the bridge at Nimy.

In the meantime, he was able to take his beloved Nellie away on holiday
with the approval of his employers, and they could get to know each other
all over again. It was midwinter and freezing by then, but they didn't care
about that. The time they spent indoors together was more precious anyway.
The strange patches of skin on his back and all those battle scars didn't make
Nellie love Sid any less. Somehow there wasn't a single scar on that handsome face – and whatever scars he was hiding psychologically, he seemed to
her to be the same old Sid she had known before the war.

Soldiering could never be the same for Godley, though. There was no
shortage of dignitaries waiting to rub shoulders with the VC hero, something
he clearly found a little daunting at first. Not that he was averse to risking the perils of London's public transport system along with everyone else.
But, after learning that he would receive his VC from King George V in the
ballroom at Buckingham Palace, he couldn't hide his excitement, or indeed
his frustration at not yet knowing when the ceremony would take place. You

sense all these emotions in his letter to Nellie from his barracks in January 1919. Above all, you feel the enormous amount of love he had for Nellie, a love which sustained him during all those years in captivity, and had found its outlet at last:

My Dearest Darling,

Just a note to let you know that I am going out to dinner tonight at the Cannon Street Hotel at the invitation of the Right Honourable Marquis Camden – so think of me going through the hoop. I had an invitation yesterday at the Apollo and quite enjoyed it. Soldier Boy was played – it is lovely.

Well my little darling I am afraid it will be late in the month before I am decorated. I have received a letter from the War Office to say that my name is in the next list for decoration but no date has yet been fixed. Darling I have a terrible cold. I hope you feel no effects of our holiday.

Darling on Sunday night I had to walk from New Cross Gate home. The trams were full up and no possible chance of getting on. Well my little darling I've more news to write but will tell you all when I see you so goodbye till tomorrow and God Bless you my little love so will close with

Love and Kisses
your Loving Boy,
Syd
xxxxxxxxxxx

It must have been hard even for a level-headed character such as Godley to keep his feet on the ground in the midst of all this attention. He had already received a letter from King George V. On paper headed by the royal crest and the words 'Buckingham Palace,' it read:

The Queen joins me in welcoming you on your release from the miseries and hardships, which you have endured with so much patience and courage.

During these many months of trial, the early rescue of our gallant Officers and Men from the cruelties of their captivity has been uppermost in our thoughts.

We are thankful that this longed for day has arrived, and that back in the old country you will be able once more to enjoy the happiness of a home and to see good days among those who anxiously look for your return.

George R.I.

'Syd' had wanted to set up home with Nellie, and now he would be able to do just that. They'd go to Buckingham Palace together first, to collect his decoration. The proud day soon arrived. Colin explained that, 'He went to the Palace with his two step-brothers and my Nan to get his VC (William and Reginald were two step-brothers). One step-brother was in the Royal Flying Corps. Not a pilot, ground crew, but they tended to get bombed too!'

On 15 February 1919 Godley was shown into the ballroom of Buckingham Palace to meet the king in person. And while Private Sidney Frank Godley was rightly proud, he wasn't overawed at the prospect of meeting the king. Eileen maintained, 'He took it in his stride like it was an everyday event. He never made a big thing about the VC.' Andy added, 'He didn't look overwhelmed by anything, though, did he? I've seen pictures when he was walking down a row of soldiers and he never seemed fazed by anything like that.'

He may not have been overawed, but that's not to say he wasn't emotional. He must have spared a thought for Lieutenant Maurice Dease, whose family had lobbied for more personal investitures. Poor Maurice couldn't be there to accept his own decoration. His life had been ended by the Germans. For Maurice there were no personal rewards for his valour, other than the sure knowledge that in his final moments he had done his duty and more. For Maurice there was no celebrity, at least none he could enjoy; no time to marry or feel the thrill of starting a family either. These pleasures were taken away from countless young British men in the violence across the water, denied forever.

Sidney was one of the lucky ones and he continued to enjoy life, accepting his time in the limelight as part of his duty, to the army and all those who had fallen. On 26 February 1919, he was welcomed home by the Mayor of Lewisham and presented with 50 guineas – a significant sum of money back them – and a copy of the Lewisham Roll of Honour. He could put the money towards a new life with Nellie, while the Roll of Honour was a sobering antidote to any sense of self-importance.

'He knew how lucky he was to be alive,' said Andy Slade. Sid must have realised it in that church, as he and Nellie said their vows. Private Godley, VC, was in one piece, against all the odds. Strictly speaking, his skull was now more than one piece, because the Germans had rather crudely added some lead to it. And his back, rather than being one piece, was more accurately several little pieces all sewn together. Still, it made a work of art every bit as miraculous as Nellie's wedding dress – some would say even more so, given the circumstances.

The loving couple were married in style. Linda Godley, Colin's wife, said, 'They had a lovely big wedding. We've got a lovely big wedding photo of them.' The marriage certificate made it all official:

MARRIAGE CERTIFICATE

Marriage Solemnized at The Parish Church of St Mark. Harlesden. August 2nd, 1919.

Sydney Frank Godley, 29, Bachelor, Plumber, 25 Battlefield Street, Lee, Kent.
Father's name: Frank Godley, House Decorator.

Ellen Eliza Norman, 34, Spinster, 53 Fulmers Road, Harlesden, NW.
Father's name: George Norman, Farm Labourer.

In the presence of William George Norman and Rosina Elizabeth Nunn.
Vicar: Ernest Reynold Whalley

Although Reverend Whalley presided over proceedings and did all the official paperwork, since it was his church, there is a suggestion that another man took much of the service. And there can be little doubt that Reverend Noel Mellish was the true spiritual leader on the day, the man the groom looked up to most. That's not to say that there was anything wrong with Whalley. It was just that Reverend Mellish was a war hero in his own right. As the first member of the chaplaincy to win the VC, something he achieved while attached to none other than the 4th Royal Fusiliers, there was no one whose blessing Godley wanted more on the day of his wedding to his beloved Nellie. You could make a wedding as fancy as the bride wanted, but for a groom it was also about the quality of the men present.

Sidney's father was there, just as he should be, whatever difficulties there had been in Sidney's childhood. However much Frank had failed as a father, however unstable Sidney's formative years had been, the groom showed that sons have an extraordinary capacity for forgiveness, especially once they have matured into adults themselves. Many of Sidney's family were there, including his paternal grandfather, who sported a spectacularly long white beard. How Sidney must have wished that his mother were still alive to enjoy his big day. But he had long ago been forced to come to terms with not having a mother. Perhaps she would be looking down on him now, from Heaven. Although Reverend Mellish couldn't compensate for the absence of a mother, his presence was both comforting and inspiring. Very few men had shown quite the sort of bravery Godley and Mellish had shown during the Great War.

Noel Mellish was a little older than Godley, though he too knew north London as a youngster, having been born in Oakleigh, Barnet, in 1880. Before Godley even thought about joining the army, Mellish saw action in the Boer War as a member of Baden-Powell's police. He didn't take long to display his extraordinary bravery in battle, though killing other people was something he would never relish. Nor did it form part of the reason why he was considered so courageous. A colleague explained that:

> On one occasion, his unit being surrounded by Boers, there seemed little hope for them. Mellish was given the task of summoning help. Somehow he got through but then, his duty done, he returned to his comrades to tell them help was on the way and to assist with the defence until reinforcements arrived.

Mellish already felt a calling, because while he was in Africa he assisted at a local church and native mission. 'It is such men as Mellish who restore one's faith in mankind,' it was said of him during that period of his life. The longer Godley's life went on, the more you could say the same about him, as we shall see. As for Mellish, he returned home and took holy orders in 1912, becoming curate at St Paul's church in Deptford. Just as Sidney Godley would show with increasing regularity as his life went on, Mellish showed a remarkable ability to relate to troubled boys. He helped his Church Lads Brigade to take over a former pub and turn it into a Boys' Club. The youngsters called it the 'Noel Club' in honour of the man who was trying to keep them on the straight and narrow.

Though he offered his services to the army chaplaincy on the outbreak of the First World War, Mellish didn't serve until May 1915. He soon made up for lost time, and like Godley he would suffer the personal pain of losing a brother. Second Lieutenant Richard Coppin Mellish was killed in action while serving with the 1st Middlesex Regiment at the Battle of Loos on 25 September 1915. Early the following year, Noel Mellish was attached to the 4th Royal Fusiliers, where he quickly followed Dease and Godley into regimental legend with his selfless bravery.

He found himself in the notorious Ypres Salient in Belgium, at the start of what became known as the 'Action of the St Eloi Craters'. Situated about 3 kilometres east of Ypres, St Eloi was an area where a section of the German trenches jutted out into British lines, a situation that couldn't be allowed to continue. The British attempted to take the German positions and had some success at the opening line of German trenches before becoming bogged down. There were many British casualties, wounded men stranded in areas that hadn't been properly secured, almost as vulnerable as if they were stuck in no-man's land. This was where Reverend Mellish came in. His citation reads:

On three consecutive days, the 27 to 29 March 1916, during the heavy fighting at St Eloi, Belgium, he went to and fro continuously between the original trenches and the captured enemy trenches, attending to and rescuing wounded men. The first day, from an area swept by machine gun fire, he rescued ten severely wounded men.

How proud the deeply religious Maurice Dease would have been, had he lived to see Mellish go about his courageous work among the wounded of the battalion. Dease was a Catholic and Mellish an Anglican, but it would have made no difference whatsoever. They were both prepared to sacrifice their lives trying to help their comrades. The Mellish citation went on:

Although his battalion was relieved on the second day, he returned and rescued twelve more of the wounded. Taking charge of a group of volunteers on the third day, he again returned to the trenches in order to rescue the remaining wounded.

This excellent work was done voluntarily and was far outside the sphere of his normal duties.

An officer of the Northumberland Fusiliers had also witnessed Mellish and his heroic work. He wrote:

Nothing could be finer than the way Captain Mellish did his duty and more than did his duty during the time he was near us. Immediately the troops captured the trenches and while the wounded were picking their way painfully back, the enemy's guns were turned on full blast and the intervening ground was deluged with shell and machine-gun fire. Into this tempest of fire the brave parson walked, a prayer book under his arm as though on church parade in peace time.

He reached the first of the wounded and knelt down to do what he could for them. The first few he brought in himself without any aid and it made us think a bit more of parsons to see how he walked quietly under fire assisting the slow moving wounded and thinking more of saving them from discomfort than of his own safety.

It was only during a lull in the fighting when the ambulance parties could get out that he finally took a rest. Next day he was out again as unconcerned as ever. Some of the men would not have survived the ordeal had it not been for the prompt assistance rendered to them by Mr Mellish.

The first Reverend VC of the war had returned to London to be presented with his award by the king at Buckingham Palace on 12 June 1916. Though Godley had earned his award almost two years earlier, he'd had to wait three more years to walk those same proud steps into the palace before meeting the grateful king. Yet Mellish had gone back to the war after receiving his VC, and had somehow survived until the Armistice.

Like Godley, all Mellish really wanted to do, when he knew he had played his part and was going to survive, was to return to his sweetheart back home. Unhindered by captivity, Mellish was even quicker off the mark than Godley, and married Elizabeth Wallace at his home church of St Paul's in Deptford in December 1918. Now here he was at Sidney's wedding, and he couldn't have been happier for his fellow VC. Both men knew that it was something of a miracle that they were both standing in this Harlesden church, with so much to celebrate and so much to look forward to.

By now Noel Mellish was Vicar of Lewisham, about 12 miles from Harlesden, so it was no bother for him to attend and at the very least assist with the wedding. If ever there was a time to thank God for his mercy, it was now. While Mellish prayed for Sidney and Nellie, the wedding photographer prepared his equipment. The loving couple couldn't have looked happier when they had their photograph taken. It is a beautiful picture.

Nellie didn't brag about her fancy wedding, certainly not to her grand-children. 'She never said much,' Colin recalled, thinking how similar she was to her husband in that respect. 'My Nan was another one who didn't

*Ag Infms Oct*

Any further communications on this subject should be
addressed to
The Secretary,
War Office,
London, S.W.1.

MEMORANDUM.

| From. | To. |
|---|---|
| A.G.4.a., War Office, London, S.W.1. 11 Feby 1919. | *Privak S. Godley VC. Royal Fusiliers 25 Batterfield Street Lee S.E* |

Following reference should
be given in reply :- } (A.G.4.a.)          Room O11.

You are required to attend at Buckingham Palace at *10·0*
a.m. on the *15 February 1919* to receive the *Victoria*
Cross from His Majesty the King.

You should report yourself to the Regimental Sergeant
Major 3rd (Res) Battalion Scots Guards, Wellington Barracks, S.W.
on the *15 February 1919* before at *9.30 am*

*You are requested to acknowledge the receipt of
these orders.*

Brigadier-General.
Deputy Director of Personal Services.

Ordered to the palace: Godley gets the good news that he is to receive his VC from the king.

say much about things.' Sidney didn't go around bragging about Mellish's appearance at his wedding either. There was a difference between respect and trying to make capital out of another man's fame. He would come to know that difference all too well, though he was only just starting to make sense of his newfound celebrity and how to use it wisely for the common good. Perhaps Mellish even gave Godley some advice on that front. Whether he did or not, Mellish would have reason to be proud of his fellow VC and the way he conducted himself for the rest of his life.

But, in that moment on their special day, what mattered most to Sidney and Nellie Godley was that they could begin their new life together. They had a future – one which had seemed most unlikely on 23 August 1914, and for most of the war years. They had been separated for so long that there was no way anything was going to split them up again – except of course death itself, as their vows had foretold. They could enjoy the present, and then they could start a family. Sidney Godley was going to give his children a stable start in life, quite unlike the one he had known as a small child. He would give them a future, while respecting the past.

Exactly how much Sidney told his beloved Nellie about what he had been through at Nimy bridge and beyond, only they knew. There is no evidence that Sid Godley was badly scarred psychologically by the horrors he had witnessed on the very first day of the fighting. However, if Sid and his wife thought they could walk out of the church into an entirely new type of life, where peace would always hold sway, they were wrong. If they thought they had left Mons or even war behind forever, they would soon have cause to think again.

# 16

# Gunner Godley and Old Bill

Sidney Frank Godley had a contented smile on his face as he watched another Arsenal match at Highbury with his daughter Eileen. It was 1930 and Godley was enjoying the peaceful interlude before another war. Trust Godley to support a team whose nickname was 'The Gunners'. Eileen recalled:

> From the time I was seven, I was introduced to football. My father was an Arsenal fan, even though we lived at Leigh Green, down Lewisham way, I used to go to Highbury with him for football matches. I used to stand right against the fence and he used to stand there with me. It was all boys, there were hardly any girls in the stadium in those days. My dad used to say, 'Don't start arguing with anyone.'

Her elder brother Stan would also have been urged to concentrate on the action on the field, because these were glorious days for Arsenal. A young striker called Cliff Bastin was taking English football by storm, even though he was still only 18 years old. The manager was Herbert Chapman, and he too had begun to earn his place among the game's legends.

Arsenal had beaten Huddersfield 2–0 in the FA Cup final that year. The crowd booed when a German airship called the Graf Zeppelin hovered over the stadium for a while. LZ 127 was the largest Zeppelin ever built at the time. It was 776ft in length, big enough to darken the skies when it passed above you. It almost scraped the hair of spectators as it floated seemingly just inches above row Z of the roofless old stadium. That kind of daring might not have provoked such a furious response among the fans under other circumstances. After all, the Graf Zeppelin was destined to smash all the records in a career of almost 600 flights. It became the first aircraft to fly more than a million miles, before being retired in 1937. But for those who had lived in London during the First World War, the Zeppelin airships had signified atrocity. Godley didn't have direct experience of seeing these monsters in the sky during the war, because he was imprisoned on the other side of Europe. But he would have heard all about them by 1930, and would have known some of the dreadful history of what they did. English civilians suffered fifty-one air raids in the First World War and some 5,000 bombs dropped on them. Apart from £1.5 million worth of damage, there was a much more tragic cost to human lives, and a high one at that. In 1915 alone, while Sidney was getting used to life as a prisoner of war, the Zeppelins discovered how immune they were from aircraft defending London and from anti-aircraft fire. By flying far higher than any level at which a British shell or plane could follow, they were able drop bombs at will, albeit relatively indiscriminately. You couldn't achieve any accuracy from up there, but you could certainly rain terror down on the innocent citizens below. In twenty raids in 1915, the Zeppelins dropped 37 tons of bombs, killing 181 people and injuring 455. They were nicknamed 'baby-killers' and became a symbol of all the British hated about Germany.

The feared successor to the Zeppelins in the bombing of London was the Gotha G.V. – a bi-plane but an equally destructive and indiscriminate executioner of the innocent. In a maiden daylight raid on London on 13 June 1917, these bombers caused 162 deaths and 432 injuries. In the very worst case, a bomb fell on a primary school in Poplar, killing eighteen children.

So a Gotha would have attracted the same hostility as the Graf Zeppelin's extraordinary appearance at the 1930 FA Cup final, which left a blemish on what was otherwise a happy day for Arsenal fans such as Sidney and Eileen. Godley wouldn't have liked to see a German aircraft darkening London skies like that. Sadly, a decade later, German intrusions into British air space would prove far more deadly, and Godley would place himself in fresh danger to deal with the destruction below.

For the moment, however, watching Arsenal with his daughter brought joy to Godley's life, as he took advantage of the season ticket the club gave to distinguished war veterans. And the only territorial disputes might be over a certain spot on the Highbury terracing. Sidney would never allow his daughter to be pushed around. Neither did he want to have to use his fists for no good reason. He never picked a fight that wasn't necessary. He had won the Victoria Cross for his bravery, and of course he was still well equipped to step in ferociously if anyone should be stupid enough to threaten his daughter in any way. But that didn't mean he wanted to have to prove how tough he was in trivial situations. If there was any trouble, he had to know it wasn't his daughter who had started it by annoying someone or by saying the wrong thing if she was accidentally shoved. Eileen smiled as she said:

> My dad used to say, 'Don't argue with them!' He just wanted us to watch the football and enjoy ourselves. I don't remember any particular player, I liked them all. If they got goals, even better! And if that pleased my dad, that pleased me. I remember knitting my dad a red and white scarf and it was so long I think it could have gone round him several times and kept his feet warm!

There were plenty of occasions when Eileen would see the delight on her father's face that season. Having won that FA Cup in 1930, Arsenal bagged the league title in the 1930–31 season. And they would take the title three more times in the mid-thirties. Highbury was buzzing every time father and daughter went there. Godley had always loved his football, even before he played centre-half for the 4th Royal Fusiliers. That wasn't going to change.

But the world was changing in the 1930s and a new menace was developing in Germany as Adolf Hitler's Nazi party seized control of Germany with an increasingly oppressive grip. When all their enemies were dealt with in Germany, they would start to look abroad. It was only a matter of time. So moments of peace were to be enjoyed, and savoured. God knows, Sidney Godley had earned them.

Not that he had ever forgotten the war. As a humble winner of the Victoria Cross, Godley was a highly respected figure among the Old Contemptibles Assiociation, formed for the veterans of the First British Expeditionary Force of 1914 and a reference to the Kaiser's alleged description of 'General French's contemptible little army,' though the Kaiser later claimed he had never used the phrase.

The Old Contemptibles Association was founded by Captain J.P. (John Patrick) Danny, of the Royal Artillery, on 25 June 1925. All members were known as 'chums', to remove any element of class and prejudice. What mattered was that you had seen active service between 5 August and 22 November 1914. These dates marked the key campaign fought by the first BEF, as they gradually came to terms with the German onslaught. Their bravery at Mons, the Marne, the Aisne and Ypres had helped to keep the enemy from the Channel ports and also from Paris. To have been part of the BEF during those opening months of war and come under fire entitled you to a medal which became known as 'The Mons Star'. But precious few had the medal Godley had been awarded and had lived to tell the tale. No wonder he was in demand. Colin explained:

> When they came home from the war, these soldiers, Captain Danny could see their plight. Some of them had lost their limbs and Danny said, 'We've got to do something.' So he set up the Old Contemptibles Association. They must have got in touch with my grandfather and at one stage he did a term as president and chairman. He was president of the founder-branches of the Old Contemptibles Association. He was doing his bit all the time.

The Association grew quickly until it had 178 branches in Britain and a further fourteen abroad. During those tough economic times of the mid-1920s, the Old Contemptibles made sure they were not forgotten. Above all, they ensured they were not forgotten by one another. There were many functions for Sidney to attend, and he did so dutifully. As Colin explained, there were consequences:

> He had all his medals including the Victoria Cross and they ended up getting knocked around a bit. They got bent, because he used to stuff them in his pocket when he went out and only put them on when he got close to where he was going. He was like that, even about the Victoria Cross. 'I'd better put it on I suppose.' That sort of attitude. Don't get me wrong, he was very proud to be a VC. But he was also very humble.

'Quite nice, really, that he never bragged about it,' commented Andy, his other grandson.

Colin's wife, Linda, confirmed, 'Even when there was a parade somewhere, he didn't put his medals on until that parade was about to start.'

Colin knew his grandfather's routine after these veterans' get-togethers were over. Once again, the medals didn't stay out on show longer than they had to. 'Then he'd shove them back in his pocket on the way home again. Ellie would have to restitch the ribbons.' Eileen knew he cared more for his comrades than his own prestige:

My dad used to run sweepstakes for the Old Contemptibles to raise money. The ticket sales used to fly, all these people used to bring their counterfoils and their money, and I don't know how my mother ever managed making all those cups of tea. He used to have a good old sum of money by the end of it. I know there was one 'Old Contemptible', he was in a poor way health-wise, and my dad did help him a lot. And if any of them died and the families were hard-put, dad used to say to them, 'A few quid wouldn't help, you know?' And he'd make sure a few quid would go, and he'd say, 'I think I've done the right thing.'

A character called 'Old Bill' had been created towards the end of the war by humourist and cartoonist Bruce Bairnsfather. 'Old Bill' was a British soldier with a wry sense of humour, which he applied to life in the trenches. The cartoon character had a walrus moustache a bit like Sidney's, so it wasn't hard for Godley to play the role when he was asked to do so. Some even claimed that the creator had seen a picture of Godley after his VC award became public knowledge and based his character on Sidney. It seems more likely that it came from soldiers he had come to know himself, because he had seen action in France. Whatever the truth, Godley took to the role naturally and became even more popular during his 'personal appearances' as a result. Colin was at pains to point out that the real-life hero was only prepared to adopt the fictional stereotype because he thought it would help raise money for his old comrades:

That 'Old Bill' comparison, it wasn't Sidney's idea, that was put on him as an Old Contemptible. They used to put a lot on for ex-servicemen who weren't in as good a position as they were, injured and all that. Some of them were really suffering and down. What my grandfather used to do was to go around the different Legions, and they'd put on a little show. He'd dress up as 'Old Bill' to help out. It just used to raise a pound or two for the bucket. He didn't do it to say, 'Oh, look at me.' I would imagine he didn't really like doing it, but he thought, 'We need to do something for other people.'

Godley had a framed medal on his wall, 'To "Chum" Godley, from the Old Contemptibles'. This was the only rank they recognised.

They didn't place any emphasis on rank, but they did value bravery. And there was none braver than Sidney Frank Godley. The others recognised it, and it was inevitable that he became a living symbol of the bravery of the Old

Contemptibles as a whole. Eileen explained, 'Everywhere dad went he was welcomed. When he used to go anywhere with the Old Contemptibles, it was always like that. He used to go up to this Old Contemptibles club up north, and he used to get a really good welcome up there too.' Andy confirmed, 'He was a well-liked person and he didn't brag about what he'd done at all.' Colin isn't convinced that his grandfather enjoyed the constant attention:

> I don't think he wanted the publicity, but he would attend dos out of respect, if he was asked to go. He had a mate from the Middlesex regiment called Harry Light. By all accounts they were a right little pair. They used to go to reunions in London, sink a few pints then walk all the way home. They always ended up sitting on the police station steps at Bethnal Green to give them a breather. A couple of old constables who knew them told me that. They were characters, Sidney and Harry. I wish more people from today had met my grandfather.

The 'chums' of the Old Contemptibles continued to do all they could to help each other, and also continued to embrace each other's families. These men had fought hard to survive, they were thankful that they had been able to come home and start those families. They knew how lucky they were, and they were mindful of all the young men, Maurice Dease among them, who had given their lives and would never have the indescribable satisfaction of children. So this was no time to exclude those children, now that they were growing big enough to be able to understand, if the chance arose to involve them too. Eileen recalled:

> He used to go off to various dos with the Old Contemptibles, and I enjoyed going off with them too on various outings. My dad just took it all in his stride. He wasn't a man to put the word about in terms of what he'd done. He didn't go around saying 'I've got this medal' or 'I've got that.' He'd rather talk about football. He got to know lots of people and the conversation would often turn to football, because he was comfortable with that and he knew that once he started talking to anyone about football, well … That was it!

Warm-hearted and generous of spirit, Sidney saw the good in everyone and had time for everyone. But if his good nature was abused, and he could no longer avoid the conclusion that someone was a bad type, that person generally had reason to regret his nastiness, because no malicious adult would get a second chance to mess with Godley. Eileen explained, 'My dad was a man that … he was very easy to get on with, but … and the "but" is important because anyone who crossed him, that's where the "but" came in. He could wipe the floor with anybody after that.' He didn't need a violent solution most of the time. Once Godley decided he didn't like someone because of something they'd said or done, or because they hadn't kept their word or pulled their weight in a certain situation, they'd soon know about it – because he wouldn't give them much more than the time of day:

> He was the kind of man that if he didn't get on with a person, he didn't ignore them, but … you know what I mean. My dad had no time for people who couldn't face up to things and try to put them right. Whatever he did, his whole heart was in it.

Sid Godley was big-hearted and he had enough kindness for everyone who seemed decent. Above all he was a man who enjoyed his peace and adored his children. There was no way he would ever allow them to be subjected to the trauma and instability he had suffered as a child. In a way, they benefited from his suffering. He gave his children love in abundance and firm boundaries which weren't to be crossed. Eileen explained:

> He was a lovely dad, he really was. I never knew him ever to smack us … but to get a telling off from him, well! You were more than told off! You were really torn off a strip! If he told you off, you knew you had been told off!

Eileen and her brother Stan knew it was for their own good and it didn't make them love their father any less. She explained, 'He and I got on far better than my mother and I did. I didn't get on too well with my mother. But my father and I, we weren't just father and daughter, we were friends.' Eileen recalled this with a tear in her eye as the memory of her father's warmth came flooding back to her. Sidney was clearly a man who possessed considerable sensitivity. What he thought might hurt his daughter, he appears to have kept from her. He didn't want to explain to a small girl the horrors of what he had been through. He tried to make light of the way he had suffered physically:

> He just thought having two different colours of skin from those skin grafts was a bit comical. If I know my dad as well as I think I know him,

then there was another reason for him finding it comical – because he knew where the grafted skin had come from!

As she laughed, Eileen confirmed that she thought much of it might have come from his backside. At least that was the impression she had been given by her father. 'He had a wonderful sense of humour,' she said, adding in sheer delight, 'He did, he did!' As for the horrors of Nimy bridge, they never talked about it, although they were so close that Eileen believed he would have been prepared to do so if she had really made it clear that she wanted to understand everything:

> I think he would have told me about that day on the bridge if I'd wanted to know, but I never got to the point of pressing him about things. If he wanted to tell me something, he would tell me. That's the understanding we had as I started getting older. When I was younger we'd got so close partly because my father and I had all the children's illnesses at the same time. He had whooping cough the same time as me. We shared all those things.

Colin revealed that Sidney was reluctant to talk about Mons in much detail. He smiled as he said, 'Sidney was a bit of a sod really because we would probably have known a bit more if he had talked more about it. He didn't confide much to my father, Stan, on it.'

Godley hoped his children would never need to understand the horrors of war. Sadly those hopes were to be dashed before very long. In the meantime, Sidney had taken a job as a school caretaker at Cranbrook in Bethnal Green. It was a rough area and there were many disadvantaged children, some of whom had gone off the rails. Sidney could have scared the life out of them to try to keep them in line when there was conflict. In fact, he took the opposite approach. Eileen remembered:

> If there were any kids being a bit difficult, my dad would only have to say, 'What football team do you support?' He'd get talking to them about football and do you know what? He used to win those kids over. He really did. He had that way. He'd talk to them about football. He was a wonderful man. Sometimes these kids they would come into the school grounds and especially at the weekend, if they thought my dad wasn't there. And they had a way of climbing up to the blessed top of the school, and somebody knocked on the door and said to my dad, 'These boys are

up there.' My dad went out, he didn't shout, he didn't do anything, he just stood there. I think it amazed people that he didn't do anything, not even when one of those kids stayed up there on the roof for a bit. But when I was talking to him afterwards, my dad said, 'If I'd shouted, that child would have fallen and been killed.' And that was my dad's way of dealing with the thing. Just seeing my dad still standing there was enough for that child to come down. That child came down to the ground unhurt and didn't get the clip round the ear which my dad said he deserved. But he got a good telling off and I don't think he did it again.

Although it might sound strange for a tough old soldier, Sidney took a non-confrontational approach to life whenever he could. The same applied to his marriage to Nellie. If she nagged him about anything, he took it in his stride, knowing she loved him deep down. 'I suppose in her way she did, yes,' admitted Eileen. 'He was a man who would get along. And I suppose he loved her too, he did. I wouldn't say anything different to that. Yes, I think he did. But she was just a person who was difficult to get on with.'

Nellie had to accept the fact that, although Sidney was married to her, he was also married to the Old Contemptibles. 'If she felt bad I don't suppose she ever said anything,' Colin explained:

I don't think my Nan ever drank but my granddad had a few some-times. He used to go to some of those Old Contemptibles functions with his friend Harry and it could turn into a boys' night out. They'd have a laugh and a joke. That was normal, but I think my granddad and my Nan were happily married, and their life was their own.

Their life was their own but the war was always there in the background, it had never really gone away. The subject was unavoidable when you were a VC winner. Naturally Godley's name was often mentioned in the same breath as Maurice Dease, who had won the highest award at the same time. As she grew a little older, Eileen began to notice a pattern. If something had been written about her father and the battle at Nimy bridge, it was always 'Dease and Godley'. It was never 'Godley and Dease'. Eventually Eileen plucked up the courage to ask her father why. 'I asked, "Why is he always, in anything written or talked about, always first?" And dad said to me, "Well, he was an officer and I was a private." Those were his words.'

The words weren't spoken with any bitterness. But Eileen told the story in such a way that it wasn't hard to imagine a wry smile on Sidney's face, as he accepted the 'natural order' of things. It was as though he knew that, whatever he had done he would always have been overshadowed by a man of superior rank, because that was the way of the world.

Sometimes, if asked directly whether he was the first man to win the VC in the First World War, he would answer in the affirmative. He may have been under the impression that his citation had been processed before that of Dease, which would have made him the first VC winner in his own mind, even if he knew that Dease had fired the machine gun before he did at Nimy. Some described Godley as the first private to win the VC, others as the first to win it regardless of rank. He was certainly the first man to win the VC in the First World War and live to tell the tale. It may all have become blurred in the mind of an uncomplicated man. Judging by the following letter, he had also been fed other incorrect information, and may have grown used to repeating it parrot-fashion, particularly if he was tired and keen to complete yet another reply to his heavy mailbag as quickly as possible. Written from 49 New Cross Rd, SE 14, on 13 June 1920, Sidney wrote this to an anonymous correspondent:

Dear Sir,
In answer to your letters and inquiries, it is quite correct about Daniels, he was the first man to win the V.C. with bar. I was the first man to win the V.C. It was on August 23 at Nimy bridge, which was the first point the Germans attacked. It is about two miles advance of Mons. My dispatches are timed at 7.35 p.m., 10 p.m. and 1.40 a.m., which are in the care of the late Mayor of Lewisham. They were taken from my Colonel after he was killed, by the Rev. Noel Mellish, V.C. and presented to me by him. Will you kindly tell your father that I have sent to Records for the card he requires; will send it on as soon as it arrives. I have a very heavy week-end with invitations. On Friday I take tea with the Honourable The Lady Gavagh. On Saturday I luncheon with the Officers of the Brigade of Guards and then to Buckingham Palace for the King's Garden party, and then to the Alhambra for the Evening, all for gaining the V.C. The wife and baby are going on lovely so I will close now.

I remain yours truly
S.F. Godley, V.C.

There is no reference in the Victoria Cross register to a soldier called Daniels winning the VC and bar. Lt Col. Harry Daniels, VC, MC (The Rifle Brigade), had won his VC in March 1915, but no bar. Perhaps the addition of the Military Cross had confused Godley somehow. Indeed, only three men have won a bar to their VC. These are Arthur Martin-Leake, who was awarded the highest honour in February 1902 and October 1914; Noel Godfrey Chavasse, August 1916 and August 1917; and Charles Hazlitt Upham, May 1941 and July 1942.

Such facts didn't exercise Godley unduly. It didn't matter to Sidney who was the first VC of the war either, because he had quite enough attention already. No one respected the memory of Maurice Dease more than he did. The poor man had given his life for the cause. But if Godley had been told enough times that he was the first VC of the war, he was prepared to believe it. Furthermore, it was common among the working classes to raise a philosophical eyebrow at the higher esteem in which the officer class was generally held, when the rank and file had faced at least as much danger during that terrible war.

So Sidney could be forgiven for telling his daughter that 'Dease was an officer and he was a private,' and therefore her dad would always come second in any mention of the pair.

# 17

# Remembering ...
# and Learning Nothing

Sid Godley had some grounds for poking fun at snobbery as he perceived it. Official documentation five years after his own letter showed there was more than a grain of truth to his suspicions.

Back in 1926 Stonyhurst College had been in the process of preparing their own official war record. On 22 August Rev. Frank Irwin of Stonyhurst wrote to Captain T.B. Trappes-Lomax at the War Office to get a definitive statement that Dease had been the first VC of the First World War. The informal handwritten note gave a clue that 'Tom' Trappes-Lomax was himself a Stonyhurst old boy. Irwin wrote:

> Dear Tom,
> IMPORTANT
> Can Maurice Dease be called the 'First V.C. of the Great War'? The Director of the Air Historical Branch, War Office informed us that Dease was the First OFFICER VC of the great war: three other ranks were awarded the V.C. on the same day.
>
> If you can manage to get it I should like a terse official statement with leave to publish same on authority of War Office.
>
> Sorry to bother you again but this is really a point which thoroughly deserves full elucidation.

The War Office, or more precisely Colonel G.C. Williams, CMG, DSO, replied on 1 October that year:

Sir

With reference to your letter addressed to Captain TB Trappes-Lomax, on the subject of awards of the Victoria Cross, I am to inform you that the question has been carefully examined, and the following questions arrived at.

It has definitely been established that, reckoning from the outbreak of the Great War, the first acts of gallantry to be eventually awarded by the grant of the Victoria Cross took place at Mons on August 23rd 1914.

The first German attack fell on two bridgeheads held by the 4th Battalion Royal Fusiliers, at about 9.10 a.m. Lieutenant MJ DEASE was in action at one bridgehead, Private SF GODLEY at the other.

Lieutenant Dease and Private Godley earned the VC about 9.10 a.m., whilst engaged in repelling the attack in question.

About 4.30 p.m. the question of destroying the bridges over the MONS–CONDÉ CANAL, in order to safeguard retreat, became most important. Captain T WRIGHT, Royal Engineers, and Lance Corporal CA JARVIS, Royal Engineers, devoted themselves to this task, and earned the VC about 4.30 p.m.

The British forces retired southwards in the course of the evening, and the retreat was duly covered by cavalry. The 15th Hussars were in action for this purpose at the village of Harmignies, southeast of the canal. Corporal CE GARFORTH, 15th Hussars, earned the VC at this period; hour uncertain, but certainly after the incidents described above.

The order of priority is therefore –

1. Lieutenant MJ Dease, VC, Royal Fusliers.
1. Private SF Godley, VC, Royal Fusiliers.
2. Captain T Wright, VC, Royal Engineers.
2. LanceCorporal CA Jarvis, VC, Royal Engineers
3. Corporal CE Garforth, VC, 15th Hussars.

I am to inform you that, in virtue of his rank, Lieutenant MJ Dease, VC, may be considered primus inter pares [first among equals], and it may safely be assumed that, as Battalion Machine Gun Officer, he had trained PRIVATE GODLEY, and formed that military character which at the opening of the first action vindicated the training received.

I am Sir, Your obedient Servant,

(Signed) GC Williams, Col,

For Lieutenant General, Military Secretary

The attitude of the War Office seemed to be this: if an officer acted bravely, it was to the officer's credit. If a private acted bravely, it was to the officer's credit. This seemed to contradict the spirit in which the award was created, because the original warrant for the VC, section 6, stated that 'all persons shall be placed on an equal footing for eligibility for the decoration regardless of rank or service.'

Eileen remained convinced that such snobbery as demonstrated by the War Office lasted well into the Second World War. She insisted, 'Even if my dad had been first, Dease would still have been mentioned first, because I know what happened with ranks, I was in the forces (WW2) and an officer will always take precedence over a private.'

In the case of their reply to Stonyhurst College, however, the War Office had been right in stating that Dease was first, albeit for the wrong reasons. They weren't quite right about the time-frame or respective locations. But Maurice had clearly won the first VC of the First World War, because he was dead or dying by the time Godley's own heroics began on that Belgian bridge. But did it really matter? And should it matter now? Sidney and Maurice won the highest bravery award in the same action and they should always be mentioned in the same breath, regardless of class.

Sidney realised the meaninglessness of class, especially when they had all faced such dreadful danger together. Maurice's bravery was what had impressed Sidney, not his background. If others wanted to put Dease before him, Godley wasn't the sort of person who would really mind. After all, there were far worse people to be overshadowed by than Maurice Dease. And, if Sidney was asked about him, there can be little doubt that he honoured his memory in the most glowing terms possible.

Though Colin didn't have any personal experience of this, he said, 'I assume granddad talked about Dease quite a lot.' But Sidney lacked the eloquence to speak to large audiences about what his fellow VC had done, or do justice to that bravery in the public arena.

Eileen said of her father, 'He wasn't very good at speeches. If he could get out of doing one he would. He liked to talk to people but if you asked him to stand up and speak to a crowd, no.'

So Godley might have felt awkward when he was pressed to do so. You could have displayed all the bravery in the world in battle, but still feel terribly nervous about public speaking if you knew you weren't any good at it.

Deep down Sidney was still a man of action – and a kind one at that. He couldn't change the inequality he saw in society, but he and his wife could still do something to help the needy in his own little world. Colin explained:

Bethnal Green was very poor, and there were still people suffering from the First World War, even in the 1920s and 1930s, because a lot of the women had lost their husbands in that one and they were still struggling. You used to feel sorry for the kids going to school, because a lot of them didn't even have breakfast, they weren't appropriately dressed for the weather. My Nan used to make some toast, when the children went to school. This was in the 1930s. That's why a lot of the elderly still remember Nellie and Sidney in this area today.

Sid and his beloved Nellie did what they could in their own community, yet the wider world still came calling. And it must have been with a mixture of pride and trepidation that he accepted an invitation to return to Mons in 1938, twenty years after the war had ended. How could he refuse to return to the scene of battle, when there were so many others to honour too? If he had to address a crowd there, he probably kept his speech short and to the point. The following year he went back again, this time with wife Nellie, son Stan and daughter Eileen, to show them the plaque that had been erected on Nimy bridge, partly for the VC recipients and partly for the others who had defended the area against the German attack.

The terrible irony was that the Second World War was now just months away, and the Germans were about to attack again. Sidney and his family didn't know just how imminent war was during that Easter of 1939. As far as they were concerned at the time, the year simply represented the approach of a quarter of a century since the battle at Nimy.

Eillen recalled, 'This plaque was put on the bridge the first time we went, that was before the war. It was early 1939, that was.' The plaque reads:

TO THE GLORIOUS MEMORY OF
THE OFFICERS, N.C.O.s AND MEN OF
THE 4TH BATTALION, ROYAL FUSILIERS,
WHO HELD THIS SECTOR OF THE
BRITISH FRONT IN THE DEFENCE
OF THE TOWN OF MONS
AUGUST 23RD, 1914.

THIS MEMORIAL
MARKS THE POSITION WHERE
THE FIRST V.C.s AWARDED DURING
THE WAR 1914-18 WERE GAINED BY

LT. M.J.DEASE,V.C.
AND
PTE S.F. GODLEY,V.C.

Maud Dease was there to witness the unveiling of the plaque too. Maurice's sister, who had suffered so much in the aftermath of his death, had never forgotten her loving 'Badge'. She hadn't forgotten the letters, Maurice's bravery or indeed his humour. She remembered the grim sense of humour which Maurice had displayed when he put his affairs in order before leaving for France, explaining to the family that this simply wasn't a good time to be in debt. She remembered their idyllic childhood in Ireland, the fishing, the beautiful animals that had surrounded them. She hadn't forgotten anything. How could she?

And yet for her life had gone on, just as it would have done for Maurice, had he been as lucky as Sid Godley and survived all his wounds. Maud had married, just as Maurice would surely have done. In fact, she had married into nobility, because her husband, Hon. Bertram Leo French, was the son of Arthur French, 4th Baron de Freyne of Colavin. The wedding had taken place on 18 January 1927. Maud had soon had children, just as Maurice would surely have done. Lavinia Marie French had arrived on 28 October 1928. Maurice Aloysius French (later Major) followed on 5 March 1930. Arthur Edmund French was born on 10 January 1933. Maud was happy and fulfilled, but still missed her brother, and felt her grief all over again when they visited Nimy bridge in 1939. She probably witnessed Godley's tears at Maurice's grave in the St Symphorien cemetery. Indeed, her presence might even have contributed to them. That poignant moment would certainly never be forgotten by Sidney's daughter Eileen:

> We went there … We stood … It was Dease's grave. And we stood there, and I looked at my dad, and the tears were streaming down his face, and he just turned and he said, 'I should have been there.' And he was talking to the little bit of ground in between the two graves. Between Dease's grave and the one next to his. And he kept saying, 'I should have been there.'

Call it a case of survivor's guilt, or the realisation that it was a minor miracle, his presence there, standing on the ground instead of lying beneath it with the others. As his grandson Andy observed, 'He obviously thought he was lucky to be alive.' 'Yes, he really was,' chipped in the now elderly Eileen, becoming understandably upset herself:

He was absolutely in tears. He had gone back to show his respects and he knew how lucky he was to be alive. My dad did talk about Dease, because Dease's sister, she came that time. And you know ... it was something I wanted to see and do but these occasions are ... what shall I say?

The tears said it for her. Such occasions can be more than anyone can take, without the emotion overflowing. The locals made the visit all the more poignant and unforgettable. Eileen added:

It was Easter 1939. I remember it was Easter because the local children were putting flowers on all the graves. They were daffodils. That's what we call them, though the children called them 'Easter Lillies'. Just a small, little bunch of daffodils. They put them on all of the graves at Mons. And that was when granddad stood in between those two graves and said, 'I should be there.'

Something even more extraordinary happened on that visit. Two adults came up to Godley and introduced themselves, as though they were long-lost friends. They were a man and a woman and they appeared to be expecting a similar response from Godley. At first Sidney was confused by such sudden intimacy; he didn't understand quite what part he could have played in their lives. Then it dawned on him. Perhaps this was more about the part they had played in his life, rather than the other way round. Maybe they had represented his last contact with the normal, happy world, before he had been shot, blown up and taken prisoner. He did a quick calculation in his head. Yes, they looked about the right age because they were in their thirties now. And as far as he could remember, these emotional adult faces bore some resemblance to the innocent faces he had last seen twenty-five years earlier. Now he was sure, and they confirmed it for him. These were the children who had come out to give him rolls and coffee, just before the carnage started. They had given him just enough sustenance to help him survive the ordeal to come, during which he only had a water bottle for company. These were the kids he had struggled to make conversation with in French. (Nothing had changed there, because his French was no better in 1939 than it had been in 1914.) These were the brave little children who had needed to be told to get back to their families when the shelling started. 'You'd better sling yer 'ook before you get 'urt!' Sidney had told them, pointing to the rear. He had watched them reach safety, relieved at the sight, before he turned back to face his own hell. He had never seen them again. Until now.

Eileen explained, 'He met them as a grown man and woman when we went. As children, they didn't think it was anything, going out to him by the bridge. My dad had always thought it was marvellous, what those kids did. And when he met them as grown people, well!'

For a moment it appeared these happy adults were in just as much danger as they had been back in 1914. 'I think he nearly squeezed them to death!' Eileen chuckled at the memory. 'He hugged them so tight he almost squeezed the life out of them!' He really did admire what they'd done as young children, to have braved the dangers of the front to come out and bring his bread and coffee. But whether they would have done the same as adults, who knows. '"The innocence of a child," he always said.'

Sadly the bravery of these two fine people was about to be tested again, because Germany was preparing to invade for a second time. Little more than a year later, the citizens of Nimy and their country would be suffering the horrific oppression of Nazi occupation. Eileen knew how much that thought hurt her father:

> When the war started, the Germans were overrunning the low countries and my dad thought a lot about those two and the other people of Nimy and Mons. He also made a comment: 'I wonder what they'll do with that plaque,' he said. Anyway, it turned out the Belgians had taken the plaque down, and they'd buried it. I don't know where. It was all covered up so the Germans would never find it.

Even in the midst of their fresh misery, the people of Nimy and Mons had thought of Godley and Dease. Even now, those Belgians were fighting a little battle on their behalf, they felt it was the least they could do after these two had given so much to them. Godley felt powerless to do very much this time around. He had developed problems with his lungs and, besides, at 40 he was considered too old to re-enlist as a front-line fighter at that stage of the war. What he could do, however, he did. Colin explained:

> He felt sorry that Belgium had been overrun twice. He joined the Home Guard, the Sussex Regiment, but I don't know too much about that. I don't think he left the area where he was working in the East End, because he was still a school-keeper right through the war. I think it was just one of those things he joined. I don't think

they paraded like in 'Dad's Army', the TV comedy series. He wouldn't have left the school, it was partly his responsibility to keep it going during wartime.

Soon the horror of the war visited the East End too, because the bombs began to fall thick and fast in the Blitz. And the bombs which fell so casually from a Junkers Ju 88, a Heinkel He 111 or a Dornier Do 17 caused far more damage than even the Zeppelins or Gotha GVs had done during the previous global war.

The Blitz started on 7 September 1940 and signalled an onslaught which saw London bombed for fifty-seven consecutive nights. In September, in London alone, 13,000 civilians were killed and 20,000 injured. The English capital had never known anything like it, as Adolf Hitler tried to break the spirit of the British people and bully the government into surrender. It was never going to work, even though London absorbed 18,291 tons of bombs in seventy-one separate air raids during the Blitz, which carried on up to May 1941.

Londoners learned to hide in the deep shelters built into the Underground stations; sirens wailed effectively to tell them when to scurry for safety. Despite the many casualties, the resistance to this barrage endured, and Britain's leaders realised the people were going to be able to weather the storm.

With a slightly chilling objectivity, Churchill compared the effect of the German bombs in the Second World War with the deadliness of those dropped in the First World War. In late 1940, he wrote:

> We are told by the Germans that 251 tons of explosives were thrown upon London in a single night, that is to say, only a few tons less than the total dropped on the whole country throughout the last war. Now we know exactly what our casualties have been. On that particular Thursday night 180 persons were killed in London as a result of 251 tons of bombs. That is to say it took one ton of bombs to kill three-quarters of a person.
>
> [In the First World War] the small bombs of early patterns which were used killed ten persons for every ton discharged in the built-up areas. That is, the mortality is now less than one-tenth of the mortality attaching to the German bombing attacks in the last war ... What is the explanation? There can only be one, namely the vastly improved methods of shelter which have been adopted.

Even when it appeared that Britain was gaining the upper hand in the war, the bombing of London continued. Indeed, there were even more sinister devices towards the end in the shape of flying bombs. So-called 'Doodlebugs' created terror in the streets below. The engines would cut out, and a deadly silence would signal the rapid descent of the device and the explosion. Godley wasn't going to take this onslaught lying down. He was still fit enough to make some sort of difference in his area. Eileen said, 'My dad became an air-raid warden in the Second World War.' He would make sure the lights were out so that the Luftwaffe weren't guided right onto them. And, when the German bombs found them anyway, he would rush out into the danger and brave the explosions, digging away in the rubble for any signs of life.

When you are as closely attached to a community as Godley was to his own in Bethnal Green, the dead and maimed weren't just statistics. These women and children were often people he had known for years. Sidney didn't lack bravery; he had been a tough soldier and had proved what a gritty, stubborn streak he possessed at Mons. Yet he was also predominantly a gentle, sensitive soul, and what he went through in the Second World War was every bit as tough to cope with as what he endured in the first. Speaking in the East End in 2013, Colin insisted:

> My grandfather wasn't tough, that was the thing. He used to cry. What would get to him were all the civilian casualties, because, as you know, he'd had that job as school-keeper prior to the war and he knew every-one around his area. That school was only about a mile away from here. It is still there, but not a school any more, it's called Cranbrook Terrace.

Sidney's loyalty to Bethnal Green and his determination to stay there meant he was in one of the most dangerous places in England during the Second World War. Some 80 tons of explosives fell on the Metropolitan Borough of Bethnal Green during the war, damaging 21,700 houses. Of those dwellings, 2,233 were completely destroyed and 893 were left uninhabitable. The hardy citizens of Bethnal Green suffered greatly, because 555 of them were killed and around 400 were seriously injured.

The worst incident came on 3 March 1943, long after the original shock of the Blitz had passed. Psychological scars remained, however, and the bombing, though less intense, persisted. So there was no hanging around when the air raid siren wailed, urging families towards the cover of the shelter at Bethnal Green tube station. Just as the crowd was starting to hurry down the steep steps into the station, a loud blast was heard and someone screamed 'Bomb!' People surged forward down the steps in a wave and a lady tripped, sending many others crashing to the floor. Suddenly scores of others had been carried in on top of them and the crushing began. Some 300 people squeezed down into the stairwell, still hoping to avoid the bombs which seemed to have landed earlier than usual, oblivious to the life being pushed out of the people who lay beneath them. When the panic subsided, 173 people lay dead, many of them women and children. It was one of the worst civilian disasters of the Second World War, and totally unnecessary. An anti-aircraft battery had been trying out a new type of explosive shell in a nearby park, hoping to be able to boast of a fresh way to defend Londoners from the Germans. Unfortunately, no one had bothered to tell the citizens of Bethnal Green of the new technology with its extra decibels, which sounded so much like a German bomb falling nearby. Like so many disasters, a failure to communicate had played a major part. And, after that failure, not much more was needed to create a catastrophe.

What made it worse for the people of Bethnal Green was the attitude of the authorities, who decided to hide the truth. It was considered dangerous for morale to spread the news that a sudden panic had contributed to so many deaths – and a panic caused by the sound of 'friendly' shells at that. So instead they came up with another, simpler story. A German bomb had fallen directly onto the tube station stairwell, they said. Those trapped by the blast there had no chance. The people of Bethnal Green knew it wasn't true, because there were enough survivors to tell the truth to the bereaved. But they had to suffer among themselves, without the sympathy of the nation or even the wider capital. And just about everyone in Bethnal Green would have known someone caught up in the tragedy, including Godley.

Added to the suffering of people he knew and loved was a personal sense of despair, that all he and the Old Contemptibles had been through seemed to have done no good. The First World War had only spawned more violence after Germany, driven to its knees financially and humiliated at the end of the fighting, looked to Hitler for fresh pride and revenge. Colin believes his grandfather must have found all that very hard to take: 'I imagine he thought, "What did we all go through the First World War for, if they were going to have another one? It was supposed to be the war to end all wars, why did they have another one?"'

# 18

# Bombs, Dentists and the Final Battle

Sidney Godley may have been an old warrior, but he was badly affected by witnessing women and children dying in the Blitz. They weren't nameless strangers. They weren't uniformed men who had signed up to do a violent job. Eileen explained, 'It was very hard for him because he knew so many of those people. Some of them were friends and they were like family.' Godley continued to witness the carnage and brave the danger, and he knew only too well from past experience that he couldn't consider himself to be immune from the death and destruction all around him.

Then one day he had yet another brush with death. The Germans who had shot him, blown him up and put him back together at the start of the First World War tried to kill him all over again. Eileen said:

He was out doing his warden round on one occasion, and I don't know what the bomb was, but anyway this thing came down, not all that far from him, and it blew him from one side of the road, right across to the other. He just finished up with bruises.

Sidney, who still had a German bullet in his head, had defied them yet again. The patchwork skin on his back remained intact. There were no fresh flesh wounds, no more grafts necessary, he was in one piece. He might have been sore and shocked, but the Germans were not going to neutralise Sid in this particular war. While he was a free man, while Britain was holding the

Germans at bay, he would continue to do his bit. And that meant going out and dodging the bombs again, just as soon as he felt able to do so. It took him less than forty-eight hours from being blown into the air to going back out for more. With audible pride, Eileen said, 'Everybody thought it would put him off doing it, but no. Not dad. He would be out again. He was off duty for a day or two because he had some bruises. But then he was back out there.'

You could say that he lived a charmed life during wartime. That wasn't his only brush with death before Hitler was finally defeated. Eileen added:

He got away with all sorts of things during the war. They bombed the school he worked in. The bell tower at the top of the school – that was blown away. Any damage to the school was put to rights because the children were still going to their lessons again in no time.

Colin benefited from Sidney's good fortune:

I was born in his house. Prior to having me, my mum got bombed out of her own house. She moved into a couple of rooms with an elderly lady, then the back of that house got blown off and my Nan said, 'No more – come and live with us.' My grandfather said the same, and added that 'If we are going to go (meaning blown up) we will all go together.'

That solidarity had been in evidence for a good few years already. Colin said of Sidney:

My grandfather had a wonderful relationship with his daughter-in-law Ada, my mother. Her father died when she was 2 years old and, having no brother to give her away on her wedding day, my grandfather stepped in. He said, 'Ada if you're good enough to marry my son Stanley I will give you away.' He did just that, and she looked upon him as the father she never had. I think he looked upon her as having a hard start in life like he did.

While Sidney's son Stanley served abroad, the family he'd had no choice but to leave behind stood firm beneath the German bombs as they rained down on the East End. They stood together under Sidney's roof. Colin added, 'It was a school house and they tended to build them a bit heavier. The house got damaged but it was still inhabitable. So we survived there until my mum got rehoused after the war. Elisa – Nellie – was my grandmother and she had helped look after us.'

So Colin was able to spend the first few years of his life under the protective wings of Sid and Nellie. 'A lot of the time, the man in my life was my granddad and that went on for four years.' That was all part of Sidney's Second World War fight – and he fought all his battles well. Stan and Eileen were doing their bit too. Stan was out in the Far East trying in vain to prevent the advance of the Japanese. His son's efforts must have made Sidney proud, but the desperate situation there must also have worried him greatly. Colin revealed, 'My dad Stan was in the Middle East, Port Said, but he never said much about it. My dad never came home until 1948. He never said much to us about the war.'

Eileen was doing her bit too:

I was a nurse in the air force. The number of wounded RAF active service personnel that I saw … well, you wouldn't believe some of them could ever live. I went to quite a few places, but the last one I worked in was the Royal Air Force hospital in Uxbridge. Previously, I'd been in other medical units. Altogether I had nearly five years service.

Godley had to accept that his daughter would see the horrors of war close up if she was going to help put the wounded back together. This was no time to be over-protective:

If my dad was worried about me he never said so. He wouldn't have done. When he saw me, he'd just say, 'Alright?' That was it. But he would come to the underground station and see me on the train, when I was going back to work. Just to make sure I got on it OK! On one occasion I said to him, 'Do you know what? They want to see the Victoria Cross you've got.' There was a number of wounded in the hospital who said they'd never seen one. Straight away he said, 'Take mine back and show them.' I did take it back. I took it in and the Warrant Officer who was in charge of the hospital said, 'What are you doing walking around with that? Let's put it in the safe until you go home!' Next thing our Chief Medical Officer said, 'I've had a look at your dad's Victoria Cross. I've never seen or handled one before. I'd have liked one of those.'

Come the weekend, I collected it and took it home. 'Our Chief Medical Officer would have liked to win one of those,' I told my dad as I handed it back to him. He just said, 'I don't know how he would have won one here!' It was quite comical, just the way he said it. He was often like that. He'd be sitting in a room with the family and he'd start talking, and before you knew anything, you were almost doubled up laughing. It wasn't so much the thing he said that was funny; it was the way he would tell you. I always had to check whether or not his face was straight at the time. He used to pretend he was taking something very seriously, but underneath this marvellous sense of humour was at work. It's hard to explain. He was comical at times. He was a lovely dad.

But he also knew when there was serious work to be done – particularly at his beloved school in Bethnal Green. Godley relished the challenge of keeping that school open, whatever the Germans could throw at them all. He had always loved children, he had always sympathised with kids who were having a tough time. His own turbulent childhood had given him a special sensitivity and determination in that area. Cranbrook was destined to remain open, Godley was going to see to that. This was his fight and he was going to win it. Colin explained:

That's the sort of person he was, because he was the school-keeper. The school got a bit bombed and two of his cleaners got killed. He said to my mum, because I'd been born by then, 'Could you help me out for a couple of days, until I can get another cleaner?' Forty-seven years on, she was still doing it.

Godley wasn't destined to live that long, but he certainly lived long enough to see the Germans put back in their place. And when they were, he wasn't just happy and relieved for the East End, which had suffered so much but had never allowed its unique spirit to be conquered. Godley was delighted for the people of Belgium too. He had felt their suffering almost as keenly as that of his own people.

At the end of the Second World War he wrote to the Belgian ambassador to tell him how pleased he was that the country had been liberated. His own fight in the First World War clearly hadn't been for nothing, after all. Godley received a swift reply:

Ambassade de Belgique,
103 Eaton Square,
London SW1
September 13th, 1944

Dear Sir,
I received your kind letter of congratulations and good wishes on the
liberation of my country and I am most grateful to you for the friendly
thoughts that prompted you to write to me …

Colin said, 'I think he had a feeling for Belgium, because he had been there
in battle and then again in peacetime, just before the Second World War.
They're bound to imprint something on you, experiences like that.'

Godley couldn't help but wonder about the fate of the plaque on the
bridge. At that stage, he didn't even know that it had been hidden away, just
before the Germans invaded. Eileen added:

Then after the war dad heard from the Fusiliers who had been in touch
with the Belgians, and dad learned that the plaque had been found and
it was going to be put back on Nimy bridge. We went out to see it put
back. I went with him. Mum, dad, Stan and me, we went over together
once. Well, we went back with the Royal Fusiliers.

And it was during one of those post-war trips back to Mons that Sidney met
Maurice's Dease's nephew and namesake, Maurice French, who recalled:

I met Sidney Godley in Mons but I don't remember him very well. He
had a big moustache and didn't talk about the battle. I suppose he used
to come to Armistice Funding with the regiment. I would have been
in my early twenties, so it could have been about 1954. I wish to hell
I could remember more but he probably came up and said, 'Your uncle
was a very brave man,' something like that.

Among many people, at home and abroad, Sidney was revered just as much
after the Second World War as he had been after the first. Their gratitude would
be eternal.

'A medal from the people of Mons.' That was the message below one of
the honours he kept at home. He valued it as much as any. Yet he retained his
humility, because he knew he was just an ordinary mortal, not so very different from anybody else, especially in peacetime.

And Eileen revealed a little secret that reminded us all just how normal
Sidney was. 'Do you know what? He was more afraid of going to the dentist
than anything else!'

'Aren't we all?' chipped in her son Andy.

Eileen continued:

He had this toothache, his face came up, my mum said, 'You're going to the dentist's.' 'I'm not,' he said. 'I'll pull it out myself.' Anyway it finished up, my mum got him to the dentist, he had this tooth out, and the dentist said he needed more to come out … no more ever came out. He didn't want to go again! He said the next time he'd do it himself.

AMBASSADE DE BELGIQUE

103, Eaton Square,
LONDON, S.W.1.

September 13th, 1944.

Dear Sir,

    I have received your kind letter of congratulations and good wishes on the liberation of my Country and I am most grateful to you for the friendly thoughts that prompted you to write to me.

    I deeply appreciate too the kind things you say about my countrymen, and I feel quite certain that they will be eagerly awaiting an opportunity of welcoming all their old friends back to Belgium.

    With renewed thanks, I remain,

    Yours faithfully,

*E. de Cartier*

Sidney F. Godley, Esq.,VC.,
10, Cranbrook Terrace,
Bethnal Green,
E.2.

Letter from the ambassador: Belgium thanks Godley for his congratulations after liberation from the Nazis.

Andy couldn't help but smile:

> The bravery he showed in Mons, but he couldn't face the dentist's chair! Amazing really, when you think about it! He could make a last stand at his machine gun but couldn't sit in the dentist's chair. It's a remarkable twist to the story! It's a funny anecdote. A courageous man … frightened of the dentist.

In fact, Sidney was constantly being reminded of his mortality, every time he tried to draw breath, because his lung condition had deteriorated. Colin recalled this painfully. 'He was lovely, but in later years you did feel sorry, because my memories of him in later years was that you used to see him with a rubber pump and a mask, because he had bronchial problems. It sticks in your mind.'

Perhaps the First World War had finally got him after all. Colin explained:

> I always say the prison was the start of his bronchial problems, because it didn't do him any good. I suppose there wasn't too much worry about looking after them, no health and safety in those days wherever you worked – for the Germans under duress or back in England! He did smoke a bit too. Not a lot, I don't think, but a few cigarettes. But being a school keeper at one of those old schools couldn't have done his lungs any good either. It had four floors, everything was carted up manually, and the boilers were in the basement. They were coke-fired in the school and there was no ventilation. I remember going down there and everything you touched was that deep in ash and all that. So that didn't help. Coking two big boilers doesn't help your lungs. Add it all together …

Maybe that's why some of Colin's happiest memories of his granddad were when Sidney still had his health and Colin was just a small boy climbing around him and over him. He claims he still had a clear recollection of coming across the German bullet, lodged in his granddad's skull:

> You could feel it. When you're little, you can get away with things around your granddad. I can just feel it now. I used to think, 'What happens if he ever stands up under a cupboard and bangs his head? Would that kill him by pushing metal further through his skull?' Silly things go through your mind.

By the mid-1950s, Godley had moved out of London, a decision which Colin thought backfired on him horribly:

> He stayed as a school-keeper until 1951, when his health meant he had to retire. Because his lungs had deteriorated, the local health people decided the best place for him to go to would be Denton in Essex, because it was always damp. I don't know why they felt that way. My dad Stan was of the opinion that it killed Sidney, because it was so damp. It was a damp area but they went there anyway. It was a new add-on to a little enclave of rows of houses. They were quite cut off, whereas in London everyone had known them. He didn't go out much.

The *Daily Express* interview of 1954 reported that, 'He retired as a caretaker in 1951. In 1954 he lived in a three-roomed, £1 a week flat in Debden, surrounded by photos of his grown-up children and their children.'

It wasn't a glamorous way to spend his final few years, perhaps not a fitting place for a great war hero. But then again Sidney Frank Godley had never had any airs and graces. And now that he knew he was reaching the end of his life, he didn't see why he should stay away from things that might harm him a little but actually gave him pleasure – such as animals. Eileen explained:

> Really he should never have been near any animals because it used to affect his breathing. But I was living nearby and we had a dog called Spotty. We discovered our dog always went missing on a certain day and we'd discover him up at mum and dad's flat. I don't know whether it was something they always had on that day, for dinner, but he'd go up on that day and mum or dad would tell him to go home, and he'd come back home. Torrington Drive, that was.

It is easy to believe that Sidney was encouraging the dog to visit by serving its favourite food on a given day. It created some excitement in a very quiet existence. But thankfully his chums in the Old Contemptibles hadn't forgotten him. He was quoted in the *Daily Express*, 'Sometimes I meet a few friends from these times and we remember them together. One of the best things about growing older is that one forgets the bad times and remembers only the good.'

And what remained good was the enduring memory of comradeship, a solidarity that people who had never been in the services or seen action could probably never fully understand. Sidney had shown such solidarity with his fellow Contemptibles down the years. But gradually even that driving force within Sidney had to be put to one side. Eileen said, 'In the end he had to give up fund-raising for the Old Contemptibles due to his own health.' With typical understatement, Sid was quoted in that 1954 interview admitting, 'I've got asthma now. I'm not as good as I was.'

The lungs of a fine regimental cross-country runner had been destroyed by a variety of factors. Silesian salt-mines, the coke-fired boilers of his beloved Cranbrook school in Bethnal Green and, of course, cigarettes had all contributed to his downfall. A former man of action was reduced to passive pursuits in his twilight years. The newspaper described the scene in his home, 'He was a prisoner-of-war until Armistice. Now dark hair is grey and straight back bent … An asthma mask is near him on the table and a dictionary to help him with his crosswords to pass away the time.' Eileen said:

> He wasn't all that tall but he was quite solidly built, at least he was when I knew him as a little girl. He had this lung and chest complaint which got worse and over the course of time he lost a lot of weight. It didn't alter his spirit in any way – he just remained the same dear old dad. But in later years he was under the weather. He didn't talk about the salt mines but I think he had bad lungs because of the prisoner-of-war camps. They didn't have it all that good, did they? Never told me about the salt mines. I think he would have told me about that because we used to talk about anything. Having said that, there was a lot on what happened at Mons that he didn't talk about and I'm glad in a way.

There was no desire in Sidney to unburden himself by sharing his worst memories with his children or grandchildren, even when he must have known he was slowly dying. Colin confirmed:

> Nothing was ever really mentioned about the war, even though I knew he had that bullet still there in his skull and thought I'd even felt it, lodged there. I don't think he would have wanted to tell anyone about the worst of the fighting at Nimy if they weren't there. I was only thirteen in his last year but I don't think he spoke to anyone much about the war. My dad didn't know much, and, like everyone who comes back from wars, you don't get a lot out of them. The ones who speak a lot didn't do so much, that's the impression I get. Even my dad didn't know, he never said anything about how it was for his dad.

So many other things defined Sidney Frank Godley, besides what he had to do to win that Victoria Cross. For example, when his son Stan had got married, it was Sidney who walked his future daughter-in-law down the aisle. Colin's wife Linda explained, 'My mother-in-law had no one to give her away at the wedding and Sid just stepped in and said, "I'll give you away." She was thrilled because of that.' Eileen agreed. 'That's the kind of person he was. Very reassuring.'

Sidney had never forgotten his own chaotic childhood, what it felt like to not quite belong. He hadn't forgotten his mother, whose premature death had left his own life in such turmoil. Family meant everything to Godley. If Colin Godley is right, he had joined the army to join a huge family, to achieve a wider sense of belonging. He had continued to promote that sense of family long after the First World War, through his tireless work on behalf of the Old Contemptibles. And to the very last, his own family would remain the most important part of his life.

Eileen had settled down by then to have children of her own. And she will never forget the poignant events of 1957, when life and death were encapsulated in the words and wishes of a brave old soldier. Eileen was holding back the tears as she explained:

I'll always remember taking my newborn baby daughter straight from the hospital to see him. I said I want her to see dad, so he can see his new baby granddaughter. So we went to the flat and he was sitting in an armchair in the corner, and, as we walked in, he just held his arms out for her, and I don't know who wasn't in tears because we all were, and he took her and his first words were, 'You've come to take my place.'

Godley wanted to name the newborn baby before he passed away. Although Sidney's own mother had been called Ada, it seems that she had preferred to go by the name of Ann. Eileen went on:

My dad loved my children. He named my newborn daughter. So her name was Gillian Ann. Gillian is a name is that he always liked and Ann was the name his mother went by. He said to me, 'Can your new baby have that name as well?' I jumped at it. It didn't go down all that well with my in-laws because everyone had settled on the name Margaret before that, but I didn't worry about that. I wanted my dad to have a wish and that's what he wanted. She was born on 2 May 1957 and my dad died in July 1957. He had his last wish.

Godley's medal collection had grown throughout his life. By the time he passed away, he had been awarded the VC, the 1914 Star with 'Mons' Bar, the British War Medal, the Victory Medal with Mentioned in Dispatches Bar, the King George VI Coronation Medal (1937) and the Queen Elizabeth II Coronation Medal (1953). He died and was buried with the German bullet still buried in his head. They never did remove it. That's why Private Godley lived as long as he did. Otherwise he would have been buried in the cemetery at St Symphorien, just outside Mons, many decades earlier. He had looked at that spot between Maurice Dease and the next soldier and he had tearfully told his daughter that that's where he should have been lying, with his fallen comrades. When he did finally pass away, Eileen gave that moment at Mons some more thought. It has never gone away. She said:

> To be quite honest, I often wish that there'd been enough ground for him to have been buried there when he died in 1957. But there wouldn't have been, and there would have been too much of a to-do to get all the permissions for it to happen. And, besides, I don't think he really wanted to be buried over there because he had mum, and, wherever he went, he would have wanted to have mum in the plot next to him eventually.

They must have talked about it, Sid and Nellie. They had almost been denied a future by the probability of death in wartime. But, in spite of the narrow odds of Sidney surviving two world wars, they had been granted a life together. Now that death had finally parted them, they were determined that this should only be temporary, and they stuck to their plan.

Eileen said, 'At the time, we were in the graveyard at St John's church in Loughton after dad had died, and mum said, "That's where I shall be as well." I can remember it as plain as anything. That's where she ended up as well.'

So that explained the venue for Godley's funeral. With Sid, family always came first. But the funeral wasn't just a private family affair. Godley had been a family man and a soldier too – and he wasn't about to exclude his wider 'family' from his final farewell. Neither were they about to forget him in his moment of passing. The veterans and his regiment were well represented. Eileen explained, 'I can remember walking up with the Old Contemptibles, the Royal Fusiliers, walking up the road to the cemetery at Loughton, to St John's church.'

And, just as Reverend Noel Mellish, VC, MC, had been a distinguished guest at Sidney Godley's wedding, so he was at his funeral. It was fitting, because in wartime they had walked a similar path. During the First World War they had both won the Victoria Cross. During the Second World War they had both been air raid wardens. They were men of rare bravery and determination. And that's probably why Mellish, who wasn't well, and only had five years left to live himself, made the effort to travel all the way from his retirement home in Somerset across to Essex for the occasion. He was too frail to take a prominent role in the funeral service, as he had done at the wedding. It was left to Rev. B.W. Ottaway to take the service. But the very presence of Mellish was a comfort to all, for the mourners knew how much it would have meant to Sidney Frank Godley, VC.

Colin said, 'Mellish came to his funeral but was too ill to take any part of the service so he didn't officiate, but he came up from Somerset. Mellish was the one who had conducted their wedding so it was good that he was there.'

Private Godley was buried with full military honours at Grave No. 3051 in Loughton Cemetery. A large Old Contemptibles Association badge was placed on the grave. The Royal Fusiliers had provided the bearer party. Though Colin was too heartbroken to take comfort from that at the time, he appreciated it later:

They fired over his grave. It was terrible. Absolutely terrible. I cried. It was done lovely but it was terrible. All funerals are. I've still got the cartridge cases here. They collected them up for us out of respect. And I've still got the Fusilier's 'ackle which they gave us when they buried him. He was buried with an Old Contemptibles Star or something.

Godley's obituary appeared in the *Daily Telegraph* and the *Morning Post* on 2 July 1957:

Mr F.S. Godley, VC
Mr Frank Sidney Godley, VC, who has died aged 67, won his Victoria Cross while serving as a private with the 4th Battalion, Royal Fusiliers, City of London Regiment in the defence of Vimy Ridge [sic] at Mons on August 23rd, 1914.

He was the first man from the ranks to win the VC in the 1914–18 war.

The Citation stated that it was awarded for 'Coolness and gallantry in fighting his machine-gun under a hot fire for two hours after he had been wounded.'

In the same action, another VC was awarded to Lieut. M.J. Dease, of the 4th Battalion, who died of his wounds.

Mr Godley's home was in Torrington Drive, Loughton.

In death, as in life, Sidney continued to be linked inextricably with Maurice Dease. In death, as in life, there was confusion over which of Godley's first names should be most prominent. The failure to identify correctly the location for both men's heroics seems less forgivable. The memory of Godley and Dease would have to be preserved better than that, especially since both Victoria Cross winners from the Nimy railway bridge on 23 August 1914 had now passed into the next life, the second forty-three years after the first.

Nellie's time hadn't yet come, so Eileen's son Andy made sure she didn't lack for company. Andy said:

I didn't know my granddad that much, I knew my Nan a lot more because I used to go and stay with her after granddad died. I used to go up to the flat in Torrington Drive after school on a Friday, and stay up there with her. We used to stay up and play dominoes. She didn't speak much about granddad, but I always found her a warm, caring sort of person. I got on with her very well. She was a lovely person.

Six years later, she was resting in peace next to her husband.

The relatives of Dease and Godley continued to visit Mons in the spirit of remembrance. Elaine remembered, 'We went back several times and the last time I went back was with your Uncle Stan, when you children were still quite small. It might have been 1964, for the fiftieth anniversary.' Maurice French recalled:

The Belgians gave a lunch party in 1964 and Brigadier P.R. Ashburner, British Military Attaché in Brussels, son of Captain Ashburner, attended when we visited the Nimy Memorial. It was his father who had been Uncle Maurice's company commander. Anyway at the dinner party later on there was a marvellous woman, and she'd been the daughter of the station master at Nimy back in 1914. As a girl of about 14 or 16, she had warned the British troops that the Germans were coming and then she had run up and down the line, carrying messages for the regiment.

Dease and Godley were never forgotten, in Mons or back home. In London, for example, Godley was remembered in the East End. Colin explained:

They named some houses after him and some flats. All the elderly people in the borough obviously went to school when he was a school keeper, and they held him in high esteem. There is also a plaque to him in Digby Street, just down the road from Stepney Green in Tower Hamlets. There were two blocks of flats and they had to be named to commemorate someone. The name put forward by the left-wing council was Blair Peach House, after an innocent 33-year-old New Zealander who was killed by the police during an anti-fascist demonstration against the National Front in Southall in 1979. But the locals said 'No, we want a local's name to be used.' They put granddad's name up and they fought for it, which is how it happened. The block was called the Sidney Godley VC House. There's a big bronze plaque on the buildings. It was unveiled on 8 May 1992 and I was there to see it happen, along with my father Stan and some of the Royal Fusiliers. He's not forgotten in the area, my grandad. He was there thirty years at that school in Bethnal Green. People remembered him.

He was also remembered with a memorial in the Garrison church in Portsea, Hampshire, and a new block of flats were named after him in Bexley, Greater London in 1976. He was remembered at Loughton, too, where the town council placed a blue plaque on 164 Torrington Drive in the year 2000. It reads:

PTE SIDNEY GODLEY 1889–1957
AWARDED THE FIRST VC OF THE GREAT WAR
23 AUGUST 1914
LIVED HERE.

They were wrong by a couple of hours, strictly speaking, but it hardly seemed to matter.

Colin Godley took charge of making sure the Nimy bridge plaque was in the best possible condition. He knew the best men for the job:

In 2008 a group of volunteers from the Fusiliers Association, mates of mine, arranged a trip to Mons, because the plaque was in disrepair, corroded. They brought it back to England to repair and they sandblasted it, all good as new. They put it back but the original plaque got stolen in 2010, and now there's a fibre glass one, but it still looks good.

When Sidney's son Stan died in 1996, Colin started to take more responsibility for preserving his grandfather's memory:

> My father died sixteen years ago. I took over the reins then. I've tried
> to do as much as I can in my grandfather's name and for the Fusiliers.
> As a battalion, the 4th Royal Fusiliers died as a result of the First World
> War, because there were so many casualties. There's no 4th battalion
> today – but the memory of all who served in it lives on. I've tried to
> keep granddad's memory alive. I get invited to VC functions and I go in
> his name. There's no glory for us, it's in his memory.

Colin was on the verge of tears as he said those words, and so was Eileen
as she gazed at the painting on her wall – the same painting that graces the
cover of this book, a superb picture by David Rowlands, depicting the action
that won Dease and Godley their VCs so dramatically. 'Look up there!' Eileen
says, pointing at the picture she holds in such reverence:

> No one is going to have that off me. My brother Stan got the original
> and he had one done for me. And I gave each of my three children a
> copy too, and a nice frame for it. What you see in that picture; that is
> what my father did.

Stan's son Colin did the same for his own children, Sidney's great-grand-
children, and the tradition, you suspect, will live on through the generations
to come. It is a gripping picture. Two brave men fighting for all they were
worth. One survived the action, the other didn't.

Maurice's sister Maud lived to the age of 83. She died in 1974. There is no
reason to suppose that Maurice Dease wouldn't have lived to a ripe old age
too, had he survived the war. Like so many of his generation he died in his
prime – one of millions.

# Postscript: The Centenary

At the time of writing, Colin Godley was preparing to go to Mons on 23 August 2014 for the centenary of the action. Twenty-eight members of his family were ready to be there, and the youngest of these was Sidney Frank Godley's great, great granddaughter Maggie Godley, just 1 year old. Meanwhile Eileen Slade, Sidney's daughter, was wondering if she'd be well enough to go.

Major Maurice French was doing much of the organising for the Dease descendants and also for the Royal Fusiliers. Their trip to Mons would mark the end of the regiment's retreat from the area on 5 September and the beginning of their fresh advance.

What the authorities in Mons had prepared by way of a welcome for them all remained to be seen, though there had been rumours of a new plaque on Nimy bridge. Colin explained, 'They did intimate that there will be a stone one for the centenary but I've heard no more. The one there now looks nice. We'll see.'

There were no plans for the Dease and Godley relatives to meet again, since they wouldn't be in Mons at the same time. Colin was relaxed about that:

We'll do what we see fit with respect to my grandfather, we won't do anything derogatory to Dease at all. Their two names are on the plaque. Whatever Major French wants to do and arrange, so be it. We decided years ago what we were going to do and we booked a number of rooms and transport accordingly. The 23rd of August is the day to go from our point of view; we were always going to be there for that day.

Maurice French and Colin Godley met at a VC memorial service in Westminster Hall in 2003, but it would be wrong to say they are friends. They come from different backgrounds, just as the VC winners whose memory they perpetuate. But their respect for their heroic relative has been life-long. Colin said:

> I go to the Tower of London, where the Royal Fusiliers Museum is, whenever they have the Fusiliers Association meetings. Maurice is a custodian of the Royal Fusiliers Museum in the Tower of London. But our paths don't really cross because I deal with the Fusiliers Association. I know what my grandfather did, and for forty-one years I've gone on parades in his memory. I'm very, very proud of him, my family is, and I'll keep his memory alive forever – or as long as I can.

Major Maurice French had a good reason for selling his uncle's Victoria Cross – he wanted to be able to help finance the education of his grand-children. Major French wrote to the Regimental Association to give it first refusal, since the medals had been on display at the Regimental Museum in the Tower of London. An expert valued the Dease VC group at £18,000. The Victoria and Albert Museum agreed to pay one half of this sum, and the regiment paid the other. Major French received his money in instalments. 'Uncle Maurice's VC would have gone for £400,000 if I'd waited,' he later claimed.

When Colin sold Godley's VC at auction in 2012 it went for £230,000, bought by a private collector and taken abroad. Like Maurice, Colin had valid reasons for coming to that difficult decision, not least the mounting insurance costs whenever the medal was taken out of its vault, and the related stress that caused to his family. Both sets of descendants realise that the VC itself is not the most important thing, but the valour which won it, the character of the hero. They have preserved for us a sense of that character very well. The common desire to look after family, shared by Colin Godley and Maurice French, is one of which both heroes would surely have approved. We know enough about Sidney Frank Godley and Maurice Dease to be confident of that.

As the centenary of their historic action approached, the British government decided to honour all their First World War VC heroes by laying stones in their home towns, in order to mark the centenary. Twenty-eight of these stones were due to be laid in 2014, with more to be laid in each centenary year of the war up until 2018. But in the case of Dease, the very first VC, there was a complication, because he was born not in Britain but in Coole, County Westmeath, Ireland. At first the British government didn't consider it appropriate or feasible for such a stone to be laid. But, to Dease supporters, this oversight seemed an outrageous denial of his basic right to be honoured along with the rest. Even the headmaster of Stonyhurst, Andrew Johnson, weighed into the argument and asked the government to reconsider, telling the *Lancashire Telegraph*:

> We are very proud of our seven Victoria Cross winners at the college and it is not right that Maurice Dease would not be commemorated in the right way alongside everyone else.
>
> He fought and died for this country and won recognition from the army for his actions. So he should be remembered in the proper way.
>
> He sacrificed as much as the other Victoria Cross winners and it would not be right if the first winner of a VC in the First World War was not honoured with the others.
>
> I will be writing to Communities Secretary Eric Pickles about this issue and I hope it will be resolved soon.

At the time of this book's completion, it appeared that Dease supporters had carried the day, and that a commemorative stone would be laid either in the Tower of London or at Stonyhurst. Godley's stone was to be laid in East Grinstead, where his story began.

What would Maurice Dease and Sidney Frank Godley, two particularly kind men, have asked of us in centenary year? It cost them so much personally to earn their VCs. It was the start of so much slaughter. They would surely want nothing more than for their fallen comrades to be remembered with respect, and for each and every one of us to do our bit to achieve a lasting peace for the living.

# Bibliography

Arthur, Max, *Symbol of Courage: A Complete History of the Victoria Cross*, London: Sidgwick & Jackson, 2004

Best, Brian (ed.), 'The First VC of the First World War: Lt Maurice Dease, VC,' *Journal of the Victoria Cross Society*, Vol. 1, October 2002

———(ed.), 'Sidney Godley, VC,' *Journal of the Victoria Cross Society*, Vol. 16, March 2010

Bloem, Walter, *The Advance From Mons 1914: The Experiences of a German Infantry Officer*, Solihull: Helion & Co. Ltd

Doherty, Richard and Truesdale, David, *Irish Winners of the Victoria Cross,* Dublin: Four Courts Press, 2000

Farr, Don, *Mons 1914–1918: The Beginning and the End*, Solihull: Helion and Co. Ltd, 2008

Gliddon, Gerald, *VCs of the First World War: 1914*, Stroud: Alan Sutton Publishing, 1994

———, *VCs of the First World War*, Stroud: The History Press, 1994

Hastings, Macdonald, *More Men of Glory*, London: Hulton Press, 1959

Hutchinson (Publisher), *Wonderful Stories of Winning the VC in the Great War,* London: Hutchinson, c. 1916

Irwin, The Rev. Francis S. J., *Stonyhurst War Record*, Clitheroe: Stonyhurst College, 1927

Kelleher, J. P., *Elegant Extracts: The Royal Fusiliers Recipients of the Victoria Cross,* London: The Royal Fusiliers Association, 2001

Kirby, Henry L. and Walsh, R. Raymond, *The Seven VCs of Stonyhurst College*, Blackburn: THCL Books, 1987

Lomas, David, *Mons 1914: The BEF's Tactical Triumph*, Oxford: Osprey Military, 1997

MacDonald, Lyn, *1914*, Harmondsworth: Penguin, 1989

———, *1914–18: Voices and Images of the Great War*, London: Penguin, 1998

Mulholland, John and Jordan, Alan, *Victoria Cross Bibliography*, London: Spink, 1999

Neillands, Robin, *The Old Contemptibles: The British Expeditionary Force, 1914*, London: John Murray, 2004

O'Neill OBE, H.C., *The Royal Fusiliers in the Great War*, Uckfield: Naval and Military Press Ltd, 2002 [1922]

Standard Art Book Company (Publisher), *Deeds that Thrill the Empire: True Stories of the Most Glorious Acts of Heroism of the Empire's Soldiers during the Great War*, London: Standard Art Book Company, c.1917

*Stonyhurst Magazine* – Various issues

Terraine, John, *Mons*, London: Pan Books, 1972

Thornicroft, N. J., *The VCs of Gloucestershire and North Bristol*, Gloucester: Wedderburn Art, 2005

Zuber, Terence, *The Mons Myth: A Reassessment of the Battle*, Stroud: The History Press, 2010

# Index

# If you enjoyed this book, you may also be interested in…

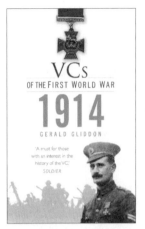

## VCs of the First World War: 1914
GERALD GLIDDON

During the opening four months of the First World War no fewer than forty-six soldiers from the British and Commonwealth armies were awarded the Victoria Cross, Britain's highest award for gallantry. In a series of biographies, Gerald Gliddon examines the men and the dramatic events that led to the award of this most coveted of medals and explores the post-war experiences of those who survived. These men, ordinary soldiers from widely differing social backgrounds, acted with valour above and beyond the call of duty. Their stories and experiences offer a fresh perspective on the opening stages of the 'war to end wars'.

978 0 7524 5908 0

## The Mons Myth
TERENCE ZUBER

Unlike conventional histories of the battles of Mons and Le Cateau, which describe how precise and rapid British rifle fire mowed down rows of German troops despite being massively outnumbered, *The Mons Myth* uses German tactics manuals and regimental histories to explore these battles. It also subjects British tactics to a critique that goes beyond admiration for rapid rifle fire and presents new and startling perspectives of both Mons and Le Cateau, showing how the Germans employed a high degree of tactical sophistication in conducting a combined-arms battle. The odds at both battles were, in fact, even, and German casualties never reached the levels described in the standard histories.

978 0 7524 5247 0

## The Real German War Plan, 1904–14
TERENCE ZUBER

This book fundamentally changes our understanding of German military planning before the First World War. On the basis of newly discovered or long-neglected documents in German military archives, the first descriptions of Schlieffen's war plans in 1904, 1905 and 1906 and Moltke's plans from 1907 to 1914 are given. Unfounded myths concerning German war planning are exploded, and the first appraisal of the actual military and political factors that influenced it prove conclusively that there never was a 'Schlieffen Plan'. Tracing the decline in the German military position, this is an essential read for anyone with an interest in the First World War.

978 0 7524 5664 5

Visit our website and discover thousands of other History Press books.

## www.thehistorypress.co.uk